Morality and Custom in Ancient Greece

These little statues, called Hermae, stood before most houses, and at many street intersections, in ancient Athens, and were felt to confer good luck. The god Hermes himself was the patron both of trickery and deception and of business transactions, as well as a protector of travellers. National Museum, Athens.

Morality and Custom in Ancient Greece

JOHN M. DILLON

INDIANA UNIVERSITY PRESS
Bloomington and Indianapolis

This book is a publication of

Indiana University Press
601 North Morton Street
Bloomington, Indiana 47404-3797 USA

http://iupress.indiana.edu

Telephone orders	800-842-6796
Fax orders	812-855-7931
Orders by e-mail	iuporder@indiana.edu

First published in the UK in 2004 by
Edinburgh University Press

Typeset in Bembo by
Koinonia, Manchester, and
printed and bound in Great Britain by
The Cromwell Press, Trowbridge, Wilts

Cataloging information is available from the Library of Congress.

ISBN 0-253-34526-x (cloth : alk. paper)
ISBN 0-253-21747-4 (pbk. : alk. paper)

1 2 3 4 5 09 08 07 06 05 04

Contents

Abbreviations

Aristotle, *Ath. Pol.* = *Athenaiôn Politeia*, or *Constitution of the Athenians*
Cicero, *Tusc. Disp.* = *Tusculanae Disputationes*, or *Conversations at Tusculum*
DL = Diogenes Laertius, *Lives of Eminent Philosophers*
Homer, *Od.* = *Odyssey*
l., ll. = line, lines (of a poetic work)
Pap. Oxy. = Oxyrhynchus Papyri
Plutarch, *Mor.* = *Moralia*, or *Moral Essays*; *De Lib. Educ.* = *De liberis educandis*, or *On the Education of Children*; *Adv. Col.* = *Adversus Colotem*, or *Against Colotes*
s., ss. = section, sections (of a prose work)
SEG = *Supplementum Epigraphicum Graecum*
Strabo, *Geogr.* = *Geography*

Note on Orthography

In the spelling of Greek names, I have in general avoided Latinised forms: so e.g. Stephanos, not Stephanus, Neaira, not Neaera, Kriton, not Crito (though I prefer to transliterate Greek *chi* as 'ch', not 'kh', e.g. Chrysilla, not Khrysilla). However, in the case of well-known Greek authors, such as Homer, Thucydides, Plato, Aristotle, Menander or Plutarch, or such figures as Croesus or Socrates, whose names have passed into the English language, I have preferred to preserve the usual Anglicised forms; similarly in the case of titles of works, such as Plato's *Euthyphro* or *Crito* (as opposed to the historical figures Euthyphron and Kriton), geographical names (Athens, Byzantium, Corinth), and names for Athenian units of currency (obol, drachma, mina, talent). I trust that this minor inconsistency will cause no serious confusion.

Note on Athenian Money

The basic unit of currency in ancient Athens was the drachma (divided into six obols). One hundred drachmae were reckoned as one mina, and sixty minae made up one talent. Values may be expressed either in minae and talents, or in hundreds or thousands of drachmae, which can occasion some confusion. As regards modern equivalences, a rule of thumb frequently resorted to is that a drachma was regarded throughout our period (mid-fifth to late fourth centuries BC) as a good daily wage for a skilled craftsman. If, however, one converts that into the going current rate for such an individual (£50–60 a day would be a very conservative estimate!), one ends up with truly monstrous totals for certain commodities or services when reckoned in minae or talents (a talent, for instance, must be reckoned as at least £300,000); so attempts at strict modern monetary equivalents for ancient prices are largely unreal.

Glossary

I include here a number of terms for basic features of Athenian society with which the reader may not be familiar. Most Greek terms are explained in the text, but some frequently occurring ones may usefully be gathered here as well.

Antidosis 'Exchange (of property)'. A remarkable provision of Athenian law whereby a citizen who had been nominated for a ***leitourgia*** could challenge another citizen, whom he considered to be wealthier than himself, but who had not been so nominated, either to take up his *leitourgia* or to undergo an exchange of properties with him.
Archon This term, meaning simply 'ruler', denotes the board of nine administrators elected each year at Athens to oversee the day-to-day administration of the state. One chief duty they had was to preside over the various courts of law. The three chief archons met with in this book are: the Eponymous Archon, who gave his name to the year (so that one expresses dates by 'the archonship of X'); the King-Archon, or *Basileus,* the surviving remnant of the kings of archaic Athens, who preserved certain of the religious functions of the earlier king; and the Polemarch, or 'War-Leader', also the remnant of an earlier military leader, subordinate to the King. The other six archons, known as *thesmothetai*, or 'law-givers', presided over various law-courts, and had various miscellaneous duties. All, as from 487 BC, were selected by lot (one from each of the ten tribes), which meant that the office came to be of little real political importance. All ex-archons, however, became members of the **Areopagus**. On the legal level, the Eponymous Archon was particularly concerned with family disputes, and the protection of orphans and heiresses; the King with religious questions, such as charges of impiety; and the Polemarch with cases involving foreigners or freed-persons.
Aretê This term is usually translated 'virtue', but may more properly be rendered 'human excellence.' It denotes the sum total of the moral, social and even physical excellence proper to a human being. It is conventionally divided into four particular 'virtues', wisdom (*phronêsis*),

courage (*andreia*), self-control (*sôphrosynê*), and justice (*dikaiosynê*). The 'virtues' of men and women were generally considered to be quite distinct, courage, for instance, being quite inappropriate for a woman, caution or timidity quite unsuited to a man.

Demos ('deme') The basic political division of the Athenian state, corresponding to something like a parish – the word is identical to that used to designate the Athenian 'people' as a whole. Set up by the political reformer Cleisthenes in 507 BC, to be the cornerstone of his rearrangement of the citizens into ten *phylai*, or tribes, the male Athenian henceforth was known by his deme (into which everyone had to be enrolled at the age of 18), as well as his father's name. Most everyday civic and religious activities took place at the level of the deme (but see also *phratria*).

Dikê Meaning literally 'justice', the general term for a case at law in Athens, though frequently denoting more particularly private cases, in contrast to a public indictment, or *graphê*. In the case of public offences, since there was no system of policing or of state prosecution in Athens, prosecution was left to 'anyone who wished' (*ho boulomenos*), a role normally filled either by vexatious busybodies representing themselves as public-spirited citizens (**sykophantai**), or personal enemies of the accused.

Hetaira 'Companion'. This was the usual term for a courtesan, something more dignified and independent than a simple prostitute (*pornê*), and accorded correspondingly more respect, though still no legal rights. Such women might be either foreign nationals who had settled in Athens (often from the Aegean islands, or the cities of Asia Minor), or former slaves who had won their freedom.

Hybris A term covering a number of offences in Greek law, but basically denoting 'insult to the person, arising from overweening arrogance, and involving an intention to humiliate'. As a specific crime, it normally covered personal assault and rape (resulting in a *dikê hybreôs*).

Kômos This is the term for a popular evening pastime among upper-class youth, involving a (mostly drunken) perambulation around the town in groups, either to gate-crash parties at friends' houses, or to call on some favoured *hetaira*. Such activities could lead to drunken brawls, and sometimes to more serious misdemeanours (such as the mutilation of the Hermae).

Leitourgia (liturgy) In Athens, in place of a regular system of taxation of property or income, certain public functions were imposed upon the richer citizens and resident aliens (**metoikoi**) – or alternatively, could be volunteered for, by public-spirited and/or ambitious individuals. These *leitourgiai,* or 'public services', included the fitting out of a warship in time of war (*trierarchia*); production of a chorus at musical and dramatic festivals (*chorêgia*); provision of a banquet for one's tribe at a festival (*hestiasis*); or leadership of a public delegation to a foreign festival (*architheôria*). All of these functions involved considerable expenditure, and most admitted of being performed either lavishly or stingily. In the later fourth century, trierarchies were generally shared, but even a half-trierarchy could come to 2,000–2,500 drachmae.

Metoikos **(metic)**   The term for a permanently resident alien in Athens – someone who 'lives with' the state. Aliens who resided in Athens (mostly for business purposes) acquired a range of rights and duties. Each metic had to have a citizen sponsor (*prostatês*), register in the deme in which he resided, and pay an annual tax (*metoikion*), amounting to twelve drachmae for males and six for females. If sufficiently rich, metics were liable for liturgies (except the trierarchy), and for other levies (*eisphorai*). They were also liable for military service. A metic could not contract a legal marriage with a citizen, and could not own a house or land unless he had received a special grant of *enktêsis* ('right of acquisition'), but, through his *prostatês,* he enjoyed the full protection of the law. Metics filled an important role in Athenian commerce and industry.

Oikos   The term for the household, comprising not only all family members, but also slaves, livestock, and physical plant. An *oikos* was presided over by a *kyrios,* 'master', the male head of the family. The Athenian house was customarily divided into men's and women's quarters, the latter being at the back of the house, or upstairs, if there was an upper storey. Most houses had a central courtyard, off which the rooms led. The most central, and sacred, part of the house was the hearth (*hestia*), around which various ceremonies took place. Most of the families with which we shall be concerned possessed a country place (*agros*) as well as a town house.

Pallakê   A term for a live-in mistress, or concubine. Such women would normally be of the courtesan class, and so non-citizens or even ex-slaves, but they could be citizen women of low social status, or of unfortunate circumstances, in which latter case their offspring, if formally adopted by the father, could be citizens.

Phratria **('phratry'),** *phrateres* **('phratry-brothers')**   In Athens, the phratry was a subdivision of the tribe, existing alongside the deme as a basic unit of association for citizens, but of a more ancient, 'organic' origin. In theory, members of a phratry were related by blood to some remote ancestor, and so were 'brothers', but in fact, in the Classical period, new members could be admitted, after due scrutiny. The most important step for being recognised as a legitimate citizen was being accepted by one's father's *phrateres* at the annual feast of the Apaturia.

Polis (**'city-state'**) The basic independent political entity in which Greeks lived, consisting normally of a central town or city (*asty*), containing a market-place (*agora*), place of assembly, law-courts and temples, ideally graced with a defensible high point, or citadel (the *polis* proper, or *akropolis*), and surrounded by a rural hinterland (*chôra*). Classical Greeks could not conceive of any other civilised mode of civic life than this; a state comprising more than one *polis* would not be conceivable, inevitably involving the enslavement of one *polis* by another.

Sykophantês A word of mysterious origin – probably an abusive term, apparently meaning 'fig-eater' or 'fig-revealer' (*sykos,* 'fig') – denoting an individual who engaged in prosecutions in cases of public concern, there being no official public prosecutors in the Athenian legal system. They thus served a legitimate purpose, but they were naturally portrayed by their victims as extortioners, or at the least vexatious busybodies. The only control on their activities was that a prosecutor who failed to gain a fifth of the votes of the jury was heavily fined, and debarred from ever bringing another case.

Preface

This book takes its origin from a seminar I have offered for some years now in Trinity College, Dublin, to the senior (fourth year) under-graduates in our Classical Civilisation programme, entitled 'Greek Popular Morality'. The title, a bow in the direction of Sir Kenneth Dover's book of that title, which I initially used as a basic background text for the course, is to a certain extent inaccurate. In the event the course became confined, more or less of necessity, to the study of the 'popular morality' of the Athenians of the second half of the fifth century BC and the whole extent of the fourth. What the Spartans, the Argives, or the Epizephyrian Locrians of that or any other age thought about anything is something that must always remain very largely a mystery to us, from simple lack of evidence, and I made no attempt to penetrate their psyches in this course.

Even in the case of the Athenians, as we shall see, there are many surprising and annoying gaps in our knowledge. For one thing, very little is heard from, or even about, that half of the population which was female. It was a convention of Greek manners that respectable women should be neither seen nor heard (even to the extent of almost never mentioning the names of mothers, wives, or daughters in public, except for offensive purposes), so that the few women we hear much of are less than respectable in one way or another. For another, we cannot expect to hear much from the perspective of slaves or even non-citizens, though both of these do figure in the literature quite frequently, viewed from the perspective of middle-class adult male Athenians. Furthermore, as we shall have cause to note again and again, many aspects of Athenian public and private life are only revealed to us incidentally, if at all, in the sources, for the simple reason that it did not occur to any of our authors that these matters needed explaining to anyone. Sometimes, indeed, we may make deductions from the very fact that a given aspect of life did *not* seem to need explaining, but that is never a very satisfactory procedure.

One large area of mystery, which is of great interest to modern historians, is that of economics. We really do not know, even in respect to Classical Athens, how many male adult citizens there were throughout the period (figures of between 30,000 as a maximum, in the mid-fifth century, to something like 20,000 in the mid-fourth would probably not be far out, but are ill enough attested), much less how many women, children, resident aliens or slaves there were. In the case of the last category, a good deal turns on the question (which will be dealt with below, in Chapter 6), since on it depends the fraught problem of how far Athens was a 'slave society', and therefore how far the direct, participatory democracy which Athens enjoyed depended for its maintenance on slave labour.

Apart from that basic question, we have no idea what might have been the Gross National Product of Athens at any stage of its history. Not only do we not know; the Athenians themselves would have had only the dimmest idea of what we are talking about. Certainly, calculations were made from time to time for the purposes of taxation, but such taxation, which was an emergency measure, generally to meet the financial demands of waging war, was based on estimated property values rather than income. It was known how much cash or treasure reposed in the Treasury of Athena on the Acropolis at any given time (though we are only very rarely vouchsafed this knowledge), and so the Athenian state would have some general notion of how rich it was, but otherwise the gathering of such statistical information remained at a pretty rudimentary level.

This little book, then, chooses to concentrate on what we do know at least something about, and attempts to illustrate this by focusing on a limited number of texts, which are examined rather extensively. A perceived weakness in Dover's magisterial work, especially in relation to prescribing it for an audience of non-Hellenists, is that it is essentially an assemblage of references, with comparatively little quotation of original sources (though enlivened by many shrewd comments and shafts of wit from Sir Kenneth). This book, if anything, goes to the other extreme, dwelling at length on a limited number of works, while being comparatively light on the references. It is my hope that, in the field of Greek social and intellectual history, there is room for both kinds of work. My approach could be summed up in the words 'salt' and 'olives', as these two items constitute the basic *opson*, or seasoning, with which the Athenians attempted to liven up their rather dreary staple diet of bread; it is my hope, that, similarly, these case-histories may help to bring to life what can otherwise become a rather tedious catalogue of customs and regulations, backed up by copious but near-inaccessible references.

As will be seen from the table of contents, I move outward from the central phenomenon of Athenian life, the *oikos,* comprising the family and extended family, with a move sideways to take in threats or alternatives to the family, in the shape of courtesans and other ladies of irregular status, returning then (Chapter 3) to the *oikos* with a chapter on problems of inheritance. After this we pass (Chapter 4) to the topic of friends and enemies, an essential feature of life in the Greek *polis,* especially in a society where surprisingly little, even in relation to such essential matters as births, deaths and marriages, was written down in any official form, and where the enforcement of judgements in the courts, in the total absence of a police force, was left up to the initiative of the plaintiff himself.

In the next three chapters, I turn to certain salient aspects of Athenian life which may seem particularly odd and even offensive to us, that is to say, pederasty (Chapter 5), slavery (Chapter 6), and religious practice (Chapter 7). In each of these cases I have tried to illustrate how the institution or practice in question really worked, and to assist modern minds to comprehend how, particularly in the case of slavery, relatively rational and humane people could behave in this way.

Finally, in an eighth chapter, I discuss the role of oral discourse, and in particular the anecdote, in the formation of the Athenian self-image. This last topic, it must be confessed, started life as an independent discourse, and to some extent still bears the marks of that, but I found that, grafted on to the seminar course, it provided a suitable coda to our investigations, so I hope that it will serve the same purpose in this book.

I am most grateful to a succession of senior Trinity Classical Civilisation classes for engaging over the years with the topics treated of here, and for raising many stimulating questions in connection with them. It is a good exercise for young persons, I think, to step mentally outside their own historical time and place, and consider how things were otherwise, at other times, and my students have always succeeded in doing that. This book is dedicated to them. I am also most grateful to my colleagues, in particular Professor Brian McGing, Dr Judith Mossman, Dr Christine Morris, and Dr Peter Liddell, for much helpful comment in areas where I am myself no means a professed expert. Any errors remaining, as the saying goes, are my own.

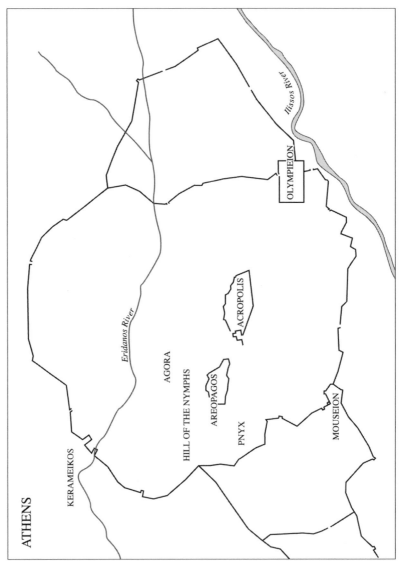

Map of Ancient Athens

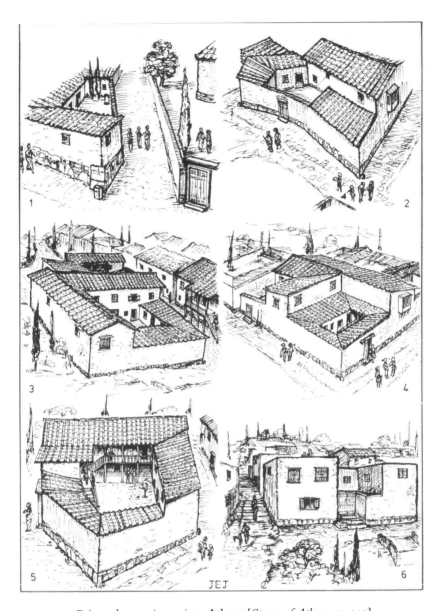

Private houses in ancient Athens [*Stones of Athens*, p. 242]

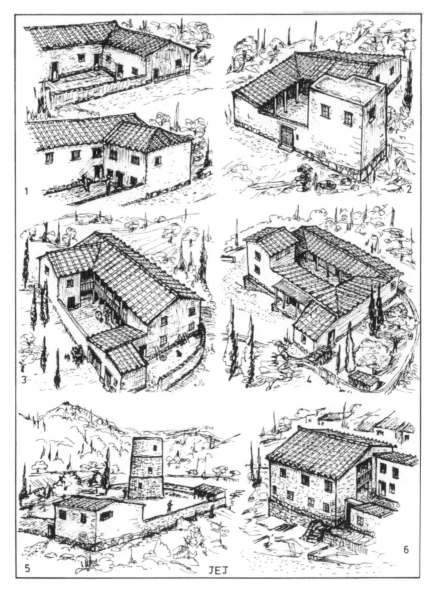

Country houses in ancient Attika [*Stones of Athens*, p. 247]

CHAPTER ONE

The Family: For Better or Worse

TWO ATHENIAN HUSBANDS: EUPHILETOS AND ISCHOMACHOS

Euphiletos

I want in this chapter to start with two perspectives on Athenian family life. The first is a somewhat dysfunctional one, in that we are concerned with an adulterous wife and an outraged husband. The second is presented to us, without apparent irony, as an ideal marital arrangement. From the study of what is common to these two households we may be able to draw some conclusions.

Our first story takes place sometime early in the fourth century BC. Since the outside world does not impinge upon the story, we cannot date it to any exact extent, except to observe that Athens does not appear to be at war (since our hero is found passing freely to and from his country property). We are indebted for our information on this incident to the speech composed by the speech-writer Lysias for the husband in the case, by name Euphiletos (no father's name or deme is supplied), who finds himself the defendant in a case brought by the relations of a gay young blade named Eratosthenes, of the deme of Oea. This gentleman seems to have made a hobby of seducing married women, and had fixed his eye some time before on the young wife of Euphiletos, who had proved susceptible to his advances. He had carried on this affair successfully for some time, before Euphiletos, acting on a tip-off conveyed to him by a dissatisfied former lover of Eratosthenes, surprised the couple *in flagrante delicto* (if we may believe his version of events), and exercised his right, under Athenian law, summarily to execute the offender.

That is the end of the story, as far as we are concerned (presumably Euphiletos got off, or Lysias would not have published the speech). Let us now go back to the beginning, and tell it, as far as possible, in Euphiletos' own words (as dictated to, and interpreted by, Lysias).[1]

---

[1] One notable aspect of Athenian forensic oratory is that, owing to the exigencies of the Athenian legal system, which required that the defendant defend himself, speeches are

When I, Athenians, decided to marry,[2] and brought a wife to my house, for some time I was disposed neither to vex her nor to leave her too free to do just as she pleased; I kept a watch on her as far as possible, with such observation of her as was reasonable. (s. 6)

We must bear in mind here, and throughout the narration, that Euphiletos is concerned to present himself to the jury as the most reasonable of husbands, so that all that he says about his marital arrangements may be taken to be entirely acceptable to an Athenian male audience. It would be likely that his wife was aged in her late teens, and had lived hitherto a thoroughly sheltered life in the bosom of her own family, hardly having set eyes on her future husband, or any other man not her immediate relative, before overtures had been made, probably through an intermediary, for an alliance between their two families. A girl in these circumstances might well turn out somewhat restless, even skittish, at the outset (if she were a girl of spirit), and all reasonable Athenian males would have agreed that she would need watching.

Euphiletos' phraseology is significant – *epei edoxe moi gêmai*, 'when I decided to marry'; there is no mention here of having become attracted to a particular girl – that would be quite improper. No, it was rather a feeling that he had sown his wild oats – he had cavorted long enough with courtesans and boys – and it was now time to settle down and start a family. His father seems by this time to be dead – at any rate he is not mentioned in the story, which makes this con-clusion virtually inevitable – but his mother is still alive when he comes to this decision, and living in the house with him, and she was doubtless nagging him in this direction.

Let us continue the narration (ss. 6–7): 'But when a child was born to me' – let us assume after about a year of married bliss – 'thence-forth I began to trust her, and placed all my affairs in her hands, considering that this was the best way of producing a sense of intimacy [*oikeiotês*].' Once again, the phraseology is significant: *epeidê de* **moi** *paidion gignetai*, 'when a child was born to *me*' – not *us*. His wife is only instrumental to the perpetuation of his line. The only significance of the baby – presumably a son, or we would have heard

composed (when they are so composed) by hired speech-writers with a degree of dramatic skill, since it has to sound as if the defendant is speaking for himself. For the translation of this speech, *On the Murder of Eratosthenes* (Lysias, Oration I), I borrow the Loeb translation of W. R. M. Lamb, with minor variations.

[2] We may assume that he was at this stage about thirty, the usual age for such a decision. Cf. W. K. Lacey, *The Family in Classical Greece*, pp. 106–7.

to the contrary – to his wife was that it tied her down suitably, and domesticated her. At any rate, Euphiletos now takes the decision to make his wife mistress of the household (*panta ta emautou ekeinêi paredôka*, 'I turned over all my affairs to her'). The significance of this can be gleaned from a comparison with our other case-history, that of Ischomachos (for which see below, p. 8). What Euphiletos means is not, of course, all of his business affairs, whatever they were, but simply the management of the household – the direction of the servants, ordering of supplies from the market, and perhaps a certain amount of administration of funds and book-balancing.

At any rate, for the period of perhaps a further year or so, life continued in the Euphiletos household on these new terms. Then, as he tells us, his mother died, and this was the beginning of his troubles, though he did not know it till some time later. For in the course of the funeral procession, or *ekphora*, in which his wife took part, she was spied by this wretched fellow Eratosthenes – who, it is suggested, spent a certain amount of his time hanging about at this sort of occasion, in the hope of picking out some promising young married woman to work his wiles on. It seems that Eratosthenes was at this juncture in between mistresses, since he was just in the process of disentangling himself from a lady whom he had seduced some time before, and whom he was now bored with. At any rate, having now fixed his eye on Euphiletos' young wife (she would certainly be not yet twenty), he lost no time about pressing his suit. This involved waylaying her maidservant (who presumably accompanied her on the *ekphora*, and was thus identifiable) as she went to the *agora* on an errand. Having caught up with her, Euphiletos says, *logous prospherôn apôlesen autên* – 'applying sweet-talk [this I take to be the force of *logoi* in this context], he subverted her.'[3]

The process is worth dwelling on a moment, as it is of the very stuff of the comedy of manners that was even at this period, perhaps, coming to be presented on the Attic stage (certainly it was a stock feature of New Comedy, a few generations later). The gallant lover seeks to approach his loved one through her maid. What, one might ask, could Eratosthenes offer the little maid for her favours as a go-between? In Renaissance comedy, he would have sent his manservant on this errand, and then the manservant could have seduced the

---

[3] The *autên* I take to refer immediately to the maid-servant, though W. R. M. Lamb, in his Loeb translation, wishes it to refer to her mistress. In any event, Eratosthenes certainly directed his *logoi* at both maid and mistress, and ultimately seduced them both. Lysias' language is perhaps deliberately ambiguous, or at least elliptical.

maidservant, and thus got the love-letters conveyed; but Eratosthenes himself can only, I suggest, have offered money or some comparable reward.

As for the *logoi*, we must presume, I think, that they were oral. For one thing, literacy rates among Athenian women cannot have been high – though we do find, for instance, in tragedy, Phaedra writing an incriminating note to her husband Theseus before killing herself,[4] and this must have at least seemed plausible to the audience; but the main consideration would have been security – better not to have notes lying around to be discovered.

And so, by whatever stages, Eratosthenes succeeded in attracting the favourable attention of young Mrs Euphiletos. We would love to know in more detail how this worked, but Euphiletos himself either does not know, or does not wish to dwell on it. Presumably Eratosthenes must have contrived to show himself to his *inamorata* once or twice, so that she could see what she was getting, so to speak, while she peeped shyly out of a window from behind a curtain, but we know nothing of this. It would seem that Euphiletos spent a certain amount of time in the country, out at the farm, and, with mother-in-law gone to her reward, life must have been pretty boring for a lively young woman, with just an infant and the slaves to talk to. This was just the sort of situation from which a predator like Eratosthenes could profit.

Let us continue the narration (ss. 9–14):

> Now in the first place I should explain to you, gentlemen of the jury, in order to make the position clear, that my house has two storeys, the upper being equal in space to the lower, with the women's quarters above and the men's below.[5] When the child was born to us, its mother suckled it; and in order that, each time it had to be washed, she might avoid the risk of descending by the stairs,[6] I used to live above, and the women below. By this time it had become such a habitual thing that my wife would often leave me and go down to sleep with the child, so as to be able to give it the breast and stop it crying. Things went on in this way for a long time, and I never

---

[4] Euripides, *Hippolytus*, 856ff.

[5] It is interesting that this detail is unusual enough to need mentioning. Naturally, in such an arrangement, the women's quarters (*gynaikonitis*) would be upstairs. In the more usual one-storey house, they would presumably normally be in the back, as would seem to be the case in the more spacious villa of Ischomachos (cf. Xenophon, *Oec.* 9. 5).

[6] The 'stairs' would be no more than a ladder – such, indeed, is the term used, *klimax* – and rather rickety.

suspected, but was simpleminded enough to suppose that my own was the chastest wife in the city.

Time went on, gentlemen, and one day I came home unexpectedly from the farm, and after dinner the child started crying in a peevish way, as the servant-girl was annoying it on purpose to make it behave like that; for the man was in the house – I learned it all later. So I told my wife to go and give it the breast, to stop it howling. At first she refused, as though delighted to see me home again after so long.[7] When I began to be angry, then, and ordered her to go, she riposted: 'Yes, so that you may have a go here at the maid. After all, before, when you were drunk, you made a pass at her!'[8] At that I laughed, and she got up and went out of the room, and, pretending to have a joke with me, pulled the key in the lock. I, without giving a thought to the matter, or having any suspicion, went to sleep quite happily, tired as I was after my journey in from the farm.

Towards daybreak she came and opened the door. When I asked why the doors had made a noise in the night, she told me that the child's lamp had gone out, and she had got a light for it from our neighbours.[9] I believed her, and said nothing. It did strike me, though, gentlemen, that she had powdered her face, though her brother had died not thirty days before;[10] even so, I made no comment on the fact, and went off without saying anything.[11]

We see Euphiletos here – and by implication the jury also – blandly oblivious to the mental cruelty, and the danger, of leaving a young wife in this way for long periods of time to run a household on her own. This was certainly an environment in which adulterers could flourish.

Nevertheless, the balloon did not go up, it seems, for some little time after that. One day, however, Euphiletos found himself accosted in the street by an old crone who had been sent to him by an

---

[7] This makes it sound as if indeed he was accustomed to spend the best part of a week at a time out at the farm, as would be reasonable if it were not that near to Athens, and this would have aggravated his wife's loneliness and sense of isolation.

[8] Presumably when she came up to clear away the dinner things. It is an interesting insight into their domestic relations that Euphiletos makes no attempt to deny this charge; he simply takes it as a joke.

[9] This detail throws an interesting light on the alleged confinement of Athenian women. It is plain that, as in contemporary conservative Mediterranean society, such confinement, while real enough, does not exclude visits to neighbours for 'borrowing' and gossip. Cf. David Cohen, *Law, Sexuality and Society*, chs 1–2.

[10] The customary period of formal mourning was thirty days, at the end of which there was a memorial feast.

[11] Sc. back to the farm, no doubt for another week or so.

aggrieved former mistress of Eratosthenes, whom he was in the process of ditching, it seems, in favour of Euphiletos' wife, and who had been doing some detective work on him. The crone introduced herself, and then told him, to his horror, that he had been cuckolded, and that his wife's maid, if put to the question, would reveal all. He went home and summoned the maid, threatened her with being whipped and sent to the mill, and finally – mainly because he convinced her that he knew the truth already – got the whole story out of her.[12]

Matters came to a head four or five days later. We must here be conscious that it is important for Euphiletos to convince the jury that he was not setting a trap for Eratosthenes, so we may accept his narrative with some caution. He claims that he happened to meet an old and close friend of his, Sostratos, coming from the country (it is not quite clear from his account whether they were *both* coming from the country, but it is probable), and, knowing that Sostratos at that hour would find no one at home (presumably he was a bachelor; but would he not have a slave or slaves?), he invited him home to dine with him. After they dined, Sostratos went home, and he himself went to bed. The point of bringing in the story about his friend Sostratos, of course, was to show that there was no premeditation; otherwise he would not have let him go home.

Some time later, Eratosthenes arrived on one of his nightly visitations, and this time the maid came up to warn Euphiletos. I now resume his narrative (ss. 23–6):

> Telling her to mind the door, I came downstairs and went out in silence. I called on one friend and another, and found some of them at home, and others out of town. I took with me as many as I could among those who were available, and so came along. Then we got torches from a nearby shop, and went in. The door was open, as the girl had it ready for us.
>
> We pushed open the door of the bedroom, and the first of us to enter were in time to see him still lying down by my wife. Those who followed saw him standing naked on the bed. I gave him a blow, gentlemen, which knocked him down, and, pulling round his two

---

[12] One of the odder details (s. 20) is that, on one occasion, after Eratosthenes had gained access to his wife, he actually persuaded her to attend the Thesmophoria in the company of *his mother*. It seems extraordinary that an Athenian matron would so connive at the misdeeds of her son, unless Eratosthenes had spun her some story about the girl being a courtesan instead of a respectable married woman; but that seems unlikely.

hands behind his back and tying them, I asked him why he had the insolence to enter my house. He admitted his guilt, and then besought and implored me not to kill him, but to take money from him instead. To this I replied: 'It is not I who am going to kill you, but our city's law, which you have transgressed and regarded as of less account than your pleasures, choosing rather to commit this foul offence against my wife and my children than to obey the laws like a decent person.'

A fine speech, indeed, though one may beg leave to doubt that Euphiletos delivered it in just those words. It is important for him to make the point, though, as the law on adultery was rather specific on the circumstances in which an indignant husband (or father, or brother – or even master of a live-in concubine) could actually exact the death penalty from an adulterer.[13] To have the right of summary execution, it was essential that one catch the culprit in the act. If he managed to escape through the window, or even as far as the family hearth, and was duly apprehended, it was necessary to go through the due processes of law; and this was what Euphiletos had not done. That is also why it was important to gather as many of one's friends together as witnesses, which is what he had judiciously done.

This is as far as the story goes. The reason that we know what happened thus far is that relatives and friends of Eratosthenes had brought suit against Euphiletos for wrongful killing, but we may assume, as I say, from the fact that Lysias published this speech, that their attempt was unsuccessful. What, however, one might wonder, was the fate of Mrs Euphiletos? Remarkably little is said of her towards the end of the speech, and this in itself shows the low regard in which Athenian womanhood was held. She was certainly disgraced and ruined (Athenian law demanded that she be divorced, even if her husband was prepared to forgive her),[14] but she is not even accorded the dignity of being blamed. She is simply considered too witless to resist the blandishments of an experienced adulterer. That is why, as Euphiletos points out (s. 32), seduction is recognised in Athenian law as a more serious crime than rape, because in the latter case 'those who achieve their ends by force are hated by the persons forced; while those who used persuasion corrupted thereby their victims'

---

[13] Cf. Cohen, *Law, Sexuality and Society*, ch. 5: 'The Law of Adultery', and Lacey, *The Family in Classical Times*, pp. 113–16.

[14] Probably in order to discourage the possibility of connivance between a corrupt husband and wife to entrap some guileless philanderer. We will see a case of this sort when we come to consider the story of Stephanos and Neaira, below pp. 38–40.

souls, thus making the wives of others more closely attached to themselves than to their husbands', and thus they corrupt and adulterate a
whole household, and introduce uncertainties of paternity.

Over the subsequent history of Euphiletos' wife, then, a veil must
be drawn. If she was lucky, she was taken back by her family, and
spent the rest of her days in miserable obscurity; if she was not, she
was turned out on the streets to seek her fortune, and that fortune
would not be pleasant.

Ischomachos

But let us turn from this family gone wrong to a more positive
situation, that of the aristocrat Ischomachos and his young wife, portrayed by Xenophon at a period some decades earlier than that of our
first story. In this case, there is no question of anything being wrong.
Xenophon presents Socrates as turning to Ischomachos as an example
of one who is universally reputed *kalos k' agathos*, a 'good chap', and
his particular question to him, when he tracks him down (sitting,
waiting to meet some friends or business associates from out of town,
in the portico of the temple of Zeus Eleutherios) and manages to
inveigle him into a discussion, is 'whether you taught your wife to be
a model wife, or whether, when you were given her by her parents,
she already knew how to manage her sphere of responsibility.'

Before we plunge into Ischomachos' reply, it would be apposite to
fill in what we can of his personal background, and that of his wife.
Unfortunately, as so often, our evidence is somewhat conflicting. At
least, however, it is clear that Ischomachos was of a family reputed
among the richest in Athens, so we are dealing here with a household
at the upper end of the spectrum of Athenian society. We learn from
a speech of Lysias (XIX: *On the Property of Aristophanes*, 46), which
must be dated to around 388 BC, that 'Ischomachos, during his life,
was considered by everyone to own more than seventy talents', but
that 'his two sons, on his death, had less than ten talents to divide
between them.' Even that, however, is a tidy enough sum.

The problem is how this item of information is to be fitted in
chronologically with the scenario presented by Xenophon. Xenophon's frame-narrative, Socrates' conversation with Kritoboulos, has
to be dated between 401 and 399, for reasons that we need not go
into here,[15] but the conversation with Ischomachos is presented as

---

[15] Briefly, Cyrus the Younger is mentioned as having died in ch. 4, s. 18, which puts the
conversation later than 401, and Socrates himself was executed in 399.

taking place considerably earlier. Since there is no problem presented in connection with Ischomachos' going back and forth to his country property, we must envisage a period of peace, certainly prior to the Spartan occupation of Decelea in 413. In fact, if we take account of certain other pieces of evidence, the conversation may have to be pushed back before the outbreak of war in 431. Ischomachos, in the conversation, is referring back to a period some years previously, when his wife first came on the scene, at the age of just less than fifteen, as a totally inexperienced young virgin. She is now considerably more mature, thanks to his careful tutoring, and is effectively running the household, but she need not even now be much more than twenty. Ischomachos, we may assume, is at this point somewhere between thirty-five and forty.

These calculations are of some importance, as we shall see, since our other piece of evidence (of a much more scurrilous nature) requires Ischomachos himself to be dead by about 420, leaving his wife (whose name, we now learn, was Chrysilla) a lusty young widow with a marriageable daughter (as well as the two sons mentioned above). We know all this from the speech by Andokides, *On the Mysteries* (124–7), composed in 399, where he is defending himself against a group of ill-conditioned persons, including the prominent plutocrat Kallias, son of Hipponikos, who want to reopen old wounds about his complicity in the mutilation of the Hermae back in 415. To get back at Kallias, he tells a most scurrilous story about how Kallias first married the daughter of Ischomachos and Chrysilla, and then, within a year (Ischomachos himself necessarily being now dead) had installed his mother-in-law Chrysilla also in his house, as his mistress. Chrysilla, if my calculations are correct, would by now be in her early forties, and still relatively nubile (in fact, Andocides alleges, she had a son by Kallias, whom Kallias was prepared to acknowledge). The fact that Lysias would thus be referring to an event that had taken place some fifteen years earlier is not a great problem, since another of his examples of misleading gossip concerns the fortune of the well-known general and plutocrat Nikias, son of Nikeratos, who had died at Syracuse back in 413.

All this is strictly by the way, however. It simply serves to put the present case-history into perspective, albeit a somewhat ironic perspective (which may or may not have been lost on Xenophon). Here we see Chrysilla as an eminently virtuous and biddable young lady, who has been fortunate enough to be blessed with a model husband, by Athenian standards.

Let us return, then, to Ischomachos' reply to Socrates' question (*Oec.* 7. 5ff):

'How on earth could she know that when I received her, Socrates?' he asked. 'She wasn't yet fifteen years old when she came to me, and in her life up to then considerable care had been taken that she should see and hear and discover as little as possible. Don't you think one should be content if all she knew when she came was how to turn wool into a cloak, and all she'd seen was how wool-spinning is assigned to the female servants? I was content, Socrates', he added, 'because when she came, she'd been excellently coached as far as her appetite was concerned, and that seems to me to be the most important training, for the husband as well as the wife.'

Here, then, is the Athenian gentleman's ideal, clearly stated. One expected as one's wife a young girl, quite untouched either physically or intellectually. The only problem was that, if one wished to have a useful helpmate and even minimally responsive companion, one had to educate her. This is what Ischomachos set out to do. He describes to Socrates his opening move (7. 10ff.):

I waited until she'd been broken in[16] and was tame enough for a conversation, and then I asked her something along the following lines: 'Tell me, my dear, have you realised yet why I married you and why your parents gave you to me? I mean, I know, and it's clear to you too, that it wouldn't have been difficult for each of us to find someone else to share our beds.[17] But for my part, I was considering whom it was in my interest to get as the best person to share home and children, and your parents had your interests at heart; so I chose you, and your parents apparently preferred me to all other eligible candidates.

He follows this with some encouraging remarks about children, and then touches on economic matters:

But what we share now is this home of ours, and we share it because I make all my income available for both of us, and you have deposited all that you brought with you in the same common pool. There's no

---

[16] He uses here the evocative term *cheiroêthês*, properly used of horses, and meaning literally 'accustomed to the hand'.

[17] This is very tactfully put. For Chrysilla, to 'find someone else's bed to share' would simply have been a matter of being bestowed by her parents upon someone else. Ischomachos' own range of options was considerably broader, including courtesans, boys, and slaves of either sex.

need to tot up which of us has made the greater contribution quanti-
tatively, but we must appreciate that whichever of us is the better
partner contributes more qualitatively.

This is a beautiful thought, but it glosses over some rather sensitive
economic realities. Once again, as in the case of sharing the bed, it is
not the same thing for the husband and for the wife to contribute
funds to a common store. Like Euphiletos, when he says that he
handed the whole running of his household over to his wife,
Ischomachos is not really saying that he handed over control of the
disposition of his wealth. Any large decisions would obviously continue to be made by him; it is merely the day-to-day running of the
household that he wishes to hand over to his wife, and housekeeping
money would no doubt be available for that, though strict accounting
would be expected. On Chrysilla's part, on the other hand, her dowry
was handed over to her husband, though it was kept notionally
separate, in case the marriage went wrong. The only constraint on an
Athenian husband who wished to divorce his wife was the necessity
of returning her dowry, possibly with interest included.[18] As it
happens, Ischomachos and Chrysilla are of good family and well provided for, so that no economic obstacles to divorce would have
arisen, if things had come to that, but many Athenian husbands who
married somewhat above themselves could find themselves rather
constrained by the fact that they were no longer in a position to pay
back their wife's dowry.[19]

At any rate, Ischomachos (speaking, no doubt, for Xenophon, and
for all right-thinking Athenian gentlemen) goes on to present us with
a classic statement of the theory of the differentiation of the sexes. He
begins by comparing his wife to the queen bee in a hive (7. 17ff.):

I'll tell you what I'm getting at, my dear. I think that the gods exercised especially acute discernment in establishing the particular pairing
which is called 'male and female', to ensure that, when the partners
cooperate, such a pair may be of the utmost mutual benefit. In the
first place, this pairing with each other is established as a procreative
unit so that the animal species may not die out. In the second place,
human beings, at any rate, are supplied with the means to have supporters in their old age as a result of this pairing. In the third place,

[18] On this question, see Lacey, *The Family in Classical Greece*, pp. 107–10.
[19] We find a complicated situation arising in respect of Demosthenes' bugbear Aphobos,
and his brother-in-law, though in this case there was an element of fraud involved.
See below, Ch. 3.

human life, unlike that of other animals, which live in the open, obviously requires shelter. But if people are to have something to store in this shelter, then they need someone to work out in the open: ploughing, sowing, planting and pasturing are all open-air jobs, and they are the sources of the necessities of life. Now when these necessities have been brought under cover, then in turn there is a need for someone to keep them safe and do the jobs for which shelter is required. Looking after newborn children requires shelter, as does making bread from corn and clothes from wool.

So far, so good. Ischomachos has presented a good case for a division of labour between men and women, on the reasonable assumption that the establishment and preservation of the family unit is a prerequisite for the survival of the race. He (or more properly, Xenophon) now proceeds to base upon this the conventional Greek doctrine that the spheres of excellence (*aretai*, 'virtues') of men and women are distinct':

> Since both of these domains – indoor and outdoor[20] – require work and attention, then God,[21] as I see it, directly made woman's nature suitable for the indoor jobs and tasks, and man's nature suitable for the outdoor ones. For he made the masculine body and mind more capable of enduring cold and heat and travel and military expeditions, which implies that he ordained the outdoor work for man; and God seems to me to have assigned the indoor work to women, since he made the female body less capable in these respects. And knowing that he had made it the woman's natural job to feed new-born children, he apportioned to her a greater facility for loving new-born infants than he did to man. And because he had assigned to the woman the work of looking after the stores, God, recognising that timidity is no disadvantage in such work, gave a larger share of fearfulness [*phobos*] to woman than he did to man. And knowing that it would also be necessary for the one who does outdoor work to provide protection against potential wrongdoers, he gave him a greater share of courage [*thrasos*].

[20] This distinction between 'indoor' and 'outdoor' (*endon* and *exô*) is replicated in other traditional societies, see the useful discussion of Cohen, *Law, Sexuality and Society*, pp. 41ff ('The Politics of Spatial Differentiation').

[21] This apparently monotheistic use of *ho theos*, in the singular (the less problematic plural has been used just above, 7. 18), is in fact quite common, in both philosophical and non-philosophical contexts. It could be taken as simply referring to Zeus, but educated Greeks did have a sense of 'the divinity' in general, corresponding somewhat to the modern use of 'nature' in similar contexts.

But because both sexes need to give as well as receive, he shared memory and awareness between them both, and consequently you wouldn't be able to say whether the male or the female sex has more of these. He also shared betwen them both the ability to be suitably responsible, and made it the right of whichever of them, the man or the woman, is better at this to reap more of its benefits. In so far as the two sexes have different natural talents [*physis*], their need for each other is greater and their pairing is mutually more beneficial, because the one has the abilities the other lacks.

We have here what amounts to a benign male chauvinist's charter. Xenophon's value in this instance, as in so many others, is precisely his unoriginality as a thinker. He is in fact thoroughly in tune with the ethos of the average Athenian male. Ischomachos continues a while longer, driving home his message that God desires that either sex stick to its own domain, and ends with a return to his image of the queen bee, since it will be an important part of Chrysilla's job to take charge of the servants.

This exhortation, he reports with satisfaction to Socrates, had a most beneficial effect, in that Chrysilla, over the next few years, exhibited a thorough mastery of household management, even to the extent of being extremely distressed when on one occasion she could not put her hand on some item he requested from the stores (8. 1–2).

As the discussion progresses, it becomes plain that, for Xenophon, Ischomachos is not only a paragon of traditional virtue, but even, in the degree of rationality he brings to bear on the question of the relation of husband and wife, considerably ahead of his time. Socrates, indeed, is made, towards the end of the account (10. 1), to utter the significant[22] compliment: 'Good heavens, Ischomachos! On your evidence, your wife has a mind as good as a man's [*andrikên ... tên dianoian*]!'

Just one little contretemps is reported in this ideally happy scenario. On one occasion, Ischomachos found it necessary to rebuke his young wife for putting on makeup, and, more remarkable still, high heels. This involves an exchange which the modern reader may well find hilarious, but which Xenophon surely only found edifying:

'Tell me, my dear', I said, 'would you love me more, as your partner in our assets, if I showed you my belongings for what they are, without

---

[22] Significant not only because of the chauvinist terms in which it is couched, but also because of Socrates' notable arguments, advanced in Plato's *Republic*, and very likely representing his own views (since they do not seem to have been Plato's), that the virtues of men and women are *the same*.

pretending that I've got more than I have, and without hiding any of them either, or would you love me more if I tried to deceive you by claiming to have more than I do, and by showing you counterfeit money and fake jewellery, and if I told you that clothing dyed with purple that will soon fade was the genuine article.'

She didn't hesitate, but exclaimed in response: 'What a dreadful thing to say! Don't you ever behave like that! I couldn't love you from my heart if you were like that.'

'Well, my dear', I said, 'our marriage means that we are also partners in each other's bodies, doesn't it?'

'So people say, at any rate', she replied.

'So would you think me a more loveable physical partner', I said, 'if I tried to present myself to you with a good natural complexion by ensuring that my body is healthy and fit, or if I presented myself to you after making up with red lead and smearing foundation cream under my eyes, so that, when we were together, I was deceiving you and making you see and touch red lead instead of my skin?'

'I'd rather touch you than red lead', she replied, 'and I'd rather see your complexion than foundation cream, and I'd rather see your eyes naturally healthy than made up.'

'The same goes for me too, my dear', I said. 'Don't think that I prefer the colour of white lead or alkanet to your own colouring. The gods have made horses to attract horses, cows cows and sheep sheep. Human beings are no different: they find an unadorned human body the most attractive. It is possible that artifice like this may deceive outsiders, but it is inevitable that people who spend all their time together will not get away with trying to deceive each other. There are several possibilities: they'll be caught out when they get out of bed in the morning before getting dressed, or the truth will be revealed by sweat or tears or washing.'

So poor young Chrysilla is well and truly put down, in the most benign and paternalistic way possible. She was not, like Euphiletos' naughty wife, making herself up to meet a lover, but only her own husband, and this is her reward. But she learned her lesson, as Ischomachos complacently tells Socrates. She never did that again.

For good measure, he gave at the same session some further advice about keeping healthy and maintaining a good figure (Greek girls of good family, we may gather, from leading a largely sedentary existence, were liable to become rather broad in the beam if they did not take care). Ischomachos suggests, to avoid this, that Chrysilla be careful to remain standing, and to move about, when supervising household tasks, such as cooking or weaving, rather than sitting down with the slaves. 'There is good exercise also to be provided,' he adds, 'by mixing water and flour and making dough, or by shaking and folding clothes or bedding'. This excellent advice also, it seems, was hearkened to, and had a salutary effect.

So there we have a vignette of upper-class Athenian family life, in a distinctly idealised mode. There are, we may note, as yet no children, but they arrived in due course – we hear of two sons, and at least one daughter – and doubtless Ischomachos had further excellent advice for their upbringing, but we do not hear it from Xenophon. From this we may judge that a shrewd and imaginative Athenian wife could actually acquire a considerable degree of influence and freedom of action within the household, with the proviso that she was always under the overall dominance of her husband, who would not usually be as considerate as Ischomachos.

THE PROBLEMS OF A SMALL (BAD–TEMPERED) ATTIC FARMER

But let us turn from this orgy of high-mindedness to examine another somewhat dysfunctional family, this time a fictional one, that of the misanthropic old Attic farmer, Knemon, in Menander's earliest surviving comedy,[23] The Grouch (Dyskolos). In turning from the sphere of forensic oratory to that of New Comedy, we must of course be mindful that we are entering a world of make-believe.[24] On the other hand, it is plain that the plots of the comedians must be based on recognisable features of everyday reality, or they would lose their point. New Comedy, by contrast to the Old Comedy of Aristophanes, is realistic. That is not to say that it is realist in the modern sense, but it is to say that it deals with scenes of everyday life, even if presented in something of a 'Hollywood' mode.

The story in this case concerns a small farmer who exhibits to an excessive degree certain characteristics of his class,[25] an extreme

[23] It was produced at the Lenaia of 316, and won first prize.
[24] Not, of course, that forensic speeches present an unbiased view of reality either, but they are within the realm of the factual.
[25] Chaireas, the friend of the young hero Sostratos, remarks at ll. 130–1: 'Poor farmers are hot-tempered – not just him, but nearly all of them.' This, of course, is a comment from a young townee of good family – though he is presented as the parasitos, 'hanger-on', of Sostratos. On the other hand, as we learn from Knemon's step-son Gorgias a little later (l. 327), Knemon was not that small a farmer – his property is estimated as being worth two talents, which is a respectable amount of money (about £250,000 in contemporary terms)! Phyle, however, where he farms, was a deme in a poorish part of Attica, on the slopes of Mt Parnes, about thirteen miles north-west of Athens.

frugality, mixed with a profound suspicion of, and antipathy to, the outside world. Knemon, we learn (from Pan, who delivers the prologue), 'married a widow, whose former husband had just died, and left her with a baby son'. This might be construed as a public-spirited thing to do, especially if the deceased husband were a relative or a fellow-demesman, but Knemon was probably after her dowry. At any rate, he proved so unpleasant that, as soon as her own son had grown to manhood and could support her (and be her *kyrios*, or 'responsible male'), she left Knemon, and went to stay with her son, Gorgias, who had inherited a tiny plot of land in the neighbourhood (supporting the assumption that the deceased first husband was at least a fellow-demesman), which barely provided sustenance for them both. There is no mention of a formal divorce here (which would have entailed at least a hearing before an arbitrator, and a return of her dowry); Pan says that she just left him (*apêlthe*), which seems to have been an option open to Athenian wives, if they had somewhere to go. She would have forfeited any dowry, however, in that case. Before she left him, she had produced a daughter, who had to be left with her husband, it seems, and who at the time of the action is of marriageable age – presumably at least fifteen.

Onto this rather miserable domestic scene there blunders a young man of good family, the rather Wodehousian[26] Sostratos. He has been out hunting on his country estate, which must be presumed to be in Phyle also, not far from Knemon's, and he has come upon Knemon's daughter, first putting garlands on the statues of the Nymphs in a shrine beside her house (l. 51), and then (ll. 189ff.) drawing water from the well – a task which women and girls of less privileged households would have to do for themselves – and which they probably welcomed, as means of getting out of the house, gossiping, and possibly even ogling boys (though the young miss in this play is far too pure and well brought up to be thinking of such things!).[27]

The young hero, Sostratos, actually offends against propriety by offering to fill her jug for her, and she accepts. This would often be the prelude to a seduction, but Sostratos' intentions are, remarkably (unlike, for instance, the vile Eratosthenes), honourable – though Gorgias' faithful slave, Daos, who spies on this encounter, naturally assumes the worst, and resolves to report on it to his master, who

---

[26] Or rather, normal young New Comedy hero. P. G. Wodehouse, of course, was simply being true to an ancient tradition.

[27] Cf. the remarks of David Cohen, *Law, Sexuality and Society*, pp. 50–1 on the situation in similar traditional Mediterranean societies.

would be expected to defend the honour of his half-sister. Daos' soliloquy (ll. 218–29) contains many significant points:

> What the devil's going on here? I don't like this at all. A young man doing a girl a service, that's not right. It's your fault, Knemon, damn you. An innocent girl, and you leave her all alone, in a lonely place, with no proper protection. Perhaps this chap knows this, and has slipped in quietly, thinking it's his luck. Well, I'd better tell her brother about this, right away, so that we can look after her.

Daos does this, and the result is a confrontation between Gorgias and Sostratos at the beginning of Act II. First, however, Gorgias scolds Daos for not intervening more actively, and in the process makes the significant point that, in spite of the break-up of the family, any scandal involving his half-sister would be a reproach (*oneidos*) to himself (ll. 243–5). This might seem to us a rather self-centred way of looking at things, but in a traditional Mediterranean society, it is a perfectly natural attitude to take up. The males of a family would all be involved in the disgrace of any of their women-folk. It is their job to protect them.[28]

Sostratos then appears on the scene, and Gorgias confronts him. There are various interesting aspects to this confrontation. First, we may consider what it tells us about distinctions of class in Athenian society. It is fair to say, I think, that, despite considerable differences in wealth, and a certain amount of attention paid to antiquity in the family tree, we do not find in the Athens of the classical period anything approaching the class distinctions which have been characteristic of Europe since the Middle Ages. The situation is, if anything, more like that in contemporary America, where enormous differences in wealth, and some pride in ancestry, co-exist with a real conviction that all men are equal, and that, so to speak, a cat may look at a king. For one thing, there do not seem to be in Athens, any more than (broadly speaking) in the contemporary United States, any strong differences of accent – along class lines, at least. This may seem a trivial point, but it is significant enough when such distinctions do exist, as in Britain and even in Ireland. This is an argument from silence, admittedly, but we never find, I think, in surviving documents, any allusion to class-based differences of accent. Other Greek accents, such as Spartan or Boeotian, are presented (mockingly), for instance, in plays of Aristophanes, but not lower-class or country Athenian accents, and that is significant.

---

[28] Cf. Cohen, *ibid.*, pp. 54ff.: 'The Politics of Reputation'.

Gorgias here is conscious of being a poor man, and he knows that he is faced with a wealthy young blood (he can tell from the expensive cloak), but he is not about to adopt a subservient attitude. He lectures Sostratos, rather sententiously, on the importance of not taking his wealth for granted, or using it as a basis for throwing his weight about.[29] He naturally assumes that Sostratos is out for a straightforward seduction. When Sostratos convinces him that his intentions are honourable, however (as he does by speaking to him frankly and openly, as an equal, without attempting to pull rank or behave with haughtiness, as a later European aristocrat undoubtedly would have if faced with an insolent peasant), Gorgias freely agrees to help him – again, as an equal. Despite the 'Hollywood' aspect of the realism of New Comedy, I think that we can draw valid conclusions from an exchange like this. This would not have seemed at all strange to Menander's audience in 316 BC – nor indeed at any time in the century and a half before that.

We gain also some interesting insights into Sostratos' comfortably upper-class family. His mother, for instance, is subject to the normal restrictions of mobility weighing on respectable Athenian ladies, but she has devised some ingenious ways to circumvent them – and we may reasonably conclude that she was not unique in this. As Sostratos explains to us in a soliloquy (ll. 260–4): 'My mother's planning to sacrifice to some god or other – no idea which. She does this every day, trailing round the whole district, making offerings, and she's sent Getas out to hire a cook, locally.'

This is plainly an ingenious wheeze to have an excuse to leave the house for frequent picnics in the country (we do not have to take literally Sostratos' claim that she does this every day). The pretext is that she is visited by ominous dreams sent by one divinity or another, requiring that she placate them by sacrifice, and this calls for an expedition to the shrine in question, accompanied by a full panoply of servants and a hired cook, and such of her friends as she can summon up. Her husband, Kallipides, no doubt sees through this, as does her son, but puts up with it good-humouredly enough. We can see here the importance of religious festivals, and religious practice generally, in relieving the tedium of female existence. Menander is gently satirising a well-recognised feature of social life.

[29] In an Athenian democratic setting, especially in the lawcourts, where the jurors would tend to be from the lower end of the socio-economic spectrum, accusations of arrogance on the part of wealthy persons were plainly quite effective – as we shall see, for example, in connection with Demosthenes' attack on Meidias (below, pp. 88–93).

In this case, the god happens to be Pan, and precisely the Pan of this shrine, and the joke is that, this time, the dream she claims to have had – she saw Pan putting fetters on her son Sostratos, and then giving him a rough country jacket and a hoe, and sending him out to dig (ll. 414–18) – has some validity in terms of the plot; but it is not to be supposed, I think, that these 'dreams' had in general much substance.

So this lady, of more or less the same socio-economic class as Ischomachos' wife, has managed, in later life, at least, to come to terms with her existence pretty satisfactorily. Her husband, as we shall see, even takes part amiably in all this. The family, it would seem, has an estate in the neighbourhood, to which he has been attending,[30] and he drops in rather late for lunch (l. 779).

His arrival (following on Knemon's providential fall down his well, and rescue by his step-son Gorgias, which changes his attitude radically for the better) brings up a topic which we will deal with in more detail later (below, Chapter 3), that of marriage contracts between families. Kallipides (as we would note immediately from his mask!) is a Nice, or Good-Natured Old Man – in contrast to Knemon – and is therefore disposed to humour his son's whims, including his sudden burning desire to get married, but even he is somewhat taken aback by the enormity of what Sostratos is proposing. One of the most basic features of the Athenian marriage contract was the bestowal of a dowry (*proix*) by the father, or family, of the bride. It was a matter of honour, and also of plain economics. It was very difficult indeed to get rid of even a very beautiful and accomplished daughter if there was no money available for a dowry, and, conversely, it was accounted a most noble act to take the daughter of a relation, friend, or fellow-demesman down on his luck – or, it might be, dead, whether in battle or from other causes – *aproikos*, 'without a dowry'.

Now Gorgias, having been adopted on the spot by his step-father Knemon,[31] and been made heir to his property, has agreed unhesitatingly to the marriage of his sister to Sostratos (we may note in passing that the girl herself is never so much as asked what she feels about this!), but he wishes to offer a dowry of one talent – which is respec-

---

[30] We can deduce this from the facts (a) that Gorgias knows of him, and indeed knows him to be a very rich man, and (b) that Sostratos, rather defensively, agrees that he is rich, but claims that he worked hard for it, as a successful farmer (ll. 773–5). One may suspect, however, that his wealth is based on more than land.

[31] It would seem that the old curmudgeon had not adopted him originally, when marrying his mother – presumably because he expected to have a son of his own, in which case Gorgias would lose out.

table, though not princely (at least by New Comedy standards), and amounts to fully half his wealth (ll. 844–5). Sostratos, however, in conversation with his father (ll. 784ff.), is proposing not only to take her without a dowry, but to give *his* sister to Gorgias *with* a dowry, to cement the alliance between the families. His father is a decent man, but this is a little too much for him (795–7): 'That's no good.[32] I've no desire to acquire *two* beggars-in-law at one go. One's quite enough for us.' However, Sostratos upbraids him for his materialism, and he gives in, good-naturedly as always. However, Gorgias' honour is at stake as well, and he insists on providing the dowry of one talent. On the other hand, he receives with Kallipides' daughter (who, we note, is not consulted either) a dowry of three talents (ll. 841–3), so all ends very well.

In dealing with a Menandrian comedy, as I have said before, we do have to discount a certain degree of Hollywood soap-opera hyperbole, but nonetheless there is much of value to be derived from these documents, particularly from what is revealed incidentally, about the values and expectations of Athenian society. We shall be making extensive further use of Menander, and some even of Aristophanes, in coming chapters.

THE CASE OF THE WICKED (OR UNFORTUNATE) STEPMOTHER

We turn now, in conclusion, to a case-history that serves to link this chapter with the next, since it involves not only an Athenian family, but one of those outside threats to it about which we shall have more to say presently, the courtesan or concubine. The story concerns the tragic outcome of an attempt to rekindle a husband's love, but in a rather unorthodox manner. It takes us back in time from the fourth to the fifth century, perhaps even to a period before the outbreak of the Peloponnesian War in 431 BC, as the author of the speech employed in the case is the early orator (and reactionary politician) Antiphon (c. 480–411 BC), and this seems to be a relatively early work of his, but there can be little doubt that the attitudes, and the domestic situation, portrayed here would be representative of the whole period we are surveying.

The narrator of this sad tale is the stepson of the accused lady, and his exact status (about which he is studiously vague, and probably for good reason) is obscure. He describes himself (ss. 1, 30) as very young

---

[32] He actually uses the adjective *aiskhron*, 'disgraceful', implying that such an alliance would compromise his honour.

and inexperienced, though his stepmother has grown-up sons (who are in fact speaking in her defence). No mother of his is mentioned, and he cannot be the son of a previous wife, since he is younger than the other children. The unavoidable conclusion must be that he is in fact the offspring of a concubine, though recognised by his father as part of the family, and we may conjecture that it was in fact the supplanting of the wife by the concubine in the affections of the husband that caused the sad sequence of events that we are about to examine. But over this embarrassing aspect of the situation a veil is industriously drawn by our speaker.[33]

Let us now follow his narrative.[34] He plunges into it rather abruptly, but certain background facts emerge as he goes along:

The was an upper room[35] in our house occupied by Philoneôs, a highly respected friend of our father's, during his visits to Athens. Now Philoneôs had a mistress [pallakê], whom he proposed to place in a brothel. My brothers' mother made friends with her; and in hearing of the wrong intended by Philoneôs, she sends for her, informing her on her arrival that she herself was also being wronged by our father. If the other would do as she was told, she said, she herself knew how to restore Philoneôs' love for her and our father's for herself.[36] She had discovered the means; the other's task was to carry out her orders. She asked if she was prepared to follow her instructions, and, I imagine, received a ready assent.

We may note, first, the characterisation of Philoneôs and his actions. On the one hand, he is kalos k' agathos, a term of high moral commendation ('a very good chap'); on the other hand, he is proposing to trade in his current pallakê, presumably after a number of years of service, and lodge her in a brothel. It is not suggested that she has done anything wrong. He is just looking for a newer model.[37] Indeed,

---

[33] It may seem strange, in this case, that the young man was in a position to bring this action, speaking as his father's son. However, if his mother had been free, and a citizen (though of humble social status), rather than a slave, and he had been formally adopted by his father, he would count as a member of the family.

[34] The text is Antiphon, Speech I: Against the Stepmother, ss. 14–20.

[35] This hyperôion would be of the same nature as that in Euphiletos' house, approached by an outside ladder, but here it was used as guest quarters.

[36] It is not clear how the speaker knows of this conversation, as it emerges later that no one was talking. One may suspect a touch of dramatic licence here, though it is indeed quite probable that some such arrangement was made.

[37] In Menander's The Girl from Samos, by contrast, which we shall look at in the next chapter, the 'nice old man' Demeas is threatening to turn his pallakê out in the street, but in this case for the good reason that he thinks (albeit wrongly) she has been having an affair with his adopted son, Moschion.

just below, the stepson unhesitatingly refers to his intentions towards her as 'injustice' (*adikeisthai emellen hupo tou Philoneou*). It is not quite clear, in fact, what the moral stance of the speaker is. He certainly does not regard the 'injustice' done to the *pallakê* as in any way constituting a justification of what she and his stepmother get up to – even if their action had the comparatively innocent purpose of reclaiming the affections of their menfolk, rather than murdering them. The truth is that a *pallakê* had no rights in the strict sense; one could 'wrong' her, as might 'wrong' a dog by kicking it just because one was in a bad temper – but this would not derogate from one's status as a *kalos k' agathos*.

So, what happened next?

> Some time after this, it happened that Philoneôs was holding a sacrifice to Zeus Ktêsios[38] in Peiraeus, while my father was on the point of leaving for Naxos.[39] So Philoneôs thought that it would be an excellent idea to make one journey of it by seeing my father as far as Peiraeus,[40] offering the sacrifice, and entertaining his friend. Philoneôs' mistress accompanied him to attend the sacrifice. On reaching Peiraeus, Philoneôs, as is to be expected, carried out the ceremony. When the sacrifice was over, the woman considered how to administer the draught: should she give it to him before or after supper? Upon reflection, she decided that it would be better to give it afterwards, thereby carrying out the suggestion of this Clytemnestra here ...[41]
>
> After supper was over, the two naturally set about pouring libations and sprinkling some frankincense to secure the favour of heaven, as the one was offering sacrifice to Zeus Ktêsios and entertaining the other, and his companion was supping with a friend and on the point of undertaking a voyage. But Philoneôs' mistress, who poured the wine for the libation, while they offered their prayers – prayers never to be answered, gentlemen! – poured in the poison with it. Thinking it a happy inspiration, she gave Philoneôs the larger draught, imagin-

---

[38] This was a periodic sacrifice to 'Zeus of the household stores', who was represented by a jar, or tokens affixed to a jar, in the storeroom of the house. A sacrifice to Zeus Ktêsios seems to have been very much of a family affair, to which only members of the family (and perhaps extended family) would normally be invited (cf. the passage from Isaeus 8, quoted below, p. 52); but Philoneôs appears to be unmarried, so he invites a close friend instead.

[39] No doubt on business; or perhaps, like Euthyphron's father in Plato's *Euthyphron*, he had an estate there which he had to supervise.

[40] Not a great journey, after all; it was a little more than 10 km from Athens to Peiraeus. It sounds, though, as if that was Philoneôs' chief place of residence, not anywhere further afield.

[41] A nice rhetorical flourish. He himself, however, is not quite in the position of Orestes.

ing, perhaps, that if she gave him more, Philoneôs would love her the more: for only when the mischief was done did she see that my stepmother had tricked her. She gave my father a smaller draught.

So they poured their libation, and, grasping their own slayer, drained their last drink on earth. Philoneôs expired instantly; and my father was seized with an illness which resulted in his death twenty days later. (ss. 18–20)

This is truly a sad little tale. The poor *pallakê* had plainly been persuaded that she was administering a love-potion, though what she really hoped to gain from it is not very clear. The logic of love-potions is obscure to me, but all they can be expected to do, one would think, would be to increase the amorousness of the partner on a temporary basis; it would hardly alter for long his fixed intention to trade her in. But no doubt in this sort of situation one grasps at straws. This objection holds in still greater measure for the stepmother herself. Her husband was off to Naxos. Did she expect him, blinded with lust, to abandon his business trip, and turn round and come straight home; and would he not then, in any case, head rather for the speaker's mother, his *pallakê* (if our conjecture about the nature of the case is correct)? Love-potions are not 'smart', presumably, in the sense that they can be directed at a particular object;[42] they would presumably tend to favour the nearest plausible one. So it rather looks as though *someone* was up to no good here – either the stepmother, or perhaps the wise woman from whom she bought the potion.

However, the *pallakê*, when arrested and tortured, behaved with exemplary nobility. She kept her mouth shut, even when broken on the wheel and hauled off to execution (s. 20).[43] Hence no case could be brought in the immediate aftermath against the stepmother. Her hands were clean; there was no smoking gun.

Nevertheless, if the girl did not talk, our speaker's father did. During the twenty days of his last illness, he seems to have made his young son fully cognisant of his conviction that his wife was behind all this. The domestic situation must have been pretty poisonous, as it seems that his own sons by his wife were not there to be confided in

---

[42] Unless, perhaps, they are combined, as they would be in the magical tradition, with suitable formulae, specifying the beneficiary or beneficiaries. But there is no mention in the narrative of the uttering of spells; and in any case, how would one do this in an intimate situation? Out in the pantry?

[43] As a slave (as we can conclude from this that she was), she was liable to torture, both to extract evidence and as punishment, and to death, as having compassed, even unintentionally, the death of her master.

by him, and are now, some years later, appearing in defence of their mother. Who nursed the father, then, in his illness? The speaker himself was perhaps in his early or mid-teens, and hardly equal to the task. Perhaps faithful slaves, then, but perhaps also that shadowy figure, the speaker's mother, on whom he does not wish our thoughts to dwell.

We do not have to concern ourselves with whether this prosecution was successful or not. On the basis of the evidence presented, I cannot see that it should have been, but, from the fact that the speech was published by Antiphon, one must conclude, regretfully, that it probably was.[44] More to the point from our perspective is what light it throws on the possible permutations of Athenian family situations. On the one hand, it reminds us of the precarious status of even legitimate Athenian wives, and of the double standard prevailing as regards extra-marital affairs; while on the other, it directs us forward to our next topic, which is the status in Athens enjoyed (if that is the word) by those women excluded from the family circle.

---

[44] This will be a generally valid rule of thumb in respect of surviving forensic speeches, since they were published primarily as advertisements for the speech-writer's prowess.

CHAPTER TWO

Outside the Fold, Beyond the Pale: Problems of Non-Citizen Women

THE ADVENTURES OF NEAIRA

The respectable Athenian household, as we have seen, is a fortress within which the womenfolk are fairly securely penned, but outside of this haven there was a jungle, in which many exotic flora and flora flourished, and into which Athenian men could, and did, wander at will. A selection of the denizens of this underworld, real and imaginary, will be examined in this chapter.

Our first case-history belongs to real life – though how near we are ever going to get to the truth in the context of an Athenian lawcase is a moot point. As in so many of these cases, the true cause of the dispute lies elsewhere, in more ancient quarrels, and Neaira, the accused, is much more of an innocent victim of a grudge against someone else (in this case, her common-law husband Stephanos), than a real malefactor. Nevertheless, it is she who gets it in the neck.

Apollodoros, the prosecutor in this case, is an interesting, but by no means loveable figure. He was the son of the noted banker Pasion, himself a freed slave, who was subsequently, for his great services (of a financial nature) to the Athenian state, granted the very rare honour of Athenian citizenship. His son took an active part in Athenian society, but, no doubt in part because of his rather jumped-up background (which many in the city who would not let him forget), was burdened with a rather prickly and litigious character (other examples of which we will take note of in a later chapter).[1] Back in 349 BC, it seems, about six to eight years before the present case is brought,[2] Stephanos, who was a minor politician, a hanger-on of the somewhat more major politician Kephisophon, had successfully prosecuted Apollodoros, who also dabbled in politics, for making an illegal proposal (a *graphê paranomôn*) – a favourite ploy of political rivals. On

---

[1] Apropos the topic of friends and enemies, in Chapter 4, pp. 94–100. His battles with his father's former slave and latterly bank manager, Phormion, whom Pasion had made guardian of Apollodoros' younger brother, Pasikles, and his part of the estate, will be alluded to in that connection.

[2] It can be dated, for reasons we need not go into now, between 343 and 339.

this occasion, Apollodoros had been lucky to get off with a fine of one talent (Stephanos had originally secured a fine of fifteen talents, designed to ruin Apollodoros utterly, and drive him out of town); and some years later Stephanos had brought a trumped-up charge of murder against him, but this time unsuccessfully. Now Apollodoros had discerned a chance to get his own back, and he was determined to make the most of it. The result is a most colourful insight into various aspects of the underside of Athenian society, which we are very glad to have, much though we may deplore the motivation behind these revelations.

Apollodoros feels that he has caught Stephanos in the heinous crime of living with a foreign woman as if she was his legitimate wife, and of passing off the children of this union as if they were legitimate Athenians. The Athenians, ever since the establishment of the extreme democracy back in the 460s, had been remarkably concerned with the exclusivity of their citizenship – mainly arising, one may suspect, from an unwillingness to extend any further than necessary the benefits of their welfare state, such as it was; certainly this extreme chauvinism is primarily a democratic phenomenon. The penalty for conviction in such a case was being sold into slavery, for the alien, and a fine of 1,000 drachmae for the delinquent citizen – but, above all, the utter ruin of any family life they had together. This is the prospect now facing Neaira.

Let us, then, turn to the story, as Apollodoros tells it (ss. 18ff.):

> There were these seven girls who were acquired while they were small children by Nikaretê, who was the freedwoman of Charisios of Elis, and the wife of his cook Hippias.[3] She was skilled in recognising the budding beauty of young girls and knew well how to bring them up and train them artfully; for she made this her profession, and she got her livelihood from the girls. She called them by the name of daughters in order that, by giving out that they were free women, she might extract the largest fees from those who wished to enjoy them.

Let us pause here a moment. What we have here is a scenario which must have been repeated frequently all over the Greek world, and which becomes a favourite motif in New Comedy. It is a sad fact

---

[3] Apollodoros does not make clear where all this is based, but from later indications we can gather that Nikaretê had her establishment in Corinth, where presumably Charisios was a resident alien. Whether Hippias continued to be his cook, or to be a slave, is not clear, but not important. For reasons that will become clearer later, I would date Neaira's birth, tentatively, in around 395 BC.

that girl-babies were frequently exposed at birth in ancient Greece, if their father declined to accept them into the family. They would be left on a hillside by their sorrowing mothers, or by a faithful family slave, sad, mewling little bundles in their cradles, with a few trinkets to go with them (which, in the Hollywood world of New Comedy, are habitually used later to identify them, and return them to their rightful parents – but rarely, we may suspect, in real life).

Such little bundles might simply die, or become the prey of wolves or birds, but they might, if they were (relatively) lucky, be found by wandering shepherds, and then either adopted into their humble households, or (more probably) sold on to hard-faced, unscrupulous ladies like this Nikaretê (who, indeed, may have had a similar start in life herself – let us not be too hard on her!). We do not know if this is how Neaira began life, but it is very probable. Of course, that is not something that Apollodoros would dwell on, in any case, since he has no desire to stir up any sympathy at all for the victim of his spite.

However, on with the story (ss. 19ff.):

When she had reaped the profit of the youthful prime of each, she sold them, all seven, without omitting one[4]... Lysias the sophist,[5] being the lover of Metaneira, wished, in addition to the other expenditures which he lavished upon her, also to initiate her;[6] for he considered that everything else which he expended upon her was being taken by the woman who owned her, but that from whatever he might spend on her behalf for the festival and the initiation the girl herself would profit and be grateful to him. So he asked Nikaretê to

[4] Apollodoros names all seven girls, in an impressive litany, but the only one of any importance to the story, besides Neaira, is Metaneira. Both of them, interestingly, have the names of mythical heroines, Metaneira being the name of the wife of King Keleos of Eleusis, who received the goddess Demeter when she was roaming the world searching for Persephone, while Neaira herself bears the name of various mythological figures, but most notably, perhaps, the beloved of Helios, and mother of the nymphs Lampetie and Phaethousa, who tend his oxen on Thrinakia. The punters plainly liked portentous names. Nikaretê (whose own name, incidentally, must mean something like 'the triumph of virtue'), we must suppose, now bought in a new supply of girls – unless she retired. She plainly specialised in *young* girls.

[5] That is, the well-known speech-writer (c. 430–c. 375), who was plainly addicted, as were many of the well-to-do gentlemen of Athens, to naughty weekends in Corinth. We may date this episode about 383, perhaps, supposing Neaira to be about twelve. One would have to be pretty young to be regarded as 'not old enough' (cf. s. 22) in this game. The story, we must note, takes a jump backwards here, as it is plain from the narrative that the girls are not yet sold off, though Lysias has already a special interest in Metaneira.

[6] That is to say, into the Eleusinian Mysteries, which were quite broadminded as to who was admitted to them. Metaneira, we may conjecture, was about fifteen years of age at this time. Lysias himself, incidentally, was not an Athenian citizen, though a highly respected resident alien.

come to the Mysteries bringing with her Metaneira that she might be initiated, and he promised that he would himself initiate her.

When they got here, Lysias did not bring them to his own house, out of regard for his wife, the daughter of Brachyllos and his own niece, and for his own mother, who was elderly and lived in the same house;[7] but he lodged the two, Metaneira and Nikaretê, with Philostratos of Colonos, who was a friend of his and was as yet unmarried. They were accompanied by this woman Neaira, who had already taken up the trade of a prostitute, young as she was; for she was not yet old enough.[8]

The only purpose of this little bit of gossip, it would seem, is to establish that Neaira was indeed in the service of Nikaretê, and this is duly established by calling Philostratos as witness that they stayed at his house. Apollodoros now turns to detailing a later excursion, in which a certain Simos of Thessaly brought Neaira and Nikaretê up for the Great Panathenaia, perhaps the following July. On this occasion, Apollodoros is able to produce evidence that they stayed with a certain Ktesippos, son of Glaukonides, and that Neaira joined the men at dinner, as only a courtesan would do (ss. 24–5).

Following on this, he tells us (s. 26), 'she plied her trade openly in Corinth and was quite a celebrity, having among other lovers Xenokleides the poet and Hipparchos the actor, who kept her on hire.'[9] It is not clear here from Apollodoros' narrative whether Neaira was already an independent operator or not; but from what imme- diately follows we gather that she is still under the control of Nikaretê, who presumably reserved her in some way specially (though not, it would seem, exclusively) for these two gentlemen, when they came down from Athens. The great sell-off prefigured in s. 19 has plainly not yet taken place.

This did, however, occur, it seems, though not in the blanket way that Apollodoros earlier suggested, and we now learn how (ss. 29ff.).

---

[7] This is a nice touch – Lysias the perfect gentleman! Presumably his wife knew pretty well what he was up to, but was in no position to protest, unless the evidence was lodged under her nose.

[8] Presumably what Apollodoros means by (literally) 'her *hêlikia* was not yet upon her' is that Neaira had not yet attained puberty. Exactly what her role was in this expedition, however, he does not make clear. Since it was Metaneira who was Lysias' girlfriend, Neaira may be supposed to have come along just for the adventure. Apollodoros plainly wants to suggest something more, but he does not specify what.

[9] We may note, by way of general background to all this activity, Plato's mention in the *Republic* (III 404D), composed more or less contemporaneously with these events, of 'having a girlfriend in Corinth' (or possibly, from Corinth) as one of the conventional luxuries to be avoided by the 'guardians' of his ideal state.

In the process, we see Neaira passing through all the possible stages of a courtesan's life, as repeatedly portrayed in New Comedy: life in a brothel; life in a brothel, but in some way 'reserved' for a certain customer or customers; life, still as a slave, but kept as the mistress of a patron or group of patrons; and finally, if one is (comparatively) lucky, life as an independent operator – technically, a freedwoman – but still under the protection of a patron. None of these situations, however, was either permanent or pensionable (as we saw in the case of the unfortunate *pallakê* of Philoneôs in the last chapter), so a girl had to watch out for herself. This Neaira did quite successfully – at least until she, or rather her partner Stephanos, fell foul of Apollodoros.

But on with the story (ss. 29–30):

> After this, then, she had two lovers, Timanoridas of Corinth and Eukrates of Leukas.[10] These men, seeing that Nikaretê was extravagant in the sums she extracted from them (for she demanded that they should pay the entire expenses of the household), paid down to Nikaretê thirty minae[11] as the price of Neaira's person, and purchased the girl outright from her in accordance with the law of the city, to be their slave.
>
> They kept her and enjoyed her as long as they pleased. When, however, they were about to get married,[12] they gave her notice that they did not want to see her, who had been their own mistress, plying her trade in Corinth or living under the control of a brothel-keeper; but they would be glad to recover from her less than they had paid down, and to see her reaping some advantage for herself. They offered, therefore, to remit one thousand drachmae towards the price of her freedom, five hundred drachmae apiece; and they told her, when she found the means, to pay them back the twenty minae.

---

[10] Leukas, the most northerly of the middle group of Ionian islands, was a colony of Corinth, and maintained close ties with the mother city. Eukrates was doubtless a young man of good family whose family had personal or trading ties with Corinth, and he presumably lived there.

[11] We are dealing with fairly large sums here: thirty Athenian minae is 3,000 drachmae, or half a talent, and therefore, according to the reasonable calculation which makes a drachma equal in contemporary purchasing power to £50, about £150,000. One must bear in mind that a basic unskilled slave could be purchased for 2–4 minae, so that Neaira is already a pretty hot property. One might suspect Apollodoros of reckless exaggeration here, except that he can prove a little later that she bought herself out for twenty minae – and in any case he has no particular reason to exaggerate in this context.

[12] The nemesis of all young men in New Comedy, as well as in real life. As we can see from the example, earlier, of Lysias, marriage need not put a stop to all jollification, but it did call for some discretion, and Neaira was plainly rather too notorious.

This, though Apollodoros is not disposed to dwell on it, gives evidence of a certain degree of common decency in these two young men, as well as a streak of self-interest. They could simply have sold Neaira, if not back to Nikaretê, then to some other brothel-keeper, perhaps in another city. Instead, they are prepared to give her a chance to earn her freedom, while granting her a bonus of one-third of her price in recognition of the value they had got out of her. Plainly she had commended herself to them, and they are prepared to recognise that. All they ask of her is that she leave town.

Fortunately, Neaira is not without resources, and a plan (ss. 30–2). She gets in touch with a former admirer, another Athenian member of the naughty-weekend-in-Corinth brigade, Phrynion of Paiania,[13] 'a man who was living a licentious and extravagant life, as the older ones among you remember'. Before approaching him, she had organised a whip-round among other former lovers, and contributed to this her own savings, so what she was asking Phrynion was simply to make up the difference.[14] This he agreed to do, and the twenty minae was handed over to Eukrates and Timanoridas, with the condition that Neaira no longer pursue her trade in Corinth. In the company of Phrynion, then, she departs to begin a new life in Athens. This event seems, from evidence to be presented in a moment, to have taken place in around 374 BC, when Neaira, by my calculations, was in her early twenties.

Neaira now arrives for the first time on the Athenian symposiastic circuit. She had visited Athens briefly some years before, in the company of Lysias, but merely as a rather under-age hanger-on. Now she was here in her own right, no longer a slave, but still bound, by curiously informal but still rather troublesome ties, to a benefactor who had put up at least some money towards her emancipation. Sadly, though, things began to go wrong rather quickly. Phrynion was a boorish fellow, and treated her with scant respect, feeling that he owned her outright (ss. 33–4):

> When he came back here, bringing her with him, [Phrynion] treated her without decency or restraint, taking her everywhere with him to dinners where there was drinking and making her a partner in his

[13] This man, son of Demon and brother of Demochares, was probably a first cousin of the orator Demosthenes, whom we shall meet presently (assuming his father Demon to be identical with Demosthenes' uncle).

[14] Apollodoros does not specify the amounts involved, presumably because he has no definite information about them, but we must suppose, I think, that Phrynion's contribution considerably exceeded that of any other individual, since he ended up in control of Neaira. We are talking, then, probably of a sum of between five and ten minae.

revels;[15] and he had sex with her openly whenever and wherever he wished, making his privilege a display to the onlookers. He went with her on *kômoi* to many houses, including that of Chabrias of Aixonê,[16] when, in the archonship of Sokratides,[17] he was a victor at the Pythian Games with the four-horse chariot, which he had bought from the sons of Mitys of Argos, and returning from Delphi he held a victory-feast [*epinikia*] at Kolias,[18] and in that place many had sex with her while she was drunk, among them even the serving-men of Chabrias.

Apollodoros' insertion here of fiddling details, such as who Chabrias bought the chariot from, has presumably the purpose of jogging the jury's memories, since he is talking of events which took place over thirty years previously. He is able, however, to come up with two witnesses, Chionides of Xypetê and Euthetion of Kydathenaion, who were at the party, and could still remember even some of the slaves going over to have sex with Neaira.

This, plainly, could not go on. Neaira had not clawed her way out of sex-slavery in Corinth to have to submit to this sort of indignity. She lasted the best part of a year after that, and then she broke loose (ss. 35–6):

> Since, then, she was treated with wanton outrage by Phrynion, and was not cherished as she expected to be, nor did he provide her with what she wanted, she packed up his household goods and all the clothing and jewelry with which he had adorned her person, and taking with her two maid-servants, Thratta and Kokkalinê, she ran off to Megara.

This occurred, Apollodoros specifies, in the archonship of Asteios (373/2 BC), probably in the autumn of 373. He also deliberately allows it to seem as if Neaira actually stole property from Phrynion, though it is really more likely that she confined herself to what was at

---

[15] The verb used is *kômazein*. The *kômos*, or revel-rout, was a favourite after-dinner occupation of Athens' gilded youth. One wandered round the town in a group, gate-crashing parties or breaking into the houses of courtesans, and generally causing mayhem. That is what Alcibiades is engaged in when he barges in on the end of Agathon's victory party in Plato's *Symposium*.

[16] Chabrias (c. 420–357 BC) was one of the foremost generals of Athens in the first half of the fourth century. He had won an important sea-battle against the Spartans at Naxos in 376, which helped to establish the second Athenian League, and more recently (in 375) had beaten the Triballoi in Thrace, which brought various northern towns into the League. He was at this time more or less at the height of his influence. Phrynion was moving in distinguished circles.

[17] That is, 374/3 BC. This would be the late summer of 374.

[18] Cape Kolias (present-day Hagios Kosmas) is a promontory on the coast of Attica just south-east of Phaleron, where, presumably, Chabrias had an estate.

least conventionally, if not legally, hers (she herself, after all, was still technically under contract to Phrynion, and arguably his slave).[19] Even the maid-servants could be regarded as part of her proper entourage.

She remained in Megara, we are told, for the best part of two years, into the following archonship, that of Alkisthenes, and so probably to the spring of 371, trying to make ends meet as a courtesan. However, as Apollodoros tells us with some glee (s. 36), business was not good, as the Megarians were a rather stingy lot, and in any case there was a war on between the Spartans and the Athenians, which meant that fun-loving Athenians were unlikely to venture as far as Megara.

Later in 371, however, her luck took a turn for the better. Peace was made between Athens and Sparta (the second 'Peace of Callias'), and then the Spartans were sensationally defeated by the Thebans at Leuctra. Shortly after this, this man Stephanos turned up in Megara, and checked in to Neaira's boarding-house (s. 37). They began a relationship, and Neaira told him all about her troubles with Phrynion. She was angling to get back to Athens, but she was (justly) afraid of the trouble that Phrynion could make for her. She needed a protector (*prostatês*), and Stephanos looked just the ticket.

Stephanos was plainly much smitten by Neaira, and Apollodoros represents him as making rash promises (s. 38):

> He on his part encouraged her there in Megara with confident words, boastfully asserting that if Phrynion should lay a finger on her he would have cause to regret it, while he himself would take her as his wife, and would introduce the sons which she then had to his clansmen [*phrateres*] as his own, and would make them citizens; and he promised her that no one in the world should harm her. So he brought her with him from Megara to Athens, and with her her three children, Proxenos and Ariston and a daughter, whom they now call Phano.

Now Apollodoros here is maliciously going beyond the evidence. He cannot possibly know in any detail what transpired between Neaira and Stephanos in Megara.[20] He certainly calls no witnesses to

---

[19] Which is why Apollodoros can use the deliberately offensive verb *apodidraskô*, 'run away', properly used of a slave. More probably, in fact, as will become apparent shortly, Phrynion is relying rather on a law enjoining a degree of loyalty and service by freedmen to their former masters (e.g. by putting oneself under the protection of another *prostatês*), breach of which could be prosecuted by a *dikê apostasiou*, or suit for desertion.

[20] We cannot even be certain that Neaira had any children at all at this time. There is no mention of any earlier, when she came to Athens with Phrynion, and she would have had to have been more or less continuously pregnant ever since in order to produce

support what he claims. All he can know is the outcome: that Neaira came back to Athens with Stephanos in late 371, and they set up house together 'in the cottage which he had near the Whispering Hermes, between the house of Dorotheos of Eleusis and that of Kleinomachos – the cottage which Spintharos has now bought from him for seven minae' (s. 39).[21] In fact, one of the issues of fact in dispute in the trial is the parentage of the various children. Stephanos, we gather later (ss. 121–2), is actually claiming that these children were not offspring of Neaira, nor yet of Neaira and himself, but those of a previous Athenian wife of his who had died. How he could possibly make this claim if there were no basis for it at all is very hard to see, but, as we shall have occasion to observe many times again, the keeping of this sort of record in ancient Athens was extremely haphazard.

Of course, as soon as Phrynion heard that Neaira was back in town, trouble began. His first move, it seems, was to gather a group of his friends and go round to Stephanos' house to reclaim her by force, on the grounds that she was still technically under his control. The legal situation, however, was rather murky. Stephanos was able to fight him off, both physically and legally, by making a counter-claim that she was a free woman. The outcome was that the case had to go to the Polemarch, who was the official concerned with cases of citizenship and free status. Stephanos and two friends had to post a bond on Neaira's behalf (s. 40).

The trial may have taken some time to come up, since now, according to Apollodoros' malicious account, Neaira, although living with Stephanos, 'continued to carry on the same trade as before, but she charged higher fees from those who sought her favours, as being now a respectable woman living with her husband' (s. 41). Stephanos is thus branded as a pimp, as well as Neaira being a prostitute; indeed, Apollodoros wishes to claim that he brought her back from Megara

---

them. In fact, for a prostitute, children are a disaster, and they have always had various ingenious ways of avoiding them, even before modern contraceptive devices were developed. Further, as we shall see from the tale of the *Girl from Samos*, mistresses were not generally encouraged either to have or to keep children, so Phrynion would not have welcomed any. Lastly, Neaira was planning to ply her trade in Megara, and pregnancy would have put a serious crimp in that plan. So on balance it would seem that this allegation about children is malicious rubbish, and that the boys Proxenos and Ariston at least were indeed children of Stephanos' from a previous, now deceased, Athenian wife, as he asserts.

[21] Again, we may observe the fine corroborative details, since all this happened about thirty years ago. Note the complexities of giving exact addresses in ancient Athens. We have no idea, unfortunately, where the Whispering Hermes was situated (it presumably made a whispering noise when the wind blew through it). We may also note the cost of Stephanos' modest residence – very much less than the price of Neaira!

mainly to supplement the meagre income he was making from
sykophantia (s. 43):[22]

> This fellow Stephanos was getting nothing worth mentioning from
> public business, for he was not yet a politician [*rhêtôr*], but thus far
> merely a *sykophantês*, one of those who stand beside the platform[23]
> and shout, who prefer indictments and informations for hire, and
> who let their names be inscribed on motions made by others, up to
> the day when he became a sidekick of Kallistratos of Aphidna.[24]

We may note, though, that Apollodoros is not able to produce any
witnesses to this particular allegation (although he can get considerable mileage from the incident of the blackmailing of Epainetos later,
ss. 64–71), so we are not obliged to believe this bit of mud-slinging.

In due course, at any rate, the case came up before the Polemarch
(probably as suggested above, a *dikê apostasiou*), and was referred to
arbitration, with quite remarkable results. On balance, it would seem
as if Phrynion did not feel that he had a very strong case – freed-
persons, and even slaves, could make a counter-claim, through their
new *prostatês*, that they had been treated badly by their old one, and
Stephanos could presumably have produced some telling evidence
about Phrynion's behaviour, such as we have heard – and he agreed
to a compromise:

> So then, Phrynion brought suit against [Stephanos] for asserting the
> freedom of this woman Neaira, and for receiving the property which
> she took from Phrynion's house, but their friends brought them
> together and persuaded them to submit the dispute to their arbitration
> [*diaita*].[25] And Satyros of Alopeke, the brother of Lakedaimonios, sat
> as arbitrator representing Phrynion, while Saurias of Lamptrai sat for

---

[22] This term, and the corresponding agent noun *sykophantês*, are not easy to translate
accurately. Meaning literally something like 'fig-eater', or 'fig-revealer' (whatever
either of those two terms may signify), it denoted a person who took vexatious law-
cases against prominent figures, ostensibly in the public interest, but very often on
behalf of some more distinguished politician against an enemy, as part of some political
feud or other. It comes to mean a minor politician, or political hanger-on.

[23] That is to say, the platform (*bêma*) in the Assembly.

[24] A talented orator and financier, who was prominent in Athenian politics from 377 to
361. Stephanos, we may suppose, attached himself to him at least as early as 369,
because we know from s. 27 above that he was responsible in that year for prosecuting
Xenokleides the poet, who had been one of Neaira's early lovers, in Kallistratos'
interest, Xenokleides having opposed Kallistratos' proposal that Athens should ally
itself with Sparta against the triumphant Thebans.

[25] This is in fact quite a common outcome of disputes, avoiding the perils of the
Athenian public courts, as we shall see in the following chapters. Only if arbitration
fails does one resort to open court.

Stephanos here; as impartial arbitrator they chose Diogeiton of Acharnai.[26] They met in the temple and, after hearing the facts from both parties and the woman herself,[27] they announced their decision, which the parties accepted, that the woman was to be free and her own mistress,[28] but that Neaira should give back to Phrynion all that she took with her from Phrynion's house, except for clothing and jewelry and maidservants, which had been bought for the woman herself;[29] she was to live with them each on alternate days; but any other arrangement arrived at by mutual agreement should be binding. The one who at the time had her in his keeping was to provide for her maintenance; and for the future they were to be friends and bear no grudge.

Apollodoros is able to provide depositions as to this remarkable agreement from the parties involved (s. 48), and further evidence from witnesses to the agreement that they dined subsequently, with Neaira being present 'as befits a courtesan [*hôs hetaira ousa*]', at the house of either of the parties, so we seem to be on fairly solid ground here. We are now, probably, somewhere in the year 370.

Apollodoros, however, now abruptly leaves the situation in suspense, and takes a leap in his narrative. The focus, in fact, switches from Neaira herself to her daughter Phanô, and the time perhaps fifteen years on, to the mid-350s, since Phanô is now of marriageable age, and we have seen reasons to doubt that Neaira had any children at all prior to her flight to Megara, at the earliest. We are left to assume that new arrangements were soon come to, according to which Neaira came to reside permanently with Stephanos, some compensation, perhaps, being paid to Phrynion – but we hear nothing of this.

[26] Of these gentlemen, Satyros is otherwise unknown, but Saurias is known from an inscription to have been a victorious *chorêgos* for the tribe Erechtheis at some time around the middle of the century, and thus a rich man, and Diogeiton was a respected figure who had been a Treasurer of Athene already back in 398/7, and a trierarch in 377/6. Every time we can identify a friend or associate of Stephanos, he is revealed as well-to-do, giving the lie to Apollodoros' portrayal of him as a beggarly sycophant and pimp.

[27] Interesting evidence here that women could give evidence at arbitrations, as they could not do in court; but this may only apply, paradoxically, to non-respectable women.

[28] This is an important concession: not only is Neaira now *eleuthera*, she is to be her own *kyria*. This contrasts strangely, however, with the provisions outlined just below. In any case, as an alien, she would require a *prostatês*.

[29] Again, interesting: if Neaira possessed recognised property, she was certainly not regarded as a slave. It is hard to see what else she would have brought from Phrynion's other that what is specified here. Pots and pans?

Stephanos' sons come of age, and seem to have been accepted without demur into their phratry and deme.[30] At least Apollodoros alleges nothing to the contrary. He concentrates instead on a series of interesting scandals involving Phanô (whom he persists in alleging was formerly called Strybele, s. 50).[31]

The first one, dwelt on in ss. 50–63, is that involving the marriage of Phanô to a certain Phrastor of Aigilia, whom Apollodoros describes, with elaborate tact, as a 'labouring man, and one who had acquired his means by frugal living'. We learn also later (s. 55) that Phrastor is at war with all his relatives, so that we seem to have here a true blood-brother of the Knemon of Menander's *Dyskolos*, a cantankerous and penny-pinching small farmer (or the urban equivalent). Stephanos, it seems, managed to marry the girl off to this rather unattractive-sounding person, at the cost of providing a dowry of thirty minae.[32] The marriage, however, did not go too well – again, in a manner reminiscent of Knemon. I let Apollodoros take up the story once again (ss. 50–1):

> When she came to the house of Phrastor … she did not know how to adjust herself to his ways, but sought to emulate her mother's habits and the dissolute manner of living in her house, having, I suppose, been brought up in such licentiousness.[33] Phrastor, seeing that she was not a decent woman and that she was not minded to listen to his advice, and, further, having learned now beyond all question that she was the daughter, not of Stephanos, but of Neaira, and that he had

[30] When we meet them again, towards the end of the speech (ss. 121, 124), all we learn is that Proxenos is now dead, Ariston still alive, and a third son, named Antidorides after Stephanos' father, is well-known as a *stadion* (middle-distance) runner, which implies that his citizenship was not in question either. The fact that, even after the purging of the deme-lists which took place in 346/5, Apollodoros is unable to allege anything against the sons is proof, surely, that his allegations in s. 38 are mere mud-slinging.

[31] The significance of this is not immediately clear. It was not uncommon for a child, male or female, to begin life with a pet-name of some sort, and then assume an adult name at a later stage, usually in their teens. We do not know what 'Strybele' means, but it sounds harmless enough.

[32] This, we may note, is no petty sum. Whatever Stephanos' financial circumstances may have been in 370, when he took on Neaira, he must now have been comfortable enough. Such evidence as there is indicates that dowries represent a minimum of 5 per cent to a maximum of 20 per cent of a man's total wealth, so, even taking the maximum here, Stephanos must have at this time been worth at least two and a half talents, which makes him reasonably prosperous. As we shall see presently, he possesses a country estate (*agros*) as well as a town house.

[33] This again, despite the derogatory spin put on it by Apollodoros, is an indication that Stephanos' household was prosperous enough. Whatever Neaira's habits, she could hardly have indulged them very far if no money was coming in (Apollodoros, of course, would like to suggest that any prosperity in the Stephanos household was the result of prostitution!).

been deceived in the first place at the time of the betrothal, when he had received her as the daughter, not of Neaira, but of Stephanos by an Athenian woman, whom he had married before he lived with Neaira[34] – angered at all this and considering that he had been treated with outrage and hoodwinked, he put away the woman after living with her for about a year, she being pregnant at the time, and he refused to give back the dowry.

What happened next is remarkable. It was illegal to conduct a divorce of this kind, when no adultery is alleged, but only incompatibility, without returning the dowry. Stephanos took Phrastor to court on what was termed a *dikê sitou*, an alimony suit, to compel him either to return the dowry or to pay interest on it, by way of support; but Phrastor now turned the tables on him by preferring against him a more serious charge (a *graphê*, or public indictment), charging that Stephanos had betrothed to him the daughter of an alien, passing her off as a citizen. This was indeed a serious charge, if proven. The guilty party would suffer disfranchisement and confiscation of property, with a third of it going to the prosecutor. Faced with this, Stephanos went to arbitration, and withdrew his suit, on condition that Phrastor withdrew his, which Phrastor accordingly did.

It may seem a little odd that, if Phrastor had secure knowledge of what he was alleging, he was prepared to drop his suit. Indeed, it could be said that he was laying himself open to some danger of sycophantic prosecution himself in so doing, since declining to prosecute such a breach of Athenian law might be seen as amounting to connivance at it.[35] We may perhaps conclude from this that in fact Phrastor was less than certain about Phanô's true ancestry, but felt that it was worth chancing his arm on the basis of certain rumours that had come to his ears. In the event, he struck lucky; Stephanos backed off, and decided to cut his losses. In all this, we are once again brought face to face with the remarkable lack of documentation that attended events of basic importance in Athenian life, such as birth, marriage, and death (with its attendant problems of wills and inheritance). We will have many other occasions to reflect on this in future chapters.

---

[34] An incidental admission here, I think, by Apollodoros that there is some substance to this claim of Stephanos'. Athens was a small enough place for it to be impossible to invent a citizen wife out of the whole cloth. It would be too easy for Phrastor to check up on this. There must have been such a lady, and she was doubtless the mother of his three sons. Where Stephanos is cutting corners is in trying to pass off the daughter as hers as well.

[35] This aspect of the situation is perhaps the reason that Apollodoros specifies (s. 53) that he is summoning Phrastor as a witness to these proceedings *under duress*.

This, however, was not the end of the saga. Phrastor, it seems, fell ill (s. 55), and was like to die (in his own mind, at least):

> He got into a dreadful condition, and became utterly helpless. But there was an old quarrel between him and his own relatives, towards whom he cherished anger and hatred; and besides, he was childless. Being beguiled in his illness by the attentions of Neaira and her daughter (they went to call on him, as he was sick and had nobody to treat his illness,[36] bringing all that was needed for his sickness and taking care of him; you know yourselves, I think, how useful a woman is in times of illness as a nurse to an invalid!), he was persuaded in fact to take back and acknowledge as his son the child which the daughter of this woman Neaira had borne after she was sent away by Phrastor while she was pregnant ...

One can imagine, in fact, Phrastor sitting up in bed and making a speech of rather the same tenor as that of Knemon in the *Dyskolos* after he has been rescued from the well (ss. 711ff.). He now, from his sick-bed, tried to have his son enrolled in his phratry and into his clan, the Brytidai (s. 59). But Athens was, after all, a small town, and his phratry and clan brothers could not be ignorant of the circumstances of his recent putting away of his wife. They accordingly both turned down his application, and when he threatened to bring a case against them,[37] they countered by challenging him to take an oath that the child was legitimate. This, Apollodoros gleefully relates, he declined to do, and he had to drop the case, and with it his decision to adopt his son.[38] Shortly afterwards, we are told, on his recovery, he married a citizen wife, the daughter of Satyros of Melitê, with whom, presumably, he is still living (happily?) at the time of this trial, some fifteen years later.

Stephanos now, however, had his daughter back on his hands (and presumably a grandson, though we hear no more of him).[39] Apollodoros now embarks on a further scandalous tale involving Phanô,

---

[36] It seems strange that he did not even have a competent slave or slaves to look after him; but even if he did (and he was plainly a rather dreadful old miser, who may have economised on slaves), there is nothing like a wifely hand in such circumstances.

[37] It is not quite clear what sort of suit this can have been, since phratries and clans had no proper legal status, so he may have just brought an action for damages (*dikê blabês*).

[38] We may note that at no stage is there a specific statement of his willingness also to take back Phanô, as opposed to just adopting their son. One might feel that that was assumed, but I am not sure that it necessarily is. If he did not, however, he might have had to return at least part of the dowry, or risk another lawcase, which would not have suited him.

[39] The poor child may, indeed, have been disposed of in some way, since there is no mention of him figuring in the next attempt at marriage.

which is presumably to be dated some little time after her marriage
and divorce, the attempted blackmail and fleecing of Epainetos of
Andros (ss. 64–71). He begins as follows:

> Now observe the greed and unscrupulousness of this man Stephanos,
> and you will realise from this too that this woman Neaira is a foreigner.
> Stephanos here laid a plot against Epainetos of Andros, a long-standing
> lover of Neaira's who had spent a great deal on her,[40] and who used to
> stay with them whenever he was in Athens because of his affection for
> Neaira. Stephanos here devised a plot against him. He invited him to
> his country place[41] to take part in a sacrifice,[42] and then took him in
> adultery with the daughter of Neaira here, and by intimidation extorted
> a ransom of thirty minae.

This raises interesting points of both fact and law. As we have seen
from the unfortunate adventure of Eratosthenes, an outraged husband
or father who caught an adulterer *in flagrante delicto* had the right to
kill him, or to exact a fine (which is the option that Eratosthenes
begged for in vain, as we recall from the last chapter). Plainly, if one
agreed to a fine, and the offender did not have his cheque-book handy,
it would become necessary to confine him on the premises until he
could come up with the money. This process of confinement, however, could not go on too long, or it became 'false imprisonment' –
though it was only wise to pursue this if one could shake off the
original charge of adultery. The question therefore becomes: is
Stephanos' house a genuine household, or is it in fact a bawdy-house?

Epainetos had in fact some influential friends who were prepared
to provide sureties for him (one of them, Aristomachos, has been a
thesmothetês, that is to say, one of the six junior archons who presided
over the majority of lawcourts, while the other, Nausiphilos, was the
son of the eponymous archon for 378/7, Nausinikos), so he was not a
man easily browbeaten. As soon as he was released, he took a suit
against Stephanos for false imprisonment. He admitted that he had
slept with Phanô, but claimed that this was by arrangement with her
mother, and that he had spent much money on the whole household,
and that Phanô was in effect a prostitute.

---

[40] If this is not an empty gibe, it must presumably refer to her Corinthian days; but no
doubt Apollodoros wishes to suggest that Stephanos had been prostituting Neaira in
Athens ever since he had taken her on.

[41] This is what we must understand, I think, by the phrase *eis agron*.

[42] An invitation to take part in family sacrifices was an honour reserved for members of
the extended family and close friends only. Cf. the account in Isaeus' *On the Estate of
Ciron* (VIII), 16–17, which we will deal with presently (below, p. 52).

Once again, it seems, as in face of Phrastor, Stephanos back-pedalled and went to arbitration, accepting as arbitrators the very men who had acted as sureties for Epainetos (ss. 69–70). This was odd enough, but the outcome, as Apollodoros tells it, was even odder. After some abject pleading by Stephanos, the arbitrators arranged a settlement, according to which Epainetos agreed to contribute a thousand drachmae (or ten minae) towards a dowry for Phanô – fully a third of what was being extorted from him for adultery – on condition that he was to have the use of Phanô for the future any time he was in town (until, presumably, she might be married off again!).

It is hard to resist the feeling that there is something wrong with this story as Apollodoros tells it. If Epainetos felt that he had a good case, he should have pressed it home. Instead, he seems largely to capitulate, and ends up by remaining on (presumably) quite good terms with the man who falsely imprisoned him. We seem to be in some sort of legal and social twilight zone.[43]

At any rate, if that was the arrangement to which Epainetos came, it would seem that he did not have a chance to enjoy the fruits of it for very long; for we now come to the third scandal, which Apollodoros regards as his trump card, the Theogenes Affair (ss. 72–84). We must now be some time in the late 350s, when Neaira herself was well over forty years old. This Theogenes is described as 'a man of noble birth, but poor and inexperienced in public affairs'. He had, however, been selected by lot as *archon basileus*, or 'King-Archon', the second most senior of the archons after the *archon eponymos*. The *basileus* was the dim democratic descendant of the old kings of Athens, but his duties were at this time primarily religious. They were not, however, without importance. He presided over the Eleusinian Mysteries and the Lenaia, arranged all torch-races, and administered the majority of ancestral sacrifices. Most relevantly to the present story, however, he presided at the Anthesteria, or 'Feast of Flowers', a festival with some of the characteristics of Hallowe'en, but really celebrating the beginning of spring, held over three days in mid-February. On the middle day of this festival, the so-called *Choes*, or Feast of Pitchers, his wife, called the *basilinna*, went through a ritual wedding – a sort of

---

[43] Not least of the oddities is that no attempt seems to have been made to produce Epainetos himself as a witness. Of course, he was a foreigner from Andros, and only irregularly in town, but there was a procedure called *ekmartyria* which could have been used, according to which he could have given his evidence to a proxy witness, who could then have given evidence. Apollodoros may have felt that he would not have been a very satisfactory witness, but it inevitably casts some doubt on the whole story.

fertility rite – with the god Dionysos. Hereby hangs the tale.

Stephanos, we are told (s. 72), befriended this simple soul, supported him at his *dokimasia*, or introductory examination, and got himself appointed his *paredros*, or assessor. Each of the three chief archons, the Eponymous, the King, and the Polemarch, it should be explained, had the right to appoint two 'assessors', chosen by himself, to whom he could delegate business, and whom he could consult on knotty points of law or policy. A man like Theogenes would be sorely in need of someone so street-wise as Stephanos, and no doubt valued him greatly. One thing that an *archon basileus* needed in order to carry out his duties fully was a wife, and this, it seems, was an area in which Theogenes was deficient. Stephanos now capitalised on the relationship by betrothing to him his daughter Phanô. The marriage was duly solemnised, and Phanô became the *basilinna*.

This gives Apollodoros a chance for what he hopes will be the *coup de grâce*. He makes the most of it (s. 73):

> And this woman offered on the city's behalf the sacrifices which none may name, and saw what it was not fitting for her to see, alien as she was; and despite her character she entered where no other of the whole host of the Athenians enters save the wife of the king only; and she administered the oath to the venerable priestesses who preside over the sacrifices,[44] and was given as a bride to Dionysos; and she conducted on the city's behalf the rites which our fathers handed down, rites many and solemn and not to be named. But those things about which it is not permitted that anyone even hear, how can it be consonant with piety for a chance-comer to perform, especially a woman of her character and one who has done what she has done?

Apollodoros is able here to draw on deep-seated prejudices of the Athenian people on the matter of the proper observance of rituals, which was the chief direction that their piety took, as we shall see when we get to that subject, and he goes on in this vein for some time (ss. 74–8). We may well agree that it was a rash move by Stephanos to put his daughter in that position, if there was any cloud at all hanging over her ancestry or character.[45] But once again, the outcome is not quite what one would have expected, given the heinousness of the offence.

---

[44] The *gerarai*, or 'venerable ladies', assisted with the secret rites on the second day of the Anthesteria, and participated in other festivals also, notably the *Theoinia* and the *Iobakcheia* (s. 78). They were fourteen in number, one for each altar in the sanctuary.

[45] It would seem, indeed, from Apollodoros' evidence (s. 75), that, apart from anything else, the wife of the King-Archon should be a virgin when married to him, which Phanô could not in any case claim to be.

The trouble started when the Areopagos[46] met to conduct its normal post-mortem on the festival (s. 80). Somebody, it would seem, had tipped some members of the council off that all was not right with the wife of the *basileus*:

> When these sacred rites had taken place, and the nine archons had gone up to the Areopagos on the appointed days, the council of the Areopagos, which in other matters also is most valuable to the state in what pertains to piety, immediately undertook an enquiry as to who this wife of Theogenes was, and established the truth; and being deeply concerned for the sanctity of the rites, the council was for imposing on Theogenes the highest fine in its power, but in secret and with due regard for appearances; for they have not the power to punish any of the Athenians as they see fit.

Already Apollodoros is waffling somewhat; it may indeed be that the Areopagos had limited powers to punish a citizen, but in a case as serious as this, individual members of it, if they felt strongly on the subject, would have been able to bring an indictment of impiety (*graphê asebeias*) against Stephanos in another court, or even a public accusation (*eisangelia*) in the Assembly, but nothing of this sort was done. Nor was any move made, it would seem, against Stephanos at the scrutiny he would have had to undergo at the end of his period as *paredros*. Instead, we are told, Theogenes pleaded inexperience and ignorance of the true nature of Phanô, and promised to divorce her and to sack Stephanos as his *paredros*, both of which actions, Apollodoros tells us (s. 83), he promptly took.

But this scenario seems wildly improbable. If Theogenes and the Areopagites actually knew what Apollodoros implies they knew, it was their plain duty to proceed against Stephanos and all belonging to him in the most rigorous way. The penalties for what he is alleged to have done include death, exile, confiscation of property, and enslavement for various of the parties concerned; and yet nothing occurred but a slap on the wrist for Theogenes, and yet another divorce for Phanô. Can it actually be that all we are dealing with is a falling-out between Theogenes and Stephanos, assisted by some rumour-mongering as to Phanô's civic status and past history which had

---

[46] The most august deliberative and judicial body of the Athenian state, composed at this time of ex-archons. It mainly now acted as a court to try to certain types of murder, but, since originally it would have served as an advisory council for the King when Athens was a monarchy, we must presume that it, rather than the Assembly, now served as the proper body to conduct the usual review of the Anthesteria, since that was a festival over which the King-Archon presided.

reached Theogenes' ears?[47] It seems necessary to assume that no certain conclusions were ever reached as to Phanô's true status, or else formal prosecution on the most serious charges would surely have been inevitable.

So there matters rested, it would seem, until Apollodoros decides to take on Stephanos at the very end of the 340s, about ten years after the events last described. Neaira is growing old in respectability, her daughter Phanô approaching middle age, twice married but no longer marriageable, the sons of Stephanos long since grown – one of them, sadly, now dead, but the other two respected members of society. One would like to think that Neaira survived this assault also, but, despite the shaky nature of much of Apollodoros' evidence, the danger is that he managed to persuade the jury, particularly by the torrent of rhetoric contained in his peroration. In that case, Neaira's best option was to leave town in a hurry – perhaps back to the safety of Megara, or even Corinth, where she should have been able to live unnoticed after this period of time. At all events, Neaira's career constitutes a most valuable panorama of the various vicissitudes of fortune which could befall a girl born into the situation into which she was born. She forms a vivid real-life backdrop to the stories from Menandrian comedy that we shall proceed next to look at.

THE TWO BACCHISES

We turn now to a study of the adventures that can befall an independent courtesan, drawing primarily on a lively tale first told by Menander, in a play called The Double Deceiver (Dis Exapatôn), but now, since the original survives in only a few fragments, available to us only in the version of the Roman playwright Plautus.[48] The plot is as follows. A young man, Mnesilochus (in Plautus' version – Sostratos in Menander's original), while in Ephesus on a business errand on behalf of his father, comes upon, and falls in love with, a courtesan called Bacchis. Bacchis must still have been in some way available when he met her, but she had in fact just hired herself out for a year

---

[47] It seems almost incredible that a formal wedding ceremony, with witnesses on both sides, can have taken place without Phanô's past life becoming a matter of discussion, but there it is.
[48] Plautus certainly takes liberties with the structure of the play, changes most of the names to rather more outlandish ones, and introduces a certain amount of lively slapstick effects, but he seems not to have altered the basic plot, which is what is of concern to us.

to a soldier called Cleomachus, who is now bringing her to Athens to live with him. Mnesilochus writes urgently to his friend back in Athens, Pistoclerus (Moschos in Menander's original), asking for help. What he wants Pistoclerus to do is to call on Bacchis' sister (also called Bacchis – and, it would seem, virtually indistinguishable from the other Bacchis; such are the requirements of the plot), and contrive a way of gaining her release from the soldier. Bacchis of Athens is also anxious to protect her sister, as she explains to Pistoclerus (ll. 42ff.):

> My sister here is imploring me to find someone to stand by her, so that that soldier of hers may take her back home when she's served her time with him ... so that he mayn't just keep her here as his servant. If she only had the money to pay him back, she'd be glad to do it.

This should put us in mind of the situation that Neaira found herself in in Athens with Phrynion, though her situation was somewhat less clearcut. What the exact legal status of these contracts between a courtesan and her protector may have been is obscure to us, but they plainly held dangers for the courtesan. If all went well, one was assured of an income and a roof over one's head for the duration, but there was little, if anything, to prevent one's protector from taking advantage, and reducing one to downright slavery – unless one could somehow find another protector.[49] This is what Neaira managed to do, in the person of Stephanos, and that is what Bacchis of Athens is now endeavouring to secure for her sister.

And in fact she succeeds in this by the time we reach the end of Act IV, though not without a plethora of comical adventures. Mnesilochus comes back, planning to buy out the soldier with money bamboozled from his father; but then, wrongly assuming that his friend Pistoclerus is two-timing him with *his* Bacchis – whereas he has really come upon him canoodling with the *other* Bacchis – he gives the money back to his father, and then, when he discovers his mistake, is sadly stuck. However, with the help of his clever slave Chrysalus, and the connivance of the soldier, he manages to persuade his father that the soldier has caught him with his wife, and is now about to exercise his right of summary execution (remember the fate of Eratosthenes!), if he is not paid off. Old Nicobulus, the father, pays

[49] Some indication of the indignities that could be visited upon an *hetaira* bound in this sort of contract may be gleaned from the plot of Menander's *Perikeiromenê*, or *The Girl with her Hair Cut Short*, where the slave of the soldier Polemon finds his mistress Glykera in the arms of another, and Polemon subsequently storms in and cuts off Glykera's hair. There was no legal redress against this sort of treatment – and worse.

up the money – two hundred gold *philippi*, in Plautus' version[50] – before he discovers that he has been cruelly conned, and it takes all the wiles of both sisters to mollify him.

Behind all the comic business, though, lie the harsh realities of the life of an independent courtesan. Theirs was a precarious life, with no social safety-net, and no pension. One had to live by one's wits, playing off one admirer against another, and trying to put a little by, in the way of trinkets or hard cash, for one's old age. Naturally, courtesans are portrayed on the comic stage, as in the law-courts, as scheming, mercenary creatures, more or less devoid of higher sentiments of any kind. The average Athenian gentleman never stopped to think for a moment about why they should be like that.

THE GIRL FROM SAMOS

A rather different situation is portrayed in another play of Menander's, *The Girl from Samos*. Chrysis, a girl from Samos – as far as we can see, not a slave, but a free lady of fortune – has been taken up by a gentleman of Athens named Demeas, who has also adopted a son, Moschion (who is of legitimate Athenian birth, but originally humbler social status, as he tells us himself in the prologue). Chrysis is thus a *pallakê*, or live-in mistress, and seems to have secured a more-or-less permanent arrangement, much like that of Neaira with Stephanos (though we see from the story of the Stepmother, in the last chapter, that such arrangements could be ruthlessly terminated, and this possibility is envisaged in the play). Demeas is, however, a Nice Old Man, in New Comedy terms, and he plainly treats Chrysis with respect and affection. She is also accepted for social purposes by the family of his neighbour and friend, Nikeratos. One rule, however, Demeas has made – no children. He has taken care of his *oikos* by adopting young Moschion, and he does not want the complication of illegitimate offspring around the house. He has made it clear that, if Chrysis has the misfortune to become pregnant, she must dispose of the child.

The trouble arises because of an indiscretion on the part of Moschion, who has seduced his neighbour's daughter during an Adonis festival, got her pregnant, and now is trying to conceal the resulting

[50] A gold *philippos* was the equivalent of twenty drachmae, so that this sum – 4,000 drachmae, or forty minae – is pretty considerable, and indeed hardly credible, if we bear in mind the cost of buying an average slave (perhaps three to four minae). Even Neaira was purchasable for thirty minae, as we recall. And this was only the *balance* of the 'rent'!

child, in the interval before the two old men return from a protracted business trip to the Black Sea area. Chrysis has in fact endured a pregnancy, and her child (providentially) has died, so she has decently agreed to take on the baby of Plangon, the girl next door, even though she knows that no children are allowed. Meanwhile, the two fathers have agreed to cement their friendship by arranging a marriage between Moschion and Plangon.

When Demeas returns, he overhears, and, excusably, misunderstands, a reference by Moschion's old nurse to 'Moschion's son', and then sees Chrysis suckling a baby (ll. 220 ff.), and flies into a rage, assuming that, not only has Chrysis had a baby, but she has had it by Moschion. For this, he blames Chrysis, not Moschion, assuming that, courtesan that she is, *she* has seduced *him*. He orders her out of the house, though granting her her trousseau and some servants (ll. 380–2). He then comments savagely on what her future career is likely to be:

> A fine figure *you* make! Once you're on the town, you'll very quickly find your true value. Other girls, Chrysis, to earn ten drachmae run off to dinner parties, and swallow strong drink until they die; or they starve, if they're not prepared to do this and do it smartly. You'll learn the hard way, like everyone else. And you'll realise what a stupid mistake you've made.

The miserable existence of an ordinary prostitute is held up before her, analogous to the role which Neaira found herself playing while she was with Phrynion. What the ten drachmae mentioned would be for is not specified, but it sounds like a fee for an evening's 'entertainment'. If so, it is not that bad, but admittedly very wearing on the health, as Demeas suggests – and, of course, extremely precarious.

Of course, this is comedy and not real life, so all ends happily, but the spectre of being put out on the streets remains. Demeas, on finding out the truth, takes back Chrysis on the same terms as before, and indeed is prepared to defend her against his friend Nikeratos, a more choleric old man, who is now enraged in turn, and wants to bully her into telling him the truth about the baby (ll. 557ff.). He stops him with the significant remark: 'You're taking a stick to a free woman, and pursuing her!' Chrysis cannot be treated like a slave, but her rights are very limited, and there is always the danger that she can be enslaved if she cannot find a protector to take her part.

SOME GREAT LADIES

Fantasy, in these instances from New Comedy, follows the facts of Athenian society. A lady like Neaira, if all went well with her, could find a very satisfactory niche in society, and even perhaps a measure of true love and fidelity; but such a niche could never be more than precarious, and even though she might come to be on good terms with respectable Athenian ladies, as Chrysis plainly is in the *Girl from Samos*, she can never herself cross the bridge into respectability. She has her freedom – a freedom that many of her respectable, citizen sisters may have envied – but she is dancing always near to the abyss.

Before we leave this topic, however, we should at least take note of a class of ladies who, though in fact never themselves very far from the abyss, were yet able to carve out a very respectable living for themselves, while acquiring considerable notoriety into the bargain (indeed, it could be said that the Athenians, in a curious way, took them to their hearts!): the great courtesans of Classical Athens, such ladies as the Laises,[51] Thais, Phryne, Gnathaina – and perhaps the most remarkable of them all, the mistress of the great statesman Pericles, Aspasia of Miletus. We have no surviving full-length treatment of any of them, either forensic or dramatic,[52] on which to base ourselves, but we do have considerable portions of a remarkable work by the early Hellenistic (mid-third century) comic playwright Machon, called the *Chreiai* ('Anecdotes', or 'Memorable Sayings'), retailing, in iambic verse, a selection of the witty remarks and notable doings of the great courtesans and parasites of Athens in the previous century.[53] These ladies, and others, consorted with the highest in the land, statesmen, poets, generals, and even kings, and could give as good as, and better than, they got in repartee with any of these, while collecting

---

[51] There were actually two Laises, Lais the Elder, originally from Corinth, who was active in Athens in the last decades of the fifth century, and died in 392, and Lais the Younger, from Hykkara in Sicily, daughter of one Timandra, a companion of Alkibiades, who 'flourished' in the early fourth century.

[52] Though we have record of Socratic dialogues entitled *Aspasia* by both Antisthenes and Aeschines of Sphettus, and Plato's Socrates likes to maintain the conceit that Aspasia is his instructress in rhetoric and other forms of wisdom (e.g. *Menexenus* 235E). A number of Middle Comedies bear the names of famous courtesans (e.g. Menander's *Thais*, Eubulus' *Nannion*, or the *Neaira* of Timocles – possibly about 'our' Neaira!), but they have not survived.

[53] Fully 462 verses of this are preserved by Athenaeus of Naucratis in Book 13 of his *Deipnosophistai*, or *Doctors at Dinner*. They have been given a modern edition by A. S. F. Gow, *Machon*, Cambridge, 1965. Machon, it may be noted, does not deal with Aspasia, but he celebrates all the others mentioned. Apart from this work of Machon's, there were various Hellenistic authors, such as Apollodorus and Callistratus (both only known to us through being quoted by Athenaeus), who wrote treatises *On Courtesans*.

sufficient sums to see them through their retirement from all of them.

Many of the stories are either too raunchy or too linguistically complex[54] to be relayed here, but a few may be told. Gnathaina, for instance, had a special relationship with the distinguished playwright of New Comedy, Diphilos of Sinope, who flourished in Athens in the last decades of the fourth century, and this lends itself to a certain amount of repartee. Here is Machon:[55]

> On one occasion Diphilos was invited to Gnathaina's to dine, so they say, in celebration of the festival of Aphrodite [*Aphrodisia*].[56] He, who was the most honoured of all her lovers (and who much enjoyed her passionate love for him), came with two jars of Chian wine, four of Thasian, perfume, wreaths, nuts and raisins, a kid, ribbons, relishes, a cook, and, on top of all that, a flute-girl.[57] Now it happened that another of her lovers, a Syrian gentleman, had sent her some snow and a *saperda*.[58] She, being rather embarrassed lest anyone should learn of these gifts, and especially fearing that Diphilos might punish her by putting her in one of his comedies, ordered the dried fish to be quickly taken away and given to those in need of a dinner, but the snow she ordered to be secretly sprinkled into the unmixed wine; then she ordered the slave to pour out about a pint and offer the cup to Diphilos. Delighted, Diphilos quickly drained the cup, and, astonished by the remarkable state of the wine, cried, 'By Athena and all the gods, Gnathaina, you manage to keep your wine remarkably cold!' To which she replied: 'Yes, my dear, we always take care to pour in a few of your prologues.'[59]

Gnathaina was plainly a familiar figure in Athenian society towards the end of the fourth century, as the great ladies Lais, Phryne, and Nannion had been before her. We see her here presiding in considerable state, in receipt of presents and other contributions from her various admirers, but possessing herself a comfortable establishment, with domestic help, in which to receive them. However, to stay in

---

[54] The Greeks were great lovers of word-play in their jokes, making for much tedious footnoting in modern versions, by which time the joke has largely congealed!

[55] Ap. Athenaeus, *Deipn.* XIII 579e–580a. This passage gives us incidentally a fine picture of the sort of state in which these grand ladies ran their salons.

[56] This is probably not an Athenian civic festival, but rather a function of a *thiasos*, or cult-association, of Aphrodite Ourania, to which courtesans would have belonged.

[57] Considering what flute-girls were usually employed for at Athenian symposia, this seems somewhat superfluous, but perhaps she really was there to play the flute.

[58] This is a kind of sea-perch, which the Athenians liked to eat salted.

[59] Even this, alas, requires a footnote: *psykhros*, 'cold', can also mean 'frigid'. Diphilos, though a very successful playwright, seems to have been noted for the frigidity of his prologues.

business one had to indulge in more straightforward transactions. Another of Machon's anecdotes[60] introduces us to a protégée of hers called Gnathainion (described as her 'grand-daughter', but possibly only in the same way that Neaira was initially presented to customers as Nikaretê's 'daughter') who became quite a figure in her own right, and plainly contributed to keeping Gnathaina, in her later years, in the style to which she was accustomed:

> A stranger came to live in Athens, a very ancient nabob [*satrapês*] – aged about ninety – and at the festival of the Kronia he saw Gnathainion with Gnathaina leaving the temple of Aphrodite. Admiring the curves of her figure, he asked how much she charged as a fee for the night. Gnathaina, with an eye on his purple cloak and weaponry, stated a fee of a thousand drachmae.[61] But he, struck a body-blow by this, exclaimed, 'Good God, woman, you are holding me to ransom, because of my martial accoutrements! Come now, let's make a truce – take five minae,[62] and spread a couch for us inside.' And she, since the nabob was so eager to show his capacities, took him up on this, saying: 'To me, Father, you may give as much as you like; for I know well, and indeed am convinced, that in the night you will give the double of it [*diploun*] to my little daughter.'[63]

Book XIII of Athenaeus is replete with further stories of Athenian ladies of the night. Their relations not only with actors and playwrights, artisans and businessmen, but also with distinguished statesmen and generals,[64] and even Hellenistic kings, seem to have been common knowledge, and hardly matters of moral disapproval – except for the expense sometimes involved!

And so, with these few sketches of life at the top of the world of courtesans, we may bid farewell to this topic.

---

[60] Ap. Athenaeus, *Deipn.* XIII 581a–c. The *satrapês* of the story seems to be a military man from the East, of a type popular in New Comedy.

[61] An incredible sum, one would think, but we must assume that Machon thought it was minimally plausible.

[62] That is to say, half what was proposed, but still a vast sum. It seems now, however, from what follows, that the soldier is proposing that he and Gnathaina herself bed down.

[63] Once again, this requires exegesis. There is a raunchy pun on *diploun*: the implication is that, if the old nabob manages to have his way with Gnathaina in the afternoon, he will hardly manage anything with Gnathainion that night – his tool will remain doubled over!

[64] The distinguished orator Hyperides, for instance, although involved with other similar ladies, such as the notorious Myrrhine, admitted to being devoted to Phryne, and directed her defence when she was prosecuted for impiety in a most bizarre trial by a certain Euthias. He got her off partly by arranging that she expose her breasts to the jurors (Athen. *Deipn.* XIII 590de).

CHAPTER THREE

Preserving the *Oikos*:
The Woes of Inheritance

We have seen in the preceding chapters something of the importance of the family and the household in Athenian life. I now want to focus on a question of basic significance in this connection: the mechanisms for the preservation of the *oikos* or household, and the transmission of property and family identity from one generation to the next.

It was of vital importance for the preservation of the household to secure a male heir. Against the securing of such an heir, however, two chief circumstances militated. The first was the high degree of mortality characteristic of Greek life, as indeed of ancient life in general. Women frequently died in childbirth, or as a consequence of it, and many children died in infancy. As for men, they might die in war, or on a sea voyage in the course of business, or by disease.[1] Remarriage had frequently to be resorted to, and young widows who had not yet produced a suitable heir, or whose children were still minors, had to be brought under the control of another *kyrios* from within the larger family circle, or at least, if they had an heir, be entrusted to the supervision of a trustworthy family member or friend.

But here the second circumstance supervenes. Fifth- and fourth-century Athens was to a remarkable extent a society without secure methods of record-keeping – an oral rather than a documentary society. Probably most adult male citizens were literate, but, as we have seen in the case of Neaira, records concerning such basic events as birth, marriage and death were simply not, as a general rule, kept. For all these key events of one's life one needs to have living witnesses, whom one (or one's father) was careful to invite along in the

---

[1] Accurate statistics on life expectancy in fifth- and fourth-century Athens are of course well beyond our reach, but there is an interesting calculation reported by A. H. M. Jones in his most useful little book, *Athenian Democracy*, p. 82, which indicates that, by the age of forty, only 40 per cent of a given age cohort of males would be still alive, and by sixty only 20 per cent. This is based on the observation that , in around 330 BC, a list of ephebes (i.e. young men of 18–19), numbered about 500, whereas, in 325/4, a list of citizens of hoplite class aged 60 numbered just 105. This is not much to go on, certainly, but the resulting calculation seems plausible enough.

first place, and who will now be ready to step forward to testify in open court. If the event concerned happened a long time ago, it may prove very difficult to assemble the necessary witnesses, and other convoluted arguments, often based on mere probability, must be resorted to. We do have a certain amount of evidence that wills were composed and preserved, but again and again, when it seems obvious to us that all that is needed to settle a given dispute is that the will be produced, this is not available. The will is lost, or it is in the hands of someone who will not hand it over, and one must still resort to witnesses. Indeed, one is driven to the conclusion that, even in the fourth century, Athens is still a society where oral testimony is primary, and documents, even when produced, are regarded as no more than a back-up to this necessary means of support. As for such things as birth certificates, or marriage certificates, preserved in some public, impartial, and freely accessible place – we must dismiss the idea from our minds. Here one's only hope is the freely contributed witness of friends, or alternatively the forced testimony of slaves.[2]

THE HEIRS OF KIRON

To illustrate the problems attendant on securing the succession to an estate if things become complicated by premature death or deaths, I want first to look at a case taken by the greatest of probate lawyers of the earlier fourth century, the orator Isaios, himself the teacher of the greatest of all Athenian orators, both political and forensic, Demosthenes, to whose inheritance troubles we will turn after that.

This case concerns a rich old man by the name of Kiron, of the deme of Phlya.[3] Kiron had married as his first wife his own first cousin, daughter of an aunt, and by her he had one daughter. Then this lady

---

[2] This question, to which we shall return in connection with our discussion of the position of slaves in general, is a rather unpleasant subject. Slaves, in Athenian law, could only give evidence under torture, in accordance with a convoluted line of reasoning which reckoned that only under torture would any evidence they might give against their masters be reliable. However, an odd feature of the surviving legal evidence is that no testimony of slaves is ever recorded in the transcript of any trial that we have (though we know of slave evidence being important in other trials, mentioned at second hand). All we hear is of the refusal of litigants to give up their slaves for torture, and much being made of that. Nor do we know how much real torture was actually applied before a slave was allowed to testify. It need not have been much more than a formality.

[3] The speech *On the Estate of Ciron* is no. VIII in the collection of Isaios' works. The standard edition is still that of W. Wyse, *The Speeches of Isaeus*, Cambridge, 1904, but it is most easily accessible in the Loeb edition of E. S. Forster, Harvard and London, 1927, whose translation I borrow. For Kiron and his connections, see J. K. Davies, *Athenian Propertied Families, 600–300 BC*, no. 8443.

died, when her daughter was only four (s. 7), and Kiron married again, having not yet secured an heir, and needing someone to look after his daughter. He married secondly the sister of a fellow-demesman called Diokles, and by her he had two sons, but, sadly, both of these sons predeceased him, presumably dying rather young.

His daughter he married off to one Nausimenes of the deme Cholargos, with a moderately generous dowry of twenty-five minae (s. 8). However, three or four years later, Nausimenes took ill and died, without producing any offspring, and so Kiron gave his daughter in marriage again, to a man whose name is unfortunately not given, but who is the father of the young man who is taking the present case, with a dowry, this time, of just a thousand drachmae, or ten minae.[4] According to the speaker (s. 43), he and his younger brother were both born after the archonship of Eukleides (403 BC), so that all these earlier events must be envisaged as taking place in the last decades of the fifth century, during the final phase of the Peloponnesian War – in which conflict, indeed, some of the male persons involved may well have died.

Kiron himself finally goes to his reward, full of years, and it is now that the problems begin. The estate is claimed by the son of Kiron's late brother (therefore, a nephew), egged on by the brother of his second wife, Diokles of Phlya (whom our speaker discerns as his real opponent), and by the speaker and his younger brother, as grandsons. The vital question emerges as being the legitimacy or otherwise of these latter two. According to the speaker's account, they had always been regarded by Kiron as members of his family:

> Kiron never offered a sacrifice without our presence; whether he was performing a great or a small sacrifice, we were always there and took part in the ceremony. And not only were we invited to such rites, but he also always took us to his country estate[5] for the Dionysia, and we always went with him to public festivals and sat at his side, and we went to his house to keep all the feast-days; and when he sacrificed to Zeus Ktesios[6] – a ceremony to which he attached a special importance, to which he admitted neither slaves nor free men outside his own family,

---

[4] Nausimenes, it seems, had died in reduced circumstances, so that Kiron had been unable to recover the original dowry (s. 8). It must have been used, rather improperly, for the day-to-day expenses of the household.

[5] I take this to be the meaning of *eis agron*. The estate, as we learn later (s. 35), was in the deme of Phlya (mod. Chalandri, north-east of Athens), and worth 'easily a talent'. The festival concerned will be the rural Dionysia, celebrated in the month Poseideion (December–January).

[6] We have met Zeus Ktesios before, in Ch. 1, p. 22.

at which he personally performed all the rites – we participated in this celebration and laid our hands with his upon the victims and placed our offerings side by side with his, and took part in all the other rites, and he prayed for our health and wealth, as he naturally would, being our grandfather. (ss. 16–17)

All this elaborate circumstantial evidence, we observe, has to be produced, and witnessed to by certain friends of the family – who, however, by the speaker's own evidence, could not have attended at least the feast of Zeus Ktesios, whatever about the other events.[7] Family friends and relatives must also be produced to attest to the legitimate marriage of the speaker's mother to Nausimenes, her first husband (ss. 11–14), and to her marriage to her second husband (ss. 18–20), in connection with which we find a further significant passage:

Now it is not only from these proofs that our mother is clearly shown to be the legitimate daughter of Kiron; but there is also the evidence of our father's conduct and the attitude adopted by the wives of his fellow-demesmen towards her. When our father took her in marriage, he gave a wedding-feast, and invited three of his friends as well as his relatives, and he gave a marriage-banquet [*gamêlia*] to members of his ward [*phrateres*] according to their statutes. Also, the wives of the demesmen afterwards chose our mother, together with the wife of Diocles of Pithus, to preside at the Thesmophoria[8] and to carry out the ceremonies jointly with her. Again, our father at our birth introduced us to his *phrateres*, having declared on oath, in accordance with the established laws, that he was introducing the children of an Athenian mother duly married; and none of the *phrateres* made any objection or disputed the truth of his statements, though they were present in large numbers and always look carefully into such matters.

This is then backed up by witnesses. It may seem remarkable that one should be driven to adducing this sort of 'proof' of legitimate marriage, instead of simply producing a marriage certificate, but this is what must happen in a society where such a thing was not conceived of.[9]

---

[7] Here is a case, by the way, where the evidence of household slaves has been demanded, but refused by the defence.

[8] The Thesmophoria, a women's festival in honour of Demeter and Persephone, was confined to legitimate citizen women, and so, *a fortiori*, was any position of authority at it.

[9] There is a nice example of the opposite argument to this in another speech of Isaios', *On the Estate of Pyrrhus* (ss. 79–80), where the speaker adduces the illegitimacy of a woman's liaison from the fact that no *gamêlia* was given to the *phrateres*, the child

Lastly, there is the evidence of what occurred at the actual funeral, which takes on a somewhat comical tone, certainly not intended (ss. 21–4):

> Furthermore, gentlemen, the conduct of Diokles on the occasion of our grandfather's death clearly shows that we were acknowledged as the grandchildren of Kiron. I presented myself, accompanied by one of my relatives, a cousin of my father,[10] to convey away the body with the intention of conducting the funeral from my own house.[11] I did not find Diokles in the house, and I entered and was prepared to remove the body, having bearers with me for this purpose. When, however, my grandfather's widow requested that the funeral should take place from that house, and declared that she would like herself to help us to lay out and deck the corpse, and entreated me and wept, I acceded to her request and went to my opponent[12] and told him, in the presence of witnesses, that I would conduct the funeral from the house of the deceased, since Diokles' sister had begged me to do so.
>
> Diokles, on hearing this, made no objection, but, asserting that he had actually bought some of the requisites for the funeral and had himself paid a deposit for the rest, demanded that I should pay him for these, and arranged to recover from me the cost of the objects for which he alleged that he had paid a deposit. Immediately afterwards, he casually remarked that Kiron had left nothing at all, although I had said not a single word about his money. Yet had I not been Kiron's grandson, he would never have made these arrangements with me, but would rather have said, 'Who are you? What right have you to carry out the burial? I do not know you: you shall not set foot in the house.' This is what he ought to have said, and what he has now instigated others to say. As it was, he said nothing of the sort, but only told me to bring the money next morning.

We have here the record of a rather undignified squabble over the old gentleman's corpse. If Diokles was to be believed (the speaker, however, just below (s. 25), reveals that the funeral expenses were

---

resulting from the union was *not* introduced to them; and that, although Pyrrhus had a fortune of three talents, which would have obliged him to entertain the wives of his fellow-demesmen to a feast on his wife's behalf at the feast of the Thesmophoria, he did not do so.

[10] Notice how one is always careful to bring at least one witness on such occasions. Our speaker could not be at all sure of the reception he would receive, and he needed this sort of insurance.

[11] This would have constituted a powerful presumption of legitimacy, and claim to inheritance, if he had been able to pull it off.

[12] This is the anonymous nephew of Kiron, his nominal rival claimant.

paid rather from the estate of the deceased, which was, in fact, considerable),[13] he had wasted no time at all in moving to take over the organisation of the funeral, and our friend, in his turn, had not been far behind him in this. As it turned out, it was just as well that he had brought witnesses (whom he is now able to call upon to testify), since when he came back the next morning with the money, Diokles had, on more mature consideration, changed his tune. Now he refused to accept the money, claiming that the expenses had been paid in the interval by the nephew, his protégé (in fact, as just stated, they were paid for out of the estate). Nevertheless, our friend, as he testifies (ss. 25–6), was not prevented from attending the funeral, which, again, he adduces as evidence that his claim to legitimacy was being tacitly accepted.

This, however, is not the end of his case, effective though it may seem. There ensues a quite extraordinary legal, or quasi-legal, argument, in which the speaker, instead of quoting chapter and verse of the relevant statute on the Law of Succession and Wills, has to resort to considerations of probability. Admittedly, he can quote some laws, but they do not seem to settle the question in all respects; a grey area is left, into which his opponent, it would seem, could insinuate himself (ss. 30–1):

> I suppose that you admit in principle as a self-evident fact that those who are descended from the same stock as Kiron are not nearer in right of succession [*ankhisteia*] than those who are descended from him. (How, indeed, could they be, since the former are collateral kinsmen [*syngeneis*], the latter lineal descendants [*ekgonoi*] of the deceased?) Since, however, even though this is so, they have the impudence to dispute my right, we will explain the point in greater detail from the actual laws.
>
> Supposing that my mother, Kiron's daughter, were still alive, and that her father had died intestate, and that my opponent were his brother and not his nephew, he would have the right to claim the daughter in marriage, but he could not claim the estate, which would go to the children born of the marriage when they had completed two years after puberty; for this is what the laws ordain. Since, then, the children, and not my opponent himself, would have become masters of her property if she were alive, it is obvious, since she is

---

[13] The details of Kiron's property and assets are given later, in s. 35. They amount to something over ninety minae, not counting considerable sums lent out at interest – not an enormous fortune, but well worth fighting for.

dead and has left children, namely, my brother and myself, that we, and not our opponents, have the right to succeed to the estate.

Is it unreasonable to characterise this argument as somewhat bizarre? Isaios is able to adduce some law here, but instead of being able to quote, say, section 10, sub-section 4: 'Inheritance rights of offspring of deceased heiress', he must resort to arguments from probability. The law dealt with some situations, it would seem, but not others.[14] To buttress his position, he adduces yet another piece of legislation (s. 32):

> This is the clear intention not only of this law but also of that dealing with the neglect of parents. For if my grandfather were alive and in want of the necessities of life, we, and not our opponent, would be liable for prosecution for neglect. For the law enjoins us to support our parents [goneis], meaning by 'parents' father, mother, grandfather and grandmother, and their father and mother, if they are still alive; for they are the source of the family, and their property is transmitted to their descendants, and so the latter are bound to support them even if they have nothing to bequeath to them. How then can it be right that, if they have nothing to leave, we should be liable to prosecution for neglecting them, yet that, if they have something to leave, our opponent should be their heir and not we? Surely that cannot be right.

Not right, indeed! This sort of argument, though, one feels should not have to be made at all. It should have been enough to prove that one is who one claims to be – and even that, as we have seen, can be difficult enough. Presumably our friend won his case (otherwise, one suspects, we would not have this speech preserved to us), but this passage, from the pen of the foremost inheritance lawyer of his age, may serve to remind us of the opportunities for mayhem inherent in the Athenian legal system.

A STORY OF A WICKED UNCLE/GRANDFATHER

Our second tale takes us into the centre of a sad little family row, but serves also to demonstrate how very convoluted Athenian family relationships could become, in the interest precisely of preserving the integrity of the oikos. This case is one of Lysias' (one of his earliest,

[14] This in spite of the fact that inheritance law was plainly quite detailed. We have, for example, from another speech of Isaios, VII: On the Estate of Apollodoros (ss. 20–2), evidence of comprehensive provision for what to do if a brother by the same father dies without issue and intestate; but in this case positive law fails him.

indeed), preserved for us, in part, only by courtesy of the first century BC literary critic and historian Dionysius of Halicarnassus, who admired Lysias' presentation of the case.[15]

The story is this, and it involves the wider stage of history to some extent. Back in 409 BC, in the latter stages of the Peloponnesian War, a prosperous Athenian called Diodotos, who had made a good deal of money in shipping, was called up for infantry duty, and felt that it would be prudent to make a will and settle his family affairs, in case anything should happen to him. About ten years before this, it would seem, when he was already wealthy, his less fortunate (or industrious) brother Diogeiton had persuaded him to marry his daughter (and thus his own niece) – to keep the family fortune firmly within the family. Of this union there had by 409 been born two sons and a daughter, of whom therefore Diogeiton was both grandfather and uncle.

Diodotos had amassed by this time a fortune of thirteen talents, a very tidy sum (ss. 5–6). He appointed his brother (and father-in-law) to take charge of his wife and daughter, and marry them off suitably with a dowry of one talent each. He also left to his wife a sum of twenty minae and thirty Cyzicene staters, and some furniture.[16]

In the event, Diodotos' fears were realised. He died in battle at Ephesus in 409, and his family was left to the tender mercies of his brother. After a certain interval, during which Diogeiton apparently concealed the fact of his brother's death from the family, the daughter was in fact married off to the prosecutor in the present case, and the mother to a man by the name of Hegemon (though with a dowry of only 5,000 drachmae – a thousand less than a talent). Diogeiton confiscated the documents listing Diodotos' assets, on the pretext that he needed them in connection with a shipping deal (s. 7). He looked after the family for eight years in all, until the elder son came of age – this would bring us down to around the turn of the century. Then he called the two boys into his presence (he had, it would seem, already married off their sister),[17] and told them that their father had left them only twenty minae and thirty staters – just the sum which Diodotos had in fact left to his wife – and since this sum was now exhausted, and he could no longer afford to keep them, he was going to have to turn them out on the street.

---

[15] It features as Speech 32 of his collected works (*Against Diogeiton*).

[16] A Cyzicene stater was worth 28 Attic drachmae, so this would amount to a further 840 drachmae. It is not quite clear why the money was conveyed in this form, but presumably it reflected what Diodotos had to hand.

[17] Presumably with the full dowry of one talent, or we would have heard about it from our speaker.

In despair, the children appealed to their mother, and she in turn brought them along to the speaker, their brother-in-law.[18] His first recourse was to convene a family council, and see to it that Diogeiton (who was naturally most unwilling) gave an account of himself to it. Now fortunately, in one of the house moves to which they had been subjected over the previous eight years, the boys had come upon their father's register of his assets (s. 14), which Diogeiton had mislaid, so they had an important control on him.[19] Diodotos' wife (his own daughter) is depicted by our speaker (or Lysias on his behalf) as speaking up most eloquently at this gathering (as she could not, of course, have done in open court), setting out the details of the assets left by Diodotos, and excoriating him for his heartlessness and dishonesty (ss. 15–17). Faced with these revelations, Diogeiton resorted to some highly creative accounting – which incidentally provides us with some rather interesting data as to what various aspects of daily life might be supposed to cost. Diogeiton has to try to come up with an account of how he got through a sum of eight talents and one thousand drachmae[20] for the upkeep of two boys and a girl over a period of eight years. It is worth looking at this masterpiece of calculation in some detail:

> Such is his shamelessness that, not knowing under what headings to enter the sum spent, he reckoned for food for two young boys and their sister five obols a day;[21] for shoes, laundry and hairdressing he kept no monthly or yearly account, but he shows it inclusively, for the whole period, as more than a talent of silver.[22] For their father's tomb, though he did not spend twenty-five minae of the five thousand drachmae declared, he charges half this sum to himself, and

[18] Why not to her husband Hegemon, one might ask? Perhaps because he was something of a crony of Diogeiton's, but perhaps because it was she and not he who was directly wronged.

[19] Note once again how precarious was the life of documents in Classical Athens. There was no official repository where such essential documents as this could be deposited, and the sons might very well have had no access to it, but would have had to have recourse to demanding a copy from Diogeiton, who might very well have pretended to have lost it. We shall see shortly that Demosthenes had just such a problem with his father's will, which was in the hands of his guardian Aphobos.

[20] This sum only covers the money that had been out in loans and recoverable in 409 BC, not the five talents in cash that Diodotos left on his death. This seems to be quietly forgotten.

[21] Since it is generally reckoned that an adult could feed himself on an obol a day (cf. Lysias, XXIV 13), this charge for three young children was about twice too high – a pattern which will be seen to recur!

[22] It is harder to estimate the unreasonableness of this – though we may reckon from its being mentioned that it *was* unreasonable. This would work out at 250 drachmae a year for eight years for each of the children, which does indeed seem excessive.

has entered half against them.[23] Then for the Dionysia, gentlemen of the jury – I do not think it irrelevant to mention this also – he entered sixteen drachmae as the price of a lamb, and charged eight of these drachmae to the children; this entry especially roused our anger.[24] And so it is, gentlemen: in the midst of heavy losses the sufferers of wrong are sometimes wounded as much by little things; for they expose in so very clear a light the wickedness of the wrongdoer.

Our speaker goes on (s. 22) to detail a further four thousand drachmae charged up to expenditure on festivals and sacrifices, before revealing the unkindest cut of all (s. 24):

> Most monstrous of all, gentlemen of the jury, he asserts that in sharing with Alexis, son of Aristodikos, the service of equipping a warship, he paid a contribution of forty-eight minae, and has entered half of this against these orphan children, whom the state has not only exempted during their childhood, but has freed from all public services [*leitourgiai*] for a year after they have been certified to be of age.

Our speaker reveals just below (s. 26) that, on top of this, he went along and asked Alexis' brother, Aristodikos (Alexis himself being dead) if he could check the records of this transaction, and discovered that the whole cost of the trierarchy to both of them was only forty-eight minae, so that in fact Diogeiton had charged the whole cost of the liturgy to the children.

All these sums, most interesting in themselves, provide a fairly comprehensive conspectus of the ways in which dishonest and rapacious guardians could rip off their charges. They also give some indication of the ways in which an honest guardian could look out for the property of his ward or wards. The simplest course of action was to take the ward into one's own household, and let whatever property there was (which might consist of, say, a town-house, a farm, and even a factory or two) to the highest bidder. Ideally, the income from such assets could pay for the day-to-day expenses of the ward, leaving such capital assets as there were to be put out as loans, the interest on which could be added to the capital. These are the sort of calculations we will see Demosthenes making in our next case-history. The loans, of course, should be prudent; investment in shipping enterprises, for example, should be strenuously avoided. A

---

[23] That is, the children paid the whole bill, since 25 minae is half of 5,000 drachmae.

[24] There are two grounds of grievance here: first, that the price of a lamb for sacrifice will have been only eight drachmae in the first place; and secondly, that orphans were not in any case liable for contributions to state festivals.

final example of skulduggery on the part of Diogeiton shows him contravening this rule (s. 25):

> Again, he dispatched to the Adriatic a cargo of two talents' value, and told their mother, at the moment of its sailing, that it was at the risk of the children; but when it went safely through and the value was doubled, he declared that the venture was his.

This was the ancient equivalent of investing in mining or information technology shares. It was, admittedly, how Diodotos had made most of his money in the first place, but as a way of investing the assets of widows and orphans it was simply not on.

It was fortunate indeed for the orphan boys that their sister had been married off to a young man of integrity and competence, and that he was in a position to engage Lysias as a speech-writer. We presume he won his case (otherwise we would hardly be hearing of it). But did he recover any or all of the money? That is unfortunately another matter, as we shall see in the case of Demosthenes.

THE SORROWS OF YOUNG DEMOSTHENES

Our next case-history concerns a pupil of Isaios (indeed, by far his most distinguished pupil), and one who became his pupil precisely because of his problems of inheritance.[25] At some time in the year 377 BC, Demosthenes of Paiania, a prosperous businessman and property-owner, father of the future orator and statesman Demosthenes, came to die. When it became plain to him that he was not going to recover, he acted with the prudence befitting the head of a household and owner of a respectable fortune, and summoned a small group to his bedside to witness, and subsequently administer, his testamentary dispositions.

This group comprised two nephews of his, Aphobos and Demophon (the former a son of his sister, the latter of his brother Demon), and an old friend (as he thought) and fellow-demesman Therippides.[26] To each of these he made generous bequests, designed to bind them by ties of gratitude, and also enjoined his two nephews

---

[25] The story is told, in some detail, in a series of three speeches of Demosthenes *Against Aphobos* (Orations XXVII–XXIX of his corpus), and two *Against Onetor* (XXX–XXXI). On Demosthenes' family in general, see J. K. Davies, *Athenian Propertied Families*, no. 3597; on Aphobos in particular, see ss. V to X of that entry.

[26] He also, as emerges later (*Against Aphobos* II 15), asked his brother Demon to sit in, as a further witness, though not himself a trustee. This, alas, did no good, as Demon became part of the conspiracy.

to take charge of the women of his household (*Against Aphobos* I 4–5). To Demophon he gave his daughter, to be married when she came of age (she was then only five), with a (generous) dowry of two talents, and to Aphobos his wife, with a dowry of 80 minae, and the right to make use of the house and furniture. Therippides, not being a member of the family, simply received the right to derive interest from 70 minae of the property, until young Demosthenes should come of age (he was at this time only seven).

All this was, it seems, embodied in a written will, and Demosthenes is certainly in a position to present the jury with a detailed description of his father's property at the time of his death (derived from his mother's recollection), but the will itself, if still extant at the time of the trial, is not forthcoming. Aphobos declined to produce it. He had good reason, if the depredations which Demosthenes alleged against him and his confederates are in any way accurate. At s. 40 we hear:

> I think, gentlemen of the jury, that you have now been fully informed regarding the theft and wrongdoings of each of these men. You would, however, have had more exact knowledge of the matter, if they had been willing to give up to me the will [*diathêkai*] which my father left; for it contained (so my mother tells me) a statement of all the property that my father left, along with instructions regarding the funds from which these men were to take what had been given them, and regarding the letting of the property. But as it is, on my demanding it, they admit that there was a will, but they do not produce it; and they take this course because they do not want to make known the amount of the property that was left, and which they have embezzled, and to the end that they may not appear to have received their legacies – as though they would not easily be convicted by the facts themselves.

An extraordinary situation, surely. Aphobos and his cronies admit the existence of a will, but simply refuse to produce it – and there seems to be nothing in Athenian law that precisely compels them to do so, though the fact that they do not can be used against them.

The matter is brought up again in the second speech against Aphobos (II 5–6), and here the situation, as revealed, is even odder:

> Strangest of all is that, though they allege that my father would not permit them to let the property, they should never produce this will from which one could have learned the truth, and that having

abstracted so important a piece of evidence, they should expect you to believe them on their mere word. It was their duty, on the contrary, as soon as my father died, to call in a number of witnesses and to bid them seal the will, so that, in case any dispute should arise, it would have been possible to refer to the writing itself, and so learn the whole truth. But as it is, they thought proper to have some other papers sealed, in which many items of the property left were not inscribed – papers which were mere memoranda [*hypomnêmata*]; but the will itself, which gave them possession of the papers to which they affixed their seals, and all the rest of the property, and which acquitted them of all responsibility for not letting the estate, they did not seal, nor yet produce.

We learn here a further detail about testamentary practice, that, if the executors were behaving correctly, they themselves would call in further witnesses and have the will sealed in their presence – presumably so that there could be no fiddling with it later. It would seem that, instead of doing that, Demosthenes' guardians called in the witnesses for the sealing of some subsidiary papers not central to the will. Why the witnesses put up with this skulduggery is not explained. Perhaps they were suborned by Aphobos and his associates, as were various other persons who enter the story, as we shall see.

When Demosthenes came of age, in the summer of 366, he immediately instituted proceedings against his guardians, and in particular Aphobos, who seems to have been the ringleader of the fraud, and whose offence was greatest, as the management of the *oikos* had been entrusted to him. Demosthenes asserts,[27] and it is indeed highly probable, that the misbehaviour of his guardians was well known, at least among the extended family, for many years before this, and indeed various efforts had been made (notably by his mother's brother-in-law, Demochares, *Against Aphobus* I 14–15) to get Aphobos to honour his commitments. He himself had, in preparation for his great challenge, enrolled as a student, as mentioned above, with Isaios (for which course of study Aphobos was only with great difficulty prevailed upon to pay the fees!), and he had gathered his evidence together with great expertise. It took something over two years, until the autumn of 364, before the case came to trial, but before that Demosthenes had had a favourable judgement from an arbitration, which Aphobos refused to accept; so, although even now only twenty years old, he was well prepared when he finally came into court.

[27] In his speech *Against Onetor* I 6.

The depredations of the guardians were indeed grievous. If Demosthenes is reasonably accurate (and if he wasn't, then Aphobos could have produced the will to refute him), his father's estate amounted to the hefty sum of thirteen talents and forty-six minae, comprising two factories (one making swords, the other sofas), with over fifty slaves at work in them, over nine talents in cash either out on loan or on deposit in various banks, and the family home with contents, including his wife's jewellery (ss. 9–11). Of all this, Demosthenes claims, on his majority, over ten years later, his guardians only handed over to him the equivalent of a little under seventy minae – not much more than one talent.[28]

We learn something, in the course of Demosthenes' lamentations, as we did from the sad tale of the children of Diodotos, about the rights and duties of guardians. Guardianship, if entered into conscientiously, was a fairly onerous task. In general, a guardian was not meant to be at a financial loss from his guardianship. He could deduct all reasonable expenses (though he was expected to keep a proper record of these), but he was expected to administer the estate entrusted to him with all due financial prudence, which could involve the investing of moneys and the management or rental of property such as factories, mines, or houses and lands. Demosthenes offers (ss. 58–9) a few examples of good management, for the edification of the jury (there were, apparently, laws governing the administration of the property of orphans, which Demosthenes now proceeds to quote – they have not, unfortunately, survived in the text):

In the case of Antidoros, as a result of his property having been let in accordance with these laws, there were given over to him, at the end of six years, an estate of six talents and more from an original amount of three talents and three thousand drachmae; and this some of you have seen with your own eyes; for Theogenes of Probalinthos, who leased the estate, counted out that sum in the market-place. But in my case, fourteen talents in ten years, when consideration is given to the time and the terms of his lease, ought to have more than trebled.

[28] In his attempt to prove the size of his estate, in default of the production of a will, Demosthenes is constrained to employ an argument from probability (s. 7). He can show that his guardians enrolled him for tax purposes at the top 20 per cent rate, which was restricted to those with the largest fortunes, 'such as Timotheos, son of Konon' – though he does not specify for us here what that was. However, we learn later (*Against Aphobos* II 11) that this put him in the 'fifteen talent and over' class. We happen to know, also, from the speech of Lysias dealt with below (*On the Property of Aristophanes*, 40), that Konon left his son Timotheos a fortune of seventeen talents.

This parallel seems slightly askew, but it is perhaps just elliptical. There is no mention of Antidoros' guardian or guardians, only of Theogenes who rented his estate, and paid up on it so handsomely – but the honest and efficient guardians are there in the background. Not only did Aphobos do nothing to raise some interest on the property or factories; he cannot now account for more than a fraction of the principal.

In addition to his other malpractices, Aphobos, having taken his marriage-portion of eighty minae, then failed to marry Demosthenes' mother, but instead, sometime later, married the daughter of one Philonides of Melite (s. 56), in connection with which he no doubt received another dowry (though Demosthenes does not specify this), and failed to provide any maintenance for Demosthenes' mother. When he was approached on this question by Demochares of Leukonion, the husband of Demosthenes' aunt (in fact his mother's sister, as is made clear later),[29] Aphobos had presented the excuse that 'he was having a little dispute with my mother about her jewels, and that, when he had settled this matter, he would act regarding the maintenance and all else in such a way that I should have no ground for complaint' (s. 15). This, of course, he never did, and Demosthenes now reckons that Aphobos owes him, not only the principal, but interest at a drachma a month for ten years, which would amount to about three talents. As for Demophon, he has not yet married Demosthenes' sister (who would now be of marriageable age), despite his marriage-portion of two talents, and he is therefore liable for that – but Demosthenes is not primarily concerned with Demophon at the moment.

Readers will be glad to hear that Demosthenes won his case. The jury awarded him his full claim against Aphobos, which amounted to ten talents (one third of the total of which he claimed to have been defrauded by the three guardians together). The same readers will be somewhat baffled to learn, however, that he never got back more than a fraction of his money.[30] The reasons for this lie in the vagaries

---

[29] In *Against Aphobos* II 3. Demosthenes and Demochares had married the two daughters of a prosperous Athenian trader called Gylon, who had made his money in the Crimea during the Peloponnesian War, but at the end of it had fallen foul of the state through allegedly betraying the port of Nymphaeum in the Tauric Chersonese to 'the enemy'. Whatever the truth of this may have been (the 'enemy' concerned can hardly have been the Spartans, but rather the local Bosporan kingdom), Gylon was heavily fined, and judged it wise not to come home, but settled down in the Cimmerian Bosphorus and married a local heiress. He sent his daughters back to Athens, however, to find husbands.

[30] Plutarch tells us, in his *Life of Demosthenes* (ch. 6), that he recovered about a talent in all.

of Athenian law. It was one thing, in ancient Athens, to get a judgement in court (though even that was unpredictable enough); it was quite another to get it enforced, and Aphobos was plainly a very slippery customer. Already before the case came to trial, he had tried to neutralise Demosthenes by contriving a curious legal move called an *antidosis*, or challenge to an exchange of property, about which we shall hear something more in the next chapter. This arose in Athens in the context of performing *leitourgiai*, or public services (such as fitting out a trireme, or financing a chorus at the Dionysia), which constituted a form of tax on the rich. If you were assessed for a *leitourgia*, and you had reason to believe that your neighbour up the street was even wealthier than you but had not been assessed, you could publicly challenge him either to exchange properties with you, or to take on the *leitourgia*. This device, when adopted with reasonable shrewdness, was more or less guaranteed to work. No one was at all anxious to go to the trouble of exchanging properties, unless the challenge was manifestly outrageous – and there would be little sense in that, in general. However, in Aphobos' case, there were other considerations. If he could find some crony who would challenge Demosthenes to an *antidosis*, he could afford to make it worth that person's while. The idea would be that Demosthenes, who was nominally master of a large fortune, but had in fact very minimal resources to hand, would be unable to meet the challenge, and would have to accept the smaller estate. The claim to the inheritance, however, went with the estate. The crony – Aphobos chose for this role one Thrasylochos of Anagyros[31] – would then take over Demosthenes' estate, drop the claim to the inheritance (being slipped a talent or so in compensation for this), and Bob's your uncle. That was the plan, and it was not a bad one, but Demosthenes, as he tells us (II 17), frustrated it by mortgaging his whole property and scraping together the twenty minae necessary to perform the *leitourgia* (which was a trierarchy). He thus preserved his right to meet Aphobos in court.

Demosthenes does an excellent job of setting out the case against his guardians in meticulous detail, following the precepts of his master Isaios, and adding to that a good measure of the *deinotês*, or righteous indignation, for which he later became justly famous. When it became obvious to Aphobos that he was going to lose, however, he resorted to various further ruses. First, he tried to allege

---

[31] By him hangs a tale, as he was the brother of a man called Meidias, an aggressive bully with whom Demosthenes now fell into enmity, with consequences which we will learn presently (see below, Ch. 4, pp. 88–94).

that the elder Demosthenes tried to conceal his wealth (and had even buried four talents in the back garden) because he was conscious that his father-in-law Gylon was an undischarged state debtor, and that he might have inherited liability. This preposterous but embarrassing allegation, brought up as it was at the last minute (*Against Aphobos* II 1), Demosthenes has to dispose of in his second speech at the trial, and he seems to have done so successfully. Then, in a separate action, Aphobos brought a charge of false witness (*pseudomartyria*) against one of the witnesses against him at the main trial, a certain Phanos, who had testified that, at the preliminary hearing before the arbitrator,[32] Aphobos had admitted something that he later tried to deny, namely that an old and faithful slave of Demosthenes senior, one Milyas, who had risen to the position of foreman of his sword factory, had been freed by Demosthenes in his will, and was therefore now a free man, who could not be forced to give testimony under torture, as was necessary for slaves.[33] Demosthenes demolishes this desperate move also, in *Against Aphobos* III.

Aphobos had now exhausted the resources of law, but he was not finished yet. He divested himself of all his property, maliciously destroying what he could not get rid of, and decamped to Megara, where he in effect sought asylum, enrolling as a resident alien. He left behind him a considerable property, both house and lands, which Demosthenes now moved to take possession of, as was his right. However, he soon received a nasty surprise. Aphobos, as noted earlier, instead of marrying Demosthenes' mother, as was his duty (having appropriated the dowry), in 366 married a lady who is described in the earlier speeches as the daughter of Philonides,[34] but who emerges now as the sister of a man called Onetor (her father being dead). She was already married to a prosperous figure called Timokrates, but a divorce is arranged (on what grounds we are not told, but relations seem to remain perfectly amicable between all parties concerned), and she is given by her brother Onetor to Aphobos.

However, for whatever reason, the dowry (which is variously declared to be eighty minae and one talent – Onetor prevaricates on

---

[32] As we have seen already, in the case of Neaira, most legal disputes in Athens were brought first to an agreed arbitrator (*diaitêtês*), assisted by representatives of each of the parties concerned, to see if the matter at issue could be settled out of court – as it often was.

[33] This troublesome feature of Athenian law will be dwelt on again, when we come to consider the position of slaves (below, Ch. 6).

[34] *Against Aphobos* I 56; III 48 – presumably this is the same person as the sister of Onetor; otherwise the scenario becomes impossibly complicated. On the family and status of Onetor, see Davies, *Athenian Propertied Families*, no. 11473.

this question) was not in fact handed over. Instead, Timokrates, who should have returned the dowry (it being a 'no-fault' divorce) arranged to hold onto it for the moment, and instead pay Aphobos interest on it at 10 per cent (*Against Onetor* I 7). Demosthenes, of course, alleges that this was because Onetor could already see the writing on the wall as regards Aphobos' financial standing, in view of Demosthenes' impending law-case, and wished to hedge his bets. However, this sort of arrangement with dowries was not actually unusual in Athenian society, where one or another party might not have the ready money, and agreed to pay in instalments, with due interest on the remaining principal.

In this case, though, something much shiftier took place. When it became obvious that judgement was going to go against Aphobos, he went through a process of divorce with his wife,[35] which involved the return of the dowry. This took the form of mortgaging the property to Onetor, who became thus effectively its beneficial owner. When Demosthenes came to take possession of it, he found mortgage-notices (*horoi*) posted, and Onetor ordered him off.

What Demosthenes seeks now to prove – and what we may assume he succeeded in proving – was that all this was a fraud. Onetor is now claiming that he actually paid over the dowry to Aphobos, and that, consequent on the divorce, he wants his money back. Demosthenes argues, with great plausibility, that, had this been the case, such a transaction would not have taken place without the presence of witnesses, and Onetor can produce no witnesses (I 19–21). As Demosthenes tellingly remarks:

> No man, in concluding a transaction of such importance, I will not say with such a man as Aphobos, but with anyone whatever, would have acted without a witness. This is the reason why we celebrate marriage-feasts and call together our closest friends and relations, because we are dealing with no light affair, but are entrusting to the care of others the lives of our sisters and daughters, for whom we seek the greatest possible security.

This is a suitably high-minded way of putting the matter; but the fact was that one was committing large sums of money to the control of another, and such a transaction absolutely required witnesses. Note

---

[35] This took the form of an *apoleipsis*, where the wife receives permission from the archon to divorce her husband, as opposed to an *apopempsis*, where the husband 'sends away' his wife. In either case, if the wife has not been convicted of adultery, the dowry was returnable.

once again that it is not a question of written documents; what we are talking about is witnesses. And of these there were none.

There was another suspicious aspect to all this. Even after the alleged divorce, as Demosthenes can show, Aphobos both continued to farm the land in question, and even to live with his wife. Demosthenes can produce the evidence of a doctor who tended the lady during an illness after her 'divorce', and can testify that Aphobos was there by the bedside, holding her hand (I 34). So the whole thing was a put-up job, both dowry and divorce.

One would like to be able to conclude that the whole thing ended happily, but plainly this is only so up to a point. Demosthenes won his case at law, and set himself up by this effort as a successful *logographos*, or legal speech-writer, and ultimately as a politician, but such evidence as we have indicates that he only ever recovered about a tenth of the ten talents judgement that he won against Aphobos. It is possible that after this victory he settled out of court with Demophon and Therippides, but we know nothing of that.[36] All in all, this case-history, like the previous one, serves to remind us how precarious was the lot of under-age heirs and heiresses in Athenian society, in the absence of a tradition of secure legal documents.

AN UNFORTUNATE MISALLIANCE

Our next case-history concerns a marriage alliance, entered into – if we may believe the narrator of our speech – for the highest motives, but which in the event went sadly wrong. It was, of course, a major motive for arranging a marriage that one link one's *oikos* with another which would be its equal or superior in wealth and/or political influence, and that was probably the purpose of the father of the deliverer of the speech that we are about to examine: Lysias XIX, *On the Property of Aristophanes*. The story, so far as we can unravel it, is as follows.

Some five or six years before the date of the trial for which this speech was delivered, which appears to be 388 or 387 BC, the speaker's father, a gentleman of the old school, just recently dead,[37] agreed, on

---

[36] We do at least have some indication that he either restored relations, or remained on good terms, with his cousin Demon, son of Demomeles, since we observe him being employed by him in a commercial case he brought against a certain Zenothemis some years later (*Oration* XXXII), and this might suggest some satisfactory settlement with his cousin Demophon.

[37] It is a great source of frustration that we are not given the name of either this gentleman or of his son, as he was plainly a person of some consequence in the society

the plea of the distinguished Athenian general, Konon, with whom he happened to be sailing on a naval expedition round the Peloponnese in 393, during the so-called 'Corinthian War',[38] to betroth his daughter, the speaker's sister, to the son of one of Konon's trusty lieutenants, a certain Nikophemos. The young man's name was Aristophanes, and he was certainly a bright spark. His father Nikophemos had been a staff-officer of Konon's back at the disastrous battle of Aegospotami in 405, which effectively ended the Peloponnesian War. After it, Konon, though he was the only Athenian commander who had come at all well out of the engagement, judged it prudent to retire to Cyprus, where he entered the service of Evagoras, king of Salamis. In this decision he was followed by Nikophemos.

Both Konon and his lieutenant had done rather well financially over the next decade, and Konon got back into the good graces of his native city by raising a fleet, in concert with the Persian satrap of Phrygia, Pharnabazos, and thrashing the Spartan fleet at Cnidos in August 394, effectively destroying the maritime power of Sparta and loosening their hold on the Greek cities of Asia Minor and the islands. This was strictly speaking a Persian victory, but it marked the beginning of the revival of Athens as a military power, and Konon was duly honoured for it.

Konon and Nikophemos, despite their newly enhanced status in Athens, continued to base themselves in Cyprus, for reasons of either convenience or prudence, but in either case they encouraged their sons, Timotheos and Aristophanes, to set up in Athens, and to develop considerable establishments there. In the case of young Aristophanes, part of this process consisted of marrying into a good family, and, through the good offices of Konon, this was duly arranged. For Aristophanes, this would have set the ultimate seal of respectability on a career which was flourishing in all other respects. Our speaker lets fall some suggestion of this, in the process of arguing that Aristophanes did *not* in fact have a large accumulation of cash when he died.

He has just been giving an inventory of the quantity of bronze plate that Aristophanes left behind him (ss. 28–9):

---

of the late fifth and early fourth centuries. On the other hand, as his son testifies (ss. 55–7), despite his great wealth, he was a man who largely minded his own business, so we might not be that much the wiser if we did learn his name.

[38] So called because most of the fighting, between Sparta and a coalition of its former allies Thebes and Corinth with their former enemy Athens, centred round the Isthmus of Corinth, with the allies trying to confine Sparta to the Peloponnese, and the Spartans trying to break out. But there were other dimensions to the struggle, one of which, securing the support of the Persian King, becomes an issue in this story.

Perhaps to some of you, gentlemen of the jury, they appear few: but bear in mind the fact that, before Konon won his victory at sea,[39] Aristophanes had no land except a small plot [*khôridion*] at Rhamnous.[40] Now the sea-fight occurred in the archonship of Eubulides; and in four or five years it was a difficult thing, gentlemen, when he had no wealth to start with, to be twice a producer of tragedies, on his father's account as well as his own; to equip a warship for three years in succession;[41] to have been a contributor to special levies [*eisphorai*] on many occasions; to purchase a house for fifty minae;[42] and to acquire more than three hundred *plethra* of land.[43] Do you suppose that, besides doing all this, he must have left many personal effects?

Adding all this up (the *eisphorai*, we learn in s. 42, came to a further forty minae), we get a total of at least seven talents fifty minae expended in little over four years, both on building up his private fortune and on projecting his public image. And this was not the end of it. One commission that Konon had entrusted to Aristophanes in 393 was a delicate piece of diplomacy that also involved considerable expenditure – 100 minae in all. This involved leading a delegation to Dionysios I of Syracuse, who had been favouring the Spartans, to see if he could be persuaded to abandon the Spartan cause and ally himself by marriage with Evagoras of Salamis (ss. 19–20).[44] What aspect of this cost so much money is not clear – though a number of triremes would have to have been fitted out; perhaps an element of straight bribery was involved. At any rate, that added considerably to his expenses in these years.

Aristophanes, nevertheless, was plainly able to maintain a lifestyle over these years commensurate with marrying into the aristocracy, or at least *haute bourgeoisie*. Our speaker's father gave him his younger

---

[39] Namely, the Battle of Cnidos, 394 BC.

[40] A rural deme of Attica, on the coast opposite Euboea.

[41] Each of these liturgies, as we learn a little later on (s. 42) cost twenty-five minae, and the three trierarchies together cost eighty minae, so we are talking of a total of two talents ten minae on this count alone.

[42] As we have seen from the case of Stephanos (above, p. 33), one could acquire a (modest) house for as little as seven minae, so this will have been a fairly impressive residence.

[43] About 80 acres, a fairly large spread in Attic terms. As we have seen, the average Athenian gentleman would reckon to possess a country estate (*agros*) as well as a town house. We learn below (s. 42) that this estate cost him 'more than five talents'.

[44] This effort does not appear to have been entirely successful, but our speaker claims that at least 'they prevailed on Dionysios not to send some warships which he had then prepared for the Spartans.'

daughter, with a dowry of forty minae (s. 15),[45] and they had three children (s. 9).[46] But then, in 390/89, disaster struck. Nikophemos and Aristophanes became involved in a distinctly risky adventure, getting together an expedition to join their patron Evagoras in an invasion of the Persian-ruled mainland of southern Asia Minor. This had plainly been promoted strongly by Aristophanes as a sure-fire operation, which would certainly bring in rich booty. The Athenian assembly, conscious of the dire shortage of public funds, was persuaded to take the risk of antagonising Persia in pursuit of the chimera of untold riches.[47] They voted to contribute ten triremes, with their gear, if Aristophanes could come up with the funding for the crews and for a contingent of light-armed troops. Our speaker's anxiety (ss. 22–3) is to show that at this stage Aristophanes was himself quite short of ready cash, and was having to borrow from all and sundry, including his father-in-law, to put together sufficient funds for the short term; but, in one way or another, he raised the money, and the expedition sailed.

Sadly, however, things went badly wrong. The fleet never even got to Asia Minor, but was intercepted and destroyed off Rhodes by a somewhat larger Spartan fleet commanded by Agesilaos' brother Teleutias.[48] The Athenian people were so incensed at this fiasco – in spite of the fact that Aristophanes had raised most of the finance himself – that they arrested both father and son, impeached them in the assembly, and executed them summarily, with confiscation of

---

[45] This daughter, we may note, had previously been married to the speaker's cousin, Phaidros of Myrrhine (who figures in both the *Symposium* and the *Phaedrus* of Plato), who had been denounced back in 415 in connection with the scandal of the profanation of the Mysteries (for which see below, pp. 167–76), and had retired into voluntary exile. We must suppose that he returned to Athens subsequently, perhaps under an amnesty, but he may have suffered confiscation of property at the time, which might explain our speaker's cautious reference to his having been reduced to poverty 'through no fault of his own' (*ou dia kakian*, s. 15). He was presumably now dead, but his widow would necessarily be of a certain age, by Athenian standards – perhaps 25 or so? – though still, no doubt, a little younger than Aristophanes.

[46] This seems rather a lot of children to have had in the time available, but one or more of them may in fact have belonged to Phaidros.

[47] It does indeed seem a reckless enterprise to risk antagonising Persia in this way, but Nikophemos and Aristophanes, as close associates of Konon, may well have felt, in the aftermath of his treacherous imprisonment at Sardis by the satrap Tiribazos in 392, which had hastened his death in Cyprus not long afterwards, that the Persians were no longer to be trusted, and needed to be taught a lesson. The adventure was still a rash one, though.

[48] So much we seem to learn from Xenophon, *Hell.* 4, 8, 24. It is slightly troublesome that this fleet (of ten ships) is described by Xenophon as being under the command of a certain Philokrates, son of Ephialtes, and that all the ships were captured. But in fact Nikophemos and Aristophanes may not have accompanied the expedition in person; this would explain why it was so easy for the Athenians to lay their hands on them.

their property (s. 7). Our speaker does not dare to criticise this decision; he simply laments it. The problem that ensued for him and his family was that the enraged Athenian people found much less wealth on hand to be confiscated than they had anticipated, and now turned on Aristophanes' in-laws, alleging that they had somehow spirited away the bulk of his fortune. It is this unfortunate misconception that our speaker is at pains to defuse.

He was, we hope, successful in this, but that is not our primary concern in the present context. What is interesting to us here is the high-minded attitude that our speaker is concerned to project in connection with that major preoccupation of an Athenian *paterfamilias*, that his sons and daughters should marry well – which normally meant into a good family, and with the handing over of a substantial dowry. Such an ambition was by no means reprehensible, though eccentric moralists like Plato might inveigh against it.[49] Of course, it was a virtue, on occasion, if one was quite secure in one's own consciousness of wealth and status in society, to accept a wife or daughter-in-law without dowry, or marry into a poor family, if there were other considerations operative,[50] and it is this that our speaker's father would appear to have done, on a number of occasions, though not in this particular case (ss. 13–15):

> My father, finding that these people [sc. Nikophemos and Aristophanes] had been vouched for by Konon, and were of proved respectability [*epieikeis*], and – at that time at least – in the good graces of the city, was persuaded to bestow his daughter: he did not know the slander that was to follow. It was a time when anyone among you would have been happy to be connected with them – *for it was not done for the sake of money*, as you may readily judge from my father's whole life and conduct.
>
> When he was of age, he had the chance of marrying another woman with a great fortune, but he took my mother without a dowry, merely because she was the daughter of Xenophon, son of Euripides, a man not only known for his private virtues but also deemed worthy by you of holding high command, so I am told.[51] Again, my sisters he

---

[49] As in the *Statesman* 310Bff.

[50] We may recall the good-humoured protestations of Sostratos' father Kallipides in Menander's *Dyskolos* (ll. 786f.); cf. Ch. 1 above, p. 20.

[51] We know that Xenophon was general at least in 430–429 BC, since we hear of him as one of the three generals who accepted the surrender of Potidaea that winter (Thucydides *Hist.* 2, 70). He was killed the following summer, in a fight with the Chalcidians in Thrace. Our friend's father will have taken his daughter to wife some time after that, presumably.

refused to certain very wealthy men who were willing to take them
without dowries, because he judged them to be of inferior birth: he
preferred to bestow one upon Philomelos of Paeania, whom most
men regard as an honourable rather than a wealthy man, and the other
upon a man who was reduced to poverty through no fault of his own,
his nephew, Phaidros of Myrrhine, and with her a dowry of forty
minae; and later he gave her to Aristophanes with the same sum.

Besides doing this, when I could have obtained a great fortune, he
advised me to take a lesser one, so long as I felt sure of allying myself
with people of an orderly and self-restrained character [*kosmioi kai
sôphrones*]. So now I am married to the daughter of Kritodemos of
Alopeke, who was killed by the Lacedaemonians after the sea-fight at
the Hellespont.[52]

As I say, no one would have faulted his father had he gone all out
to place his sons and daughters in the most profitable matches
possible, but one could certainly claim special credit for restraint and
beneficence in this area. In this case, the speaker is concerned to
prove that his father was far from being a money-grubber, such as
might have been tempted to appropriate Aristophanes' assets, did any
survive; but his account rings true enough – though some of the
details of the advantageous matches foregone would hardly have been
susceptible of proof! Our speaker goes on to detail his father's many
contributions to the public purse over a long career of fully seventy
years (s. 60),[53] but that is not of direct concern to us in the present
context – except to show that we are dealing here with a family of
substantial inherited wealth. All that we are concerned with here is
the light which this text throws on the paramount concern of
Athenians of substance – marrying well.

WHAT'S IN A NAME?

I will close this chapter with a slightly comical, though sad, little
family conflict, that of Mantitheos with his half-brother Boiotos. The
conflict in this instance concerns, not primarily an inheritance (though
that comes into it), but a name. What seems to have happened (as
usual, we have to pick our way carefully through the narrative of the
protagonist) is the following.[54] The father of Mantitheos, Mantias, of

[52] Sc. Aegospotami, in 405.
[53] This seems almost incredible, unless in fact the whole of his life is being counted in.
[54] We have in fact two speeches, the first (Demosthenes XXXIX), probably composed
by Demosthenes himself, and delivered in 348/347 – the battle of Tamynae, part of

the deme of Thorikos, obviously (from remarks let slip in the course of the speech) a man of considerable wealth and some prominence in society,[55] though married (and having produced Mantitheos), had had a relationship with a lady named Plangon, the daughter of a certain Pamphilos, and from this relationship there had resulted at least one son, now called Boiotos. Boiotos, who has now come of age, brought a suit against Mantias, claiming that Mantias was his father, and that he was being deprived of his patrimony, and even of citizenship,[56] by not being recognised. It is not quite clear whether this other relationship took place before or after Mantias' marriage to Mantitheos' mother, and therefore whether Boiotos and his brother are older or younger than Mantitheos. In any case, Mantitheos shows little embarrassment about the matter, but rather, if anything, directs an accusation of impropriety against Plangon. It was plainly, however, a matter of some embarrassment for Mantias himself,[57] and he had taken steps to resolve the situation. I give Mantitheos the floor (s. 3):[58]

> My father (for the whole truth shall be told to you, gentlemen of the jury) was apprehensive about coming to court, in case anyone, on the ground of having elsewhere received some injury from him in the course of his public life, should take the opportunity to confront him

the Euboean campaign of 348, is mentioned in s. 16 as 'recent' – concerning the name, the second (Dem. XL), probably composed by Mantitheos himself, fully eleven years later (cf. XL s. 18), concerning Mantitheos' attempt to recover his mother's dowry from the estate, which he now shared with his two half-brothers.

[55] We have some scattered indications of this: he married the daughter of one Polyaratos of Cholargos, with a dowry of one talent, which is fairly considerable (XL 7; the worthy father of the defendant in our last case-history, we may note, gave his daughter to Phaidros of Myrrhine with a dowry of forty minae), indicating that he moved in the best circles, and was worth forging a marriage alliance with); and he had some public or private business with Mytilene, which led to that city bestowing upon him a substantial present (XL 37).

[56] This latter would be the case if he had no one to introduce him to a phratry at the Apaturia, or to enrol him as a member of a deme.

[57] The situation here would seem to be analogous to that which I would postulate in the case of the father of the prosecutor in Antiphon's *Against the Stepmother*, where I suspect that the young man is actually the (legally acknowledged) son of a union with a citizen mistress. This would assume, I think, that Plangon was one of those little-mentioned figures, a citizen girl who was down on her luck, either through having been disgraced in some way, or simply through lacking a dowry on the strength of which to get married. In Plangon's case, as we learn in the second speech (s. 20), the problem was that her father had died owing a sum of five talents to the Treasury (for whatever reason), and thus there was plainly no money for dowries. Such girls as Plangon were vulnerable to being exploited as mistresses, but their offspring could aspire to recognition and citizenship – unlike, say, those of such a figure as Neaira, or Chrysis, the Girl from Samos.

[58] I borrow here the Loeb translation of A. T. Murray, with some alterations.

in this connection;[59] and at the same time was deceived by this man's mother. For she had sworn that if he should tender her an oath concerning this matter, she would refuse it, and that, when this had been done, all relations between them would be at an end, and that a deposit of money would be made to a third party on her behalf.

That is to say, Plangon was to be bought off.[60] But in the event – perhaps having had her resolve stiffened by her offspring – she declined to be bought off. When Mantias tendered the oath, she unexpectedly accepted it, and swore that both Boiotos and another son of hers, Pamphilos, were children of Mantias. Mantias thus found himself nailed. He had no option but to adopt Boiotos and Pamphilos, and present them to his phratry as his legitimate sons. This involved, when in due course he came to die, their inheritance of equal shares with Mantitheos in his property.[61] But Boiotos was not satisfied with this triumph; his appetite was merely whetted. He now claimed to be in fact the eldest legitimate son of Mantias,[62] and this had certain interesting consequences, notably the right to be named after his paternal grandfather. When he came in due course to register with his new-found deme of Thorikos, he put down his name, not as Boiotos, but as *Mantitheos*, son of Mantias (XL 34).

The original Mantitheos was now faced with an appalling prospect: his whole identity was being filched from him. He had grown up believing that he was his father's only son, prospective head of his *oikos*; now he was faced with the prospect of not even being the senior among three sons, and threatened with being deprived of his

---

[59] We may gather from this that Mantias had some involvement in public life, and in the process had accumulated some enemies, personal or political. We may note in this connection the mention of a Mantias as an obnoxious politician by Plato Comicus (*Fr.* 185 Kock), but that must refer to at least some time in the first decade of the century, since he is mentioned in conjunction with the politician Agyrrhios, who was active in the years following 403, and in any case Plato did not survive much beyond 390, so, if anything, this should be a reference to Mantitheos' grandfather, rather than his father; but it would at least show a certain family tradition of 'public service'. There is also a Mantitheos mentioned in Andokides' speech *On the Mysteries* (s. 43), as being a member of the Council in 415 BC, and unjustly accused of involvement in the mutilation of the Hermae, who may be an ancestor.

[60] This tale is told again in the second speech (XL 10–11), where we learn that Plangon was offered thirty minae to drop the claim, with the understanding that she would get her brothers to adopt her sons. It is not clear from the narrative whether the money was actually paid over.

[61] We must bear in mind that in Athenian law there was no right of primogeniture; all male offspring inherited equally.

[62] He may actually have been correct in this; Mantitheos himself is studiously vague on the subject, preferring to dwell on the bogus nature of Boiotos' claims to legitimacy in the first place.

very name.[63] He had to strike back, and that is the background for the lawsuit which is the subject of the present speech. In the course of pleading his case, Mantitheos (or rather Demosthenes, on his behalf) sketches rather vividly the interesting consequences of two people, within the same *oikos*, having exactly the same name. The passage is worth quoting at some length, since it provides rather a nice conspectus of the various contexts in which an individual of some prominence would be of concern to the Athenian state (XXXIX 7–9):

> To begin with – assuming that it is better to mention public matters before private – in what way will the state give its command to us, if any duty is to be performed? The members of the tribe will, of course, nominate us in the same way as they nominate other people.[64] So they will propose the name of 'Mantitheos, son of Mantias, of Thorikos', if they are nominating someone for chorus-director [*chorêgos*] or team manager for the Games [*gymnasiarchos*] or provider of the annual tribal feast [*hestiatôr*], or for any other office. How, then, will it be made clear whether they are nominating you or me? You will say it is I; I shall say it is you.
>
> Well, suppose that, consequent upon this, we are summoned by the Archon, or by any other magistrate before whom the case comes up. We do not answer the summons; we do not undertake the liturgy. Which of us is then liable to the penalties provided by law? And how will the generals enter our names, if they are enrolling people in a tax company [*symmoria*],[65] or if they are appointing a trierarch? Or, if there is to be a military expedition, how will it be made clear which of us is on the muster-roll?
>
> Or again, if any other magistrate, the Archon, the King,[66] the Stewards of the Games [*athlothetai*], makes an appointment for some liturgy, what sign will there be to indicate which of us they are appointing? Are they, in God's name, to add the designation 'son of Plangon', if they are entering your name, or add the name of my mother if they are entering mine?[67] But who ever heard of such a thing? Or by what law

[63] That Boiotos had some success with his bold attempt at usurping the name is indicated by a most interesting inscription that has survived from this period, naming Mantitheos, *Mantitheos*, and Pamphilos as sons and heirs of Mantias (*Inscriptiones Graecae* II² 1622, ll. 435–43).

[64] It should be explained, perhaps, that the performance of a range of liturgies was based on nominations of rich individuals by each of the ten tribes.

[65] *Symmoriai* were groups of prominent citizens formed to spread the burden of special taxes (*eisphorai*) or certain liturgies. The chief member of each *symmoria* had the responsibility of collecting the money due from the whole group.

[66] That is, the *archôn basileus*.

[67] Mantitheos here descends deliberately into absurdity. It was not even polite to

could this special designation be appended, or anything else, except the name of the father and the deme?

Mantitheos is milking this situation to the last drop. He goes on some way farther, imagining the two of them being elected to various public offices, or being chosen for jury duty, or being summoned to court – this last a particular problem, he suggests, as Boiotos is both disreputable and litigious!

It is not absolutely clear that Mantitheos won his case. One may take refuge in the (slightly shaky) assumption that forensic speeches which survive to be published were successful, but there is the troublesome evidence of the inscription mentioned above (n. 63) – though that may well have preceded this case; and then there is the apparent fact that Boiotos, despite whatever judgement may have been given here, went on calling himself Mantitheos, to the extent that he actually rejected a later summons laid against him by Mantitheos on the grounds that his name was not Boiotos, but Mantitheos (XL 34).

Legal battles between the two half-brothers continued for at least eleven years after this initial trial, with Boiotos either ignoring judgements registered against him, or wriggling out of them on technicalities (as in the instance of the name, just mentioned). The later subject of dispute concerned Mantitheos' attempt to recover the amount of his mother's dowry (one talent) from the common inheritance, on the ground that that belonged exclusively to him. He seems ultimately to have won that point, despite Boiotos' brazenly lodging a counter-claim (XL 20) for *his* mother's dowry, which he claimed to have been 100 minae! Whether Mantitheos ever recovered the money, however, we cannot be sure; for that, in the absence of any enforcement mechanism on the part of the state, he would have needed powerful friends. But that brings us to the subject of the next chapter.

---

mention the name of a respectable woman in public – that is why he goes out of his way to name Plangon – never mind cite her name as part of an official designation.

CHAPTER FOUR

The Best of Enemies: Patterns of Friendship and Enmity

We have observed in the previous chapter how comprehensively, in a society with a fairly rudimentary legal system, a dearth of written records, and minimal law enforcement procedures, one is dependent upon one's relations and friends. If you lack friends, or they let you down, then your position is perilous indeed. It is not surprising, therefore, that the theory and practice of friendship attracted a good deal of attention from among Athens' more thoughtful citizens. The flip side of the question, so to speak, is the accumulation of enemies, and how to deal with them. Athenians took their enmities seriously, as they did their friendships, and quite a proportion of the law cases that have come down to us are prompted ultimately by this motive. It was the unquestioned aim of any red-blooded Athenian to be 'a joy to his friends and a misery to his enemies', and his corresponding fear to be the reverse.

What I propose to do in this chapter is, first, to look at a number of texts which concern themselves with the topic of friendship, from Xenophon, Plato and Aristotle, and then to turn to two fine case-histories of enmity, the first in the shape of Demosthenes' encounter with Meidias – an enmity he had contracted from his battle with his guardians, related in the last chapter; the second a sorry tale involving Apollodoros, son of Pasion, the prosecutor of Stephanos and Neaira in Chapter 2. Between them they illustrate most of the twists and turns that a good Athenian enmity can take.

XENOPHON ON FRIENDSHIP

The Athenian gentleman adventurer Xenophon, in his *Memoirs of Socrates* (to whose outer circle, at least, he belonged in the last years and immediate aftermath of the Peloponnesian War), presents us with a Socrates very different from that of his slightly younger contemporary Plato, but one rather more useful for our present purpose, which is to penetrate, so far as possible, the mind of the ordinary non-philosophical Athenian. Xenophon's Socrates is not entirely devoid of irony, it must be said, but he has a far more orthodox mind and set of attitudes than his counterpart in Plato's dialogues – or than, we must suspect, the 'real' Socrates. Unlike Plato's Socrates, he does not abjure all claim to positive doctrine, nor is he backward in giving advice to his friends. In Book II, chapters 4–10, of the *Memoirs*, he is presented as imparting a series of homilies on theoretical or practical aspects of friendship, which can be taken at least as representing what the thoroughly sound-minded Xenophon thought on the subject.

Xenophon begins in chapter 4 by attributing to Socrates some reflections on friendship, which Xenophon plainly thought very sound, but which seem somewhat paradoxical in an ancient Athenian context:[1]

> I once heard Socrates expressing views about friendship which I thought would be extremely helpful to anyone in the acquisition and treatment of friends. He said that although he often heard it stated that a good and sure friend was the best of all possessions, he noticed that most people gave their attention to anything rather than the acquisition of friends. He saw that they took pains to acquire houses and lands and slaves and cattle and furniture, and tried to preserve what they had; but in the case of a friend, who according to them was the greatest blessing, most of them never considered how to acquire one or how to retain those that they had.

He goes on in this vein for some time longer, but enough has been quoted to make his point plain. This, as I say, seems at first sight thoroughly paradoxical, as, from all the evidence we can muster, it was plainly a primary concern of Athenians that they should be well supplied with friends. In the sort of society which we have been examining in previous chapters it could not be otherwise. One can only conjecture that what Xenophon's Socrates is maintaining is that where most people fall down is in testing the *quality* of their friends. What Socrates appears to be advocating, in fact, is an even more pragmatic and calculating approach to the acquisition of friends than was currently practised. As things were, one made do with the friends whom ancestry or chance encounters provided, and relied upon them to come through in whatever social, legal or financial emergencies one might find oneself confronted with. As Socrates reminds us,

---

[1] I borrow here, and in subsequent extracts, the Penguin translation of Hugh Tredennick, as revised by Robin Waterfield (*Xenophon, Conversations of Socrates*, London, 1990).

a good friend sets himself to supply all his friend's deficiencies, whether of private property or of public service. If it is required to do someone a good turn, he lends vigorous support; if some fear is causing anxiety, he comes to the rescue. As the occasion demands, he shares expense, joins in action, helps to persuade, or uses compulsion; he is equally effective in cheering on the successful and in raising up those who stumble.

These various categories of help in fact cover more or less all the situations in which we have seen, or shall see, friends being of use. 'Sharing expense' will cover helping out, with an interest-free loan, in the financing of *leitourgiai* or business ventures, or perhaps providing a dowry for daughter or sister; 'joining in action', accompanying one's friend as a witness in a variety of situations;[2] 'helping to persuade' might mean acting as go-between and arranging arbitration in a dispute; and 'using compulsion' could involve, say, supporting one's friend in the enforcement of a legal judgement, where nothing was to be hoped for from any state agency.[3]

This chapter of Xenophon's work seems intended to be somehow programmatic, but the following one (II 5) develops the main theme, with what must seem to us an even crasser degree of calculation. In conversation with his senior follower Antisthenes, Socrates raises the question whether one can actually put a monetary value on friendship:[4]

'Antisthenes', he said, 'do friends have values, in the same way that domestic slaves do? For instance, one slave, I suppose, is worth two minae, and another not as much as half a mina, and another five minae and another ten minae; and they say that Nikias son of Nikeratos

---

[2] Acts such as the speaker's father is attested as performing in Lysias' speech *On the Property of Aristophanes*, treated in the last chapter. In s. 59, after detailing all the liturgies his father has performed, the speaker adds: 'In addition, he also joined privately in providing dowries for the daughters and sisters of certain needy citizens; and there were men whom he ransomed from the enemy, and others for whose funerals he provided money. He acted in this way because he conceived it to be the part of a good man to assist his friends, even if nobody was to know.'

[3] It might even stretch to assisting a friend in breaking the law. Plato, in the *Crito* (44B–C), puts into the mouth of Socrates' old friend Kriton (whom we shall meet shortly) an argument to the effect that, if Kriton does not succeed in springing Socrates from prison and smuggling him into exile, 'many persons who do not know you and me well will think I could have saved you if I had been willing to spend money, but that I would not take the trouble.' The calls of friendship could be seen, then, as taking precedence over the laws of the state – a position that provokes Socrates' famous disquisition on obedience to the laws (50A–54E).

[4] Admittedly, Xenophon tells us, this was in the context of reproving another associate whom Socrates observed to be neglecting a friend who had fallen on hard times, but it still seems unattractively calculating.

bought an overseer of his silver mine for a talent.[5] What I am trying to discover is whether friends have their values too, like domestic slaves.'

Antisthenes, who was himself something of an iconoclast, and later founder of the Cynic school (insofar as that is not a contradiction in terms!), turns out to be the right man to whom to address such an outrageous question – which is doubtless why Xenophon casts him in this role, and he quite cheerfully rises to the bait, and puts a monetary value on various candidates for his friendship. This, however, gives Socrates the lead-in to his punch-line, which consists in remarking that 'it would be well for a man to examine himself and see what he is really worth to his friends, and to try to be worth as much as possible to them, so that his friends may be less likely to let him down.'

This does raise the tone of the exchange somewhat, but it still leaves a heavy emphasis on the practical utility of friendship, and in this, I think, Xenophon is being entirely normal, from an Athenian perspective. Friendship is certainly a matter of personal compatibility, but what concerns us here is rather its practical and utilitarian aspect. This is brought out further by the next chapter of the book (II 6), which features a conversation of Socrates with Kritoboulos, son of his old friend Kriton. Socrates' questions pinpoint all the qualities that an Athenian would tend to look for in a friend:

'Tell me, Kritoboulos, if we wanted a good friend, how should we set about our search? Should we first look for a man who can control his desires for food and drink and sex and sleep and idleness? For the man who is a slave to these can't do his duty either to himself or to a friend.'

'No, of course he can't.'

'So you think that one should keep away from people who are governed by their desires?'

'Certainly.'

'Well now', said Socrates, 'if a man is extravagant and can't meet all his expenses, but is always appealing to his neighbours, and if, when he gets a loan, he can't repay it, and, when he doesn't get one, he bears a grudge against the person who refused it, don't you think that this man is a difficult sort of friend?'

'Yes, indeed.'

'So one should keep away from him too?'

'Yes, one should.'

---

[5] That is to say, sixty minae. This puts Neaira's value of thirty minae in a certain perspective, and is in general a useful passage as regards the cost of slaves.

And so we go on, through various types of self-centred pest, who are of no use to man or beast, to make the point that the type of friend to strive for is 'one who is self-disciplined with regard to physical pleasures, and who proves to be good at managing his own affairs, reliable in his dealings with others, and eager not to fall short in doing services to his benefactors, so that it is an advantage to associate with him'.

The accent here is all on utility, and understandably so. One is to scout out carefully the man who has a good track-record as a friend, and set one's sights on him. Socrates' advice for snaring a good friend is slightly more high-minded than the preceding, as it comes down to making sure that one is a good man oneself, but it also involves identifying the right things to say to, and do for, prospective friends with a view to placing them in your debt.

One other section of Book II has some relevance to our present theme, and that is chapter 9, where Socrates is found giving advice to his friend Kriton, who was a man of considerable wealth, as to how to rid himself of *sykophantai*, whose attentions he had been complaining of. 'At this very moment', he said, 'some people are bringing an action against me, not because they have any grievance against me, but because they believe that I would rather pay than have trouble.'

This was certainly a major problem for rich men in the Athenian democratic system, where prosecution on all manner of charges was left up the initiative of 'public-spirited' individuals. To counter this annoyance, Socrates advocates forming what Aristotle would call (as we shall see in a moment) an 'unequal friendship', with a poor but honest politician (*rhêtor*) called Archedemos. How did one go about this? Xenophon doesn't specify, presumably because it was fairly obvious. Kriton would simply have invited Archedemos round to his house for a chat, in the course of which he would have explained his problem. We are given Archedemos' reply to these overtures, to the effect that there was no problem: it would be very easy, in his view, to spike the guns of these fellows, by giving them a taste of their own medicine.

Xenophon now continues (II 9, 4):

So whenever Kriton was getting in crops of corn, olives, wine, wool or any other useful agricultural produce, he used to set some aside and give it to Archedemos; and whenever he made a sacrifice,[6] he invited

---

[6] Which would involve dinner, with the animal sacrificed as the main course.

him; and he showed him every consideration of this kind. Archedemos regarded Kriton's house as a haven of refuge, and treated him
with great respect. He very soon found out that the *sykophantai*
threatening Kriton were far from innocent and had enemies, and he
summoned one of them to face a public trial, where he was faced with
either physical punishment or a large fine. Since the *sykophantês* was
conscious of a good many misdeeds, he did everything he could to rid
himself of Archedemos; but Archedemos refused to be shaken off
until the man abandoned his attack on Kriton, and paid Archedemos
himself a sum of money.

This, then, is an excellent illustration of how this sort of 'friendship' – really a client–patron relationship, such as we find formalised
later in Rome, but never in Classical Athens – worked. This is
certainly one of the things that friends are for, especially if you are a
rich man of quiet and retiring disposition, such as Kriton is portrayed
as being.[7] Indeed, we are told by Xenophon that Kriton's friends
were so impressed by the value that he was getting out of
Archedemos that they all wanted to borrow him, so Archedemos
ended up in clover. And all on the basis of some sound advice from
Socrates!

PLATO ON FRIENDSHIP: EDUCATING LYSIS

What Xenophon's Socrates seems to be advocating, in sum, is putting
the acquisition of friends on something of a 'scientific' basis; it is
simply a rationalising of basic Athenian attitudes to friendship. When
we turn to examine the Socrates of Plato's early dialogue, the *Lysis*,
we actually find something not too different. The context here is
much more explicitly erotic than in the *Memoirs of Socrates* – Lysis is a
beautiful boy, and Socrates is, on the surface, instructing his admirer
Hippothales as to how best to attract him – but the conversation with
young Lysis turns to an attempt to define the essence of friendship –
or, more oddly, what it takes to be 'dear' (*philos*) to someone. With
the odder aspects of the argument we are not, happily, concerned in
the present context, interesting though they are; what concerns us

---

[7] We can see Kriton offering, at least, to perform some of the things that rich friends can
do for their poorer associates in Plato's *Apology* and *Crito*: first, to pay any fine that
Socrates might propose for himself at his trial (as a counterweight to the death
sentence proposed by the prosecution); and later, offering to spring him from prison,
necessarily by bribing the relevant officials, and set him up comfortably in exile. In
both cases, Socrates (in memorable terms) declines.

rather is the emphasis put here, once again, on *utility*.

Socrates begins his line of argument at 207D, by asking Lysis whether his father and mother love him very much. Lysis replies that they do. Starting from this point, Socrates goes on to enquire why, then, they do not allow him to do as he likes (e.g. driving one of his father's chariots), but often, indeed, subordinate him to slaves. What emerges, by a circuitous chain of reasoning, is that one will only be given consideration, and so 'loved', in so far as one proves oneself to be knowledgeable in a given area, and so, useful. At 210A–D, Socrates sums up:

> 'Then it's like this, my dear Lysis', I said. 'As regards matters of which we possess knowledge, everyone, both Greeks and foreigners, men and women, will trust them to us and we shall do what we want with them, and no one will deliberately thwart us, but we for our part shall be free in those matters and masters of other people, and those things will be our business, since we shall profit from them. Whereas, as regards matters of which we have no understanding, not only will no one trust us to do what we please in them, but everyone, not just strangers, but even our fathers and mothers and anyone closer to us than they, will do their best to thwart us, and we for our part will be subject to others in those matters, and they will not be our business, since we shall not profit from them. Do you agree that it's like that?'
>
> 'Yes.'
>
> '*Shall we be dear to anyone, and will anyone love us, in matters in which we are of no benefit?*'
>
> '*Certainly not*', he replied.
>
> 'So now, your father doesn't love you, nor yet does anyone else love anyone else, in so far as that other is useless?'
>
> 'It would appear not', he said.
>
> 'So, if you become wise, my boy, everyone will be a friend to you, everyone will be close to you, since you'll be useful and good; but if you don't, neither your father nor your mother nor your close kin nor anyone else at all will be a friend to you.' (trans. Donald Watt, my italics)

This does, admittedly, have a distinctively Socratic spin to it, on the question of the importance of knowledge and wisdom; but on the question of utility it seems to me very much in the mainstream of Greek thought.

ARISTOTLE ON FRIENDSHIP

This concept is developed, in turn, in a characteristically comprehensive way by Aristotle, in Books 8 and 9 of the *Nicomachean Ethics*. He begins his discussion of friendship with the following significant remarks (1155a5ff):

> After this the next step will be to discuss friendship; for it is a kind of virtue [*aretê*], or involves virtue, and it is also most necessary for living. Nobody, after all, would choose to live without friends, even if he had all the other good things. Indeed those who hold wealth and office and power are thought to stand in special need of friends; for what is the use of such prosperity to them if they are denied the opportunity for beneficence, which is most commonly and most commendably directed towards friends? Or how can their prosperity be guarded and preserved without friends? Because the greater it is, the more precarious.[8] In poverty too and all the other misfortunes of life people regard their friends as their only refuge.

Aristotle goes on (8. 3, 1156a6ff.) to distinguish three types of friendship, that based on utility, that based on pleasure, and the highest, which is based on the good – that is, the mutual appreciation of goodness. With this highest kind, admirable though it is, we are not concerned in the present context, since it rather transcends the bounds of popular morality. Let us take a closer look, on the other hand, at the two lower ones.

First, that based on utility:

> 'Utility', reflects Aristotle, 'is not a lasting thing: it takes on a succession of guises. So with the disappearance of the ground for friendship, the friendship also breaks up, because the friendship was related to that. Friendships of this kind seem to occur most frequently between the elderly (because at their age what they are in pursuit of is not pleasure but utility), and those in middle or early life who are pursuing their own advantage. Such persons do not spend much time together, because sometimes they do not even like one another, and therefore feel no need of such an association unless they are mutually useful. For they take pleasure in each other's company only in so far as they have hopes of advantage from it. Friendships with foreigners are generally included in this class.'

---

[8] Cf. Xenophon, *Memoirs of Socrates* II 9, quoted above.

This is a common enough type of 'friendship' even now – a business relationship that may be pursued as far as the golf course or the squash court, and into the bar afterwards, but rarely as far as the home, except for strictly 'business' cocktail parties. In Classical Athens, though, as we have seen, and will see again, a network of such friendships was that much more important than nowadays simply because of the lack of policing, the vagaries of the lawcourts, and the minimal preservation of written records.

The consideration of friendships based on pleasure is less important for our purposes, but we may note Aristotle's characterisation of it, if only to admire the acuteness of his observation, which is just as apposite to the present day as to fourth-century Athens (1156a31–b6):

> Friendship between the young is thought to be grounded on pleasure, because the lives of the young are regulated by their feelings, and their chief interest is in their own pleasure and the opportunity of the moment. With advancing years, however, their tastes change too, so they are quick to make and to break friendships; because their affection changes just as the things that please them do, and this sort of pleasure changes rapidly. Also, the young are apt to fall in love, for erotic friendship is for the most part swayed by the feelings and based on pleasure. That is why they fall in and out of friendship quickly, changing their attitude often within the same day. But the young do like to spend the day and live together, because that is how they realise the object of their pleasure.

These reflections may seem rather stuffy and middle-aged, but they are surely also based on close analytic observation of the Classical Athenian teenage scene. Aristotle was a great observer of natural phenomena. On the other hand, not many Athenian teenagers are going to be figuring in these pages, so, as I say, their relevance is somewhat limited. If one extends the age-limit, however, to the early twenties, we will be observing a number of examples of such friendships, both real and fictional.

We may cast our minds back, first of all, to the friendship of Sostratos and Chaireas in Menander's play The Grouch. That is partly based on utility, no doubt, particularly in Chaireas' case, but it is plainly also based on real affection. Then we may recall those two young men about Corinth, Timanoridas and his friend Eukrates of Leucas, who clubbed together to buy Neaira from the madam Nikaretê, and seem to have shared her amicably until they wanted to settle down and get married. Again, from the fictional world once again, we find the friends Sostratos and Moschos in Menander's play *The Double Deceiver*,[9] who, despite certain unfortunate misunderstandings, remain good friends in the end. But these drinking and whoring partnerships, as in the present day, can easily come to grief, as we shall see when we come to examine the history of Timarchos in the next chapter.

A RARE OLD ENMITY: MEIDIAS AGAINST DEMOSTHENES

However, we must turn now from friendship to its converse, the more juicy subject of enmity. The Greeks, as we know, as well as being loyal friends, were also most enthusiastic enemies. For any red-blooded Athenian, it was axiomatic that one's aim in life was to be in a position both to do good to one's friends and *evil to one's enemies*. Conversely, an outcome to be particularly dreaded was that one become a source of joy, or even ribaldry, to one's enemies.

And enemies one was more or less bound to have. Even if one did not earn them oneself, one was very likely to inherit them from one's friends and relations. We find out about enmities most particularly by reason of the fact that sooner or later, Athenians being Athenians, they find their way into the lawcourts. If we cast our minds back to the battle between Apollodoros and Stephanos in Chapter 2, we will recall that the real reason for Apollodoros' vexatious prosecution of Neaira was a long-standing enmity with Stephanos. This was ultimately political, but it had become also deeply personal. Stephanos had indicted Apollodoros for moving an illegal proposal (a *graphê paranomôn*) back in 349 BC, and tried to ruin him by demanding a monstrous fine of fifteen talents, which the jury had fortunately reduced to one talent – still a hefty enough sum. But then Stephanos had compounded the provocation by bringing a vexatious charge of murder against Apollodoros in the rather murky matter of striking a woman in the deme of Aphidna and accidentally killing her while searching for a runaway slave (*Against Neaira*, ss. 9–10), an effort which, fortunately, failed comprehensively. And now Apollodoros is striking back, as he makes no bones about admitting (ibid. s. 16). We will come upon another instance of the same sort in the next chapter, in the attack of Aeschines on Timarchos – though in this case the real target of Aeschines' enmity lurks in the background, in the person of Demosthenes.

[9] Corresponding to Mnesilochus and Pistoclerus in Plautus' adaptation, *Bacchides*.

And it is to Demosthenes that we may now turn. A good illustration of how enmities could be acquired, and how they operated,
may be derived from the story of his encounter with a certain
Meidias. This long-running saga took its start from Demosthenes'
first major contest in life, the details of which we have followed in the
previous chapter, his battle with his guardians for the recovery of his
inheritance, back in 364 BC or so. What happened was that Meidias
and his brother had been nobbled by the ever-resourceful Aphobos,
who must have been an acquaintance of theirs, as his instruments in a
masterful wheeze to neutralise Demosthenes' law-case against him.
The idea was to get Meidias – or rather, his brother Thrasylochos – to
challenge Demosthenes to an 'exchange of property' (antidosis), that
remarkable provision of Athenian law which has been explained in
the previous chapter (above, p. 65). Normally, it would seem, this
device worked rather well, if the person challenged had indeed greater
(or even approximately equal) assets to oneself, as no one wanted to
submit to the enormous inconvenience of having to exchange one's
property, unless the advantages greatly outweighed the disadvantages.
In the present case, however, we may suspect that Aphobos had
promised to make it worth Thrasylochos' while to do this, since, as
we will recall, there was an estate of over thirteen talents at stake.
Aphobos' assumption was that Demosthenes, being a young man,
without ready access to cash, would be unable to contest the antidosis,
and have to take on Thrasylochos' property, whereat he would lose
all right to sue for the return of the inheritance which was tied to his
own property. It was a truly nasty trick. But let us permit Demosthenes to tell the tale in his own words (Against Meidias, ss. 78–9):[10]

> When I brought my action against my guardians for the recovery of
> my patrimony, being a mere lad, neither acquainted with Meidias nor
> even aware of his existence (as indeed I wish I were not now!), when
> my case was due to come on in three or four days, Meidias and his
> brother suddenly burst into my house and challenged me to take over
> their trierarchy. It was the brother, Thrasylochos, who submitted his
> name and made the challenge; but the real author of these proceed-
> ings was Meidias.
>   And first they forced the doors of the apartments, assuming that
> these became their property by the terms of their challenge;[11] next, in

---

[10] Trans. J. H. Vince, slightly altered.
[11] The property did not, of course, change hands by virtue of the challenge alone, but
Meidias and his brother assumed that young Demosthenes would not be able to come
up with the money to buy them off.

the presence of my sister, who was a young girl still living at home,[12] they used foul language such as only men of their sort would use – nothing would induce me to repeat to you some of their expressions – and they uttered unrestrained abuse of my mother and myself and all my family. But, what was more shocking still, from words they proceeded to deeds, and made clear that they were going to drop the lawsuits, claiming them as their own, to oblige my guardians.

In the event, Demosthenes was able to save his property, and his right to prosecute, by scraping together the sum of twenty minae, which they claimed was the cost of their trierarchy. The brothers were forced to retreat, but Demosthenes had not finished with them. He instituted a case for *kakêgoria* (a charge covering slanderous or abusive language) against Meidias (s. 81), and since Meidias declined to contest it, gained a verdict by default.[13] This gave him power to distrain on Meidias' property, to recover the value of the fine imposed (amounting to 1,000 drachmae, cf. s. 89), but he preferred, he says, instead to institute a *dike exoulês*, an action for ejectment, to force Meidias to hand over his property.

Meidias, it seems, was able to use the legal system to avoid any final judgement in this case, though Demosthenes' narrative becomes obscure at this point. If we can trust the authenticity of the depositions of the witnesses (and they do certainly present information not derivable from the body of the text), this case had still not come to trial eight years later. Meanwhile, however, events had moved on.

We cannot, as a background to this long-running feud, ignore the broader political situation. From the mid-350s onwards, in the aftermath of the unfortunate War with the Allies, or 'Social War', of 357–355, Demosthenes came to be increasingly involved in political disputes, primarily concerning Athens' proper role in opposing various foreign enemies. His attack on the prominent politician Androtion, aired in the speeches *Against Androtion* and *Against Timocrates* (an associate of Androtion), both of 355 BC, is not strictly relevant to our theme, except as exhibiting his political activism; much more so is his increasing opposition to Euboulos (c. 405–335 BC), the dominant

---

[12] Demosthenes' sister would have been fifteen or sixteen at this time, and of marriageable age by Greek standards (though doubtless not yet used to bad language!). Her betrothal to one of the guardians, her cousin Demophon, had plainly come to nothing.

[13] It emerges from the subsequent narrative (ss. 83–93) that Meidias first tried to bully or bribe the arbitrator to whom this case had been entrusted by the Archon, and then, when that failed, had the man disfranchised on a technicality. This is peripheral to the main issue, but is presented as an example of his general outrageousness.

figure of the later 350s (and indeed later, down to about 342), who was pursuing a policy of caution in foreign affairs, while building up Athens' financial position at home. Euboulos' power-base was his control (as Commissioner) of the so-called 'Theoric Fund', the surplus in state revenues, which in peace-time could be devoted to a form of social welfare, involving the distribution of a dole of three obols a day to any citizen who proposed to attend any of the major state festivals. It was this Fund on which more aggressive warriors like Demosthenes set their sights, in order to finance military expeditions against Philip of Macedon, in particular to defend the Thracian Chersonese and the cities of Chalcidike from Philip's aggression. The difficulty, however, was that Euboulos had put in place legislation making it illegal to propose the diversion of the Theoric Fund to military purposes in any contingency short of a full-scale declaration of war; and that made life very difficult for Demosthenes and his associates.

Meidias was by this time a prominent supporter of the policy of Euboulos, and this added sharpness to the edge of Demosthenes' hatred of him. However, aggravation on the personal level was not lacking. At some stage during the 350s, Demosthenes tells us (ss. 103–5), Meidias, while still under the threat of prosecution on the ejectment suit, launched a number of strikes, designed to incapacitate Demosthenes, or at least get him off his back. First

> he trumped up a charge of desertion [graphê lipotaxiou] against me, and bribed someone else to bring the action – a scoundrel ready for any dirty job, the filthy Euktemon. That blackmailer [sykophantês], admittedly, never moved for a trial, nor in fact had Meidias hired him for any other reason than to have this notice posted up before the Tribal Heroes[14] for all men to read: 'Euktemon of Lousion has indicted Demosthenes of Paiania for desertion.' Indeed, I think he would have been delighted, if it had been in order, to add that Meidias had hired him to indict me.

This charge, Demosthenes goes on to say, was not followed up, which resulted in Euktemon's disfranchisement (atimia). It certainly seems a wild and intemperate course of action on the part of Euktemon, but Demosthenes could hardly have told the story without any basis in fact, as the facts would be widely known. We must assume that Meidias somehow (presumably monetarily) made it worth the wretched fellow's while. Hardly less odd is the next incident, which once again involves Meidias trying to put a stooge up to harass

---

[14] The stoa of the eponymous heroes of the Attic tribes, in whose shrine in the market-place one posted notice of intention to prosecute.

Demosthenes. A certain Aristarchos had murdered another Athenian, named Nikodemos. Meidias tried to bribe the next of kin of Niko-demos, who were preparing a charge against Aristarchos, to direct the charge of murder against Demosthenes instead. On the face of it, this was quite preposterous (though there are in fact a few things that Demosthenes is not telling us),[15] but Demosthenes is able to bring on the kinsmen concerned, who indignantly rejected the proposition, as witnesses to this (s. 107), so, once again, there must be a basis of truth in this account.

This was mere skirmishing, however. We may now at last approach the final outrage. This was an assault on Demosthenes by Meidias during the Greater Dionysia of Spring 350 BC. Once again, we may let Demosthenes tell the story in his own words (ss. 13–14):

> Two years ago,[16] the tribe of Pandionis had failed to appoint a *chorêgos*,[17] and when the Assembly met at which the law directs the archon to assign the flute-players by lot to the choruses, there was a heated discussion and mutual recrimination between the archon and the overseers of the tribe. Thereupon I came forward and volunteered to act as *chorêgos*, and at the drawing of the lots I was fortunate enough as to get first choice of a flute-player. You, Athenians, all of you, wel-comed with the utmost cordiality both these incidents – my voluntary offer[18] and my stroke of luck; and your cheers and applause expressed your approval of my conduct and your sympathy with my fortune. But there seems to have been one solitary exception, Meidias, who in his chagrin kept up a constant fire of insults, trifling or serious, through-out the whole period of my *leitourgia*.

[15] We learn from Aeschines, in his speech *Against Timarchus* (for which see the next chapter), that this lad Aristarchos was in fact a pupil or protégé of Demosthenes, who was tutoring him in rhetoric (ss. 171–2), while the murdered man, Nikodemos, was a political associate of Meidias and Euboulos. This scandal actually had quite a long tail. Aeschines brings it up again in his speech *On the Embassy* (s. 148), in 343 BC, as does the orator Deinarchos, much later, in 323, in his speech *Against Demosthenes*, arising out of the Harpalos Affair (ss. 30; 47).

[16] This speech is being composed in 348 BC, for the court case which followed on from Demosthenes' original complaint in the immediate aftermath of the festival, for which see more below.

[17] That is to say, someone prepared, as a *leitourgia*, to foot the bill for fitting out and training a chorus for one of the major festivals, in this case the City Dionysia. Each of the ten tribes needed a wealthy patron to take on this task each year, and Pandionis was Demosthenes' tribe. The *chorêgos* was not himself required to take a very active part in the process, though he could do so.

[18] This is in contrast to being conscripted for such a *leitourgia*, which could also happen. Such a voluntary assumption of a duty would go down well with the general public, and enhance Demosthenes' political standing, which was no doubt what helped to stir up Meidias.

Meidias' various attempts at sabotage, if we are to believe Demosthenes' account, were indeed remarkable. His first effort was to oppose
the exemption of the chorus from military service during the period
of their training (s. 15), which was apparently a normal enough
request, but had to be applied for. He was frustrated in this, but then
put himself forward as a candidate for administrator (*epimelêtês*) of the
festival, which would have given him good opportunities for
annoying Demosthenes. He was also, it seems, unsuccessful in this.
He then, however, resorted to more unorthodox measures. Once
again, we may yield Demosthenes the floor (ss. 16–17):

> His subsequent conduct, which I am now going to describe, passes all
> limits; and indeed I should never have ventured to arraign him today,
> had I not previously secured his immediate conviction in the Assembly.
> The sacred clothing – for all clothing provided for use at a festival I
> regard as being sacred until after it has been used[19] – and the golden
> crowns, which I ordered for the adornment of the chorus, he plotted
> to destroy, men of Athens, by a nocturnal raid on the premises of my
> goldsmith. And he did destroy them, though not completely, for that
> was beyond his power.[20] And no one can say that he ever yet heard of
> anyone daring or perpetrating such an outrage in this city.
>
> But not content with this, men of Athens, he actually suborned the
> trainer of my chorus; and if Telephanes, the flute-player, had not
> proved the staunchest friend to me, if he had not seen through the
> fellow's game and sent him about his business, if he had not felt it his
> duty to take over the training of the chorus and knock them into
> shape himself, we could not have taken part in the competition,
> Athenians. The chorus would have come in untrained, and we should
> have been covered in ignominy.

And even this was not the end of it! Demosthenes goes on to allege
(s. 17) that Meidias tried to bribe the Archon (who would be
presiding at the festival); that he got the other *chorêgoi* to gang up on
him; and that he even tried to block the gangways onto the stage
from the wings, so that the chorus of Pandionis would be unable to
come on stage at all. And then, finally, to cap it all, having thus
robbed the chorus of the first prize which Demosthenes is convinced

[19] As we shall see, Demosthenes is making a good deal of the *impious* nature of Meidias'
actions, the better to nail him on a charge which would involve disfranchisement.

[20] The goldsmith is brought in a little later (s. 22) to testify that he came upon Meidias in
his shop trying to sabotage the crowns and robes, and prevented him, so there is
presumably some substance to this allegation.

that they deserved, Meidias marched up to him, dressed as he was in his official robes of *chorêgos*, and slapped him in the face. This was not only *hybris* (outrageous behaviour); Demosthenes wishes to claim that it was *sacrilege*, since he was dressed at the time in his official robes.

As we shall see more fully when we turn to the study of Athenian piety, Demosthenes is onto a pretty good thing here. The Athenians took festival periods very seriously, from the point of view of observing correct behaviour. As Demosthenes reminds the jury (ss. 11–12), there was even a law against trying to collect a debt from someone during a festival, never mind assaulting an official in the performance of his duties. It is in the light of this that he is emboldened to ask for the death penalty for this rather trivial assault.

However, the real offence is *hybris*, and on that subject Demosthenes presents an interesting disquisition, reminding us how important was the preservation of one's dignity, the saving of face, in Classical Athens, even as it had been in Homer's time (ss. 72–3):

> To be struck is not the serious thing for a free man, serious though it is, but to be struck in wanton insolence [*hybris*]. Many things, men of Athens, some of which the victim would find it difficult to put into words, may be done by the striker – by gesture, by looks, by tone; when he strikes in wantonness or out of enmity; with fist or on the cheek. These are the things that provoke men and make them beside themselves, if they are unused to insult. No description, men of Athens, can bring the outrage as vividly before the hearers as it appears in truth and reality to the victim and to the spectators.

Now Demosthenes, as we know, was a proud and sensitive man, even for an Athenian, but there is no reason to doubt that he is stating to the jury something that that they would recognise as valid.

This epic confrontation had a curiously downbeat ending, if we may believe Plutarch, in his *Life of Demosthenes* (12, 5–6). Despite the fact that, in the speech itself, he dismisses with contempt alleged efforts by Meidias to buy him off, he apparently finally yielded to the intercession of agents of Meidias, and settled out of court for a sum of thirty minae.[21] And yet he published the speech – though presumably

[21] The true reason for this modified climb-down may have been Demosthenes' unwillingness at this point too grievously to offend the powerful politician Euboulos, a partisan of whom, as has been mentioned earlier (p. 90), Meidias was. There was also the consideration that a united front was being formed at his time against Philip of Macedon, and Demosthenes was concerned not to rock the boat.

not until some time later! And thus ended the best-documented enmity of the classical period in Athens.

A FRIENDSHIP ABUSED: APOLLODOROS AND NIKOSTRATOS

Other records of enmity have surfaced, and will surface, in the course of this book, but, since they illustrate other themes also, they will be presented in other contexts. We have seen already, of course, the results of the grievous enmity between Apollodoros and Stephanos, an enmity, like that of Demosthenes and Meidias, that had political overtones,[22] and that had manifested itself in a series of troublesome lawsuits prior to Apollodoros' attack on Neaira. But this is by no means the only problem that Apollodoros faced in his contentious career. He battled long and hard for control of his inheritance against his father's former slave, Phormion, to whom, on the model of what his own masters had done for him, Pasion had granted his freedom and management of the bank and other property, as well the guardianship of Apollodoros' younger brother Pasikles.[23] Here, however, we turn to another of his misfortunes, which also ended up in the courts,[24] his relationship with a certain Nikostratos, who was a neighbour of his in the country.

Reading between the lines, this was what Aristotle would characterise as an 'unequal' relationship, in which the more well-to-do partner provides financial support, while the humbler one provides personal services of various kinds. In this case, though, it seems sadly as if the humbler partner, Nikostratos, together with his brothers Deinon and Arethousios, had decided that Apollodoros was a 'milch cow', who could be ripped off with impunity. This was the sort of situation that people in Apollodoros' position in society had to beware of. We have seen, earlier in the chapter (p. 82 above), how Plato's friend Kriton had taken steps to protect himself against sykophantai by taking on a friend of this sort, in the person of the popular politician Archedemos, and that had proved a conspicuous success. Apollodoros was not to be so lucky. But we may let him take up the story himself (*Against Nikostratos* 4–5):[25]

---

[22] As with Demosthenes and Meidias, Apollodoros was a partisan of Demosthenes and the war party, Stephanos a sidekick of Euboulos.

[23] A record of this is preserved in the speech *For Phormion*, composed by Demosthenes (XXXVI of the corpus), which gives a rather good picture of the troublesome and extravagant side of Apollodoros' character.

[24] The speech *Against Nikostratos* is included as LIII in the Demosthenic corpus, but certainly a composition of Apollodoros himself.

[25] I borrow here the Loeb translation of A. T. Murray, with minor adjustments.

This man Nikostratos, gentlemen of the jury, was a neighbour of mine in the country, and a man of my own age. We had long known each other, but after my father's death,[26] when I went to live in the country, where I still live, we had much more to do with one another, since we were neighbours of one another and of the same age. As time went on we became very intimate [*pany oikeiôs diekeimetha*]; indeed, I came to feel on such intimate terms with him that he never failed to win any favour he asked of me; and he, on his part, was useful to me in looking after my affairs and managing them, and whenever I was abroad on public service as trierarch,[27] or on any private business of my own, I used to leave him in charge of everything on the farm.

Now it happened that I had to serve as trierarch round the Peloponnese, and from there I had to convey to Sicily the ambassadors whom the people had elected.[28] I was forced to set sail in haste, so I wrote to Nikostratos, telling him that I had put to sea, and that I should not be able to come home for fear of delaying the ambassadors; and I charged him[29] to look after the administration of matters at home, as he had done before.

Now something rather odd happens. When Apollodoros got back from conducting the embassy, he was met by Nikostratos' brother Deinon, with a sad story. Three slaves from Nikostratos' farm (two of them actually given to him by Apollodoros) had run away, and Nikostratos had gone in pursuit of them. In some strange way, it would seem, these slaves had got away to sea,[30] and in the process of chasing them, Nikostratos was himself captured 'by a trireme', and taken away to Aegina, where he was sold as a slave.[31] Deinon, who had received distraught letters from Nikostratos, begged Apollodoros for help in freeing

---

[26] This took place in 370 BC.

[27] Apollodoros' attested trierarchies are quite numerous. In 368, he served as trierarch on a ship round the Peloponnese, which is presumably the occasion for the first incident related below. In 366/5 he was joint trierarch on two ships in succession. He was joint trierarch of a ship in the North Aegean from autumn 362 to February 360; and in 356 he served as joint trierarch of the state galley *Phosphoros*.

[28] If this refers to 368, the embassy may have been to Dionysios I of Syracuse to encourage him to send troops to aid Sparta against the Arcadians and the Thebans, which he did. At this time Athens was actually allied to Sparta against Thebes.

[29] The verb used, *prosetaxa* ('ordered', rather than 'requested'), has a somewhat imperious ring to it, as of a superior to an inferior.

[30] Usually a slave simply headed off for the border with Boeotia, that being the easiest option.

[31] It is not specified what sort of trireme this was – Aeginetan, or a privateer. If the former, and this is 368 (or indeed any time in the 360s), that is peculiar, since Aegina was not officially at war with Athens at this time, much though the two states disliked each other. But a pirate might well bring a captive to the slave-market at Aegina, which was a flourishing one. That is what allegedly happened to Diogenes the Cynic, for example, later in the century.

his brother. Apollodoros nobly stumped up three hundred drachmae to finance Deinon's journey of rescue, and Nikostratos was duly freed.

This, however, was only the beginning. After thanking Apollodoros most warmly for his help, Nikostratos revealed (tearfully) that the cost of the ransom was actually twenty-six minae, and he had not the wherewithal to meet this sum.[32] We may let Apollodoros take up the story (ss. 8–9):

> On hearing this story, I felt pity for him, and moreover I saw what a wretched state he was in: he showed me the wounds of the fetters on his calves (he has the scars of them still, but, if you ask them to show them to you, he will not be willing to do so). I therefore answered that in the past I had been a true friend to him, and that now I would help him in his distress; that I would let him off the three hundred drachmae that I had given his brother for the expenses of his journey to fetch him, and that I would make a contribution of one thousand drachmae towards his ransom.[33]
>
> Nor did I make this promise in words only and fail to perform it in act; but, since I was not well provided with funds in consequence of my quarrel with Phormion and of his depriving me of the estate which my father left me,[34] I took to Theokles, who at that time was carrying on a banking business, some cups and a gold crown, which I happened to have in my house as part of my ancestral inheritance, and told him to give Nikostratos a thousand drachmae; and that sum I gave him outright as a gift, and I acknowledge that it was a gift.

But this, alas, was not the end of the matter. A few days later Nikostratos was back (again, weeping). He now revealed that the foreigners (*xenoi*)[35] were pressing him for payment. Full settlement, it

---

[32] The situation in cases of ransom was that one might find someone to come up with the sum required in the short term, as a purely commercial venture, but unless one could repay the loan within a stated time, one became legally the slave of one's ransomer.

[33] That is, ten minae, a good proportion of the total. As for the 300 drachmae, that seems a lot of money simply for expenses, for the short journey across the Saronic Gulf to Aegina, but we may suppose that there was more than merely travel involved – perhaps a deposit on the ransom money? Deinon did after all return with Nikostratos.

[34] This is actually a rather tendentious reference to his dispute with Phormion, which actually concerned Apollodoros' attempts to get his hands on that portion of the estate which Phormion was dutifully preserving for his younger brother Pasikles; but it serves to date these proceedings to the years immediately following his father's death.

[35] It is not clear where these *xenoi* were operating. Were they resident aliens in Athens, or rather professional 'ransom brokers' attached to the slave market in Aegina? If the latter, though, it is not clear how enforcible their legal claim would be; so they must at least have had agents in Athens. (The fact that this whole procedure was a scam, as will be revealed shortly, does not invalidate this question; Nikostratos must be playing on known procedures for getting ransomed.)

seems, was demanded within thirty days, or the debt was doubled; and thereafter, enslavement would inevitably follow. Nikostratos claimed that he had been trying to raise the balance (sixteen minae) through either selling or taking out a mortgage on his farm, but an insurmountable problem had arisen. Another brother of his, Arethousios, now claimed to be the beneficial owner of the slaves who had run away, and had put a lien on the property, refusing to allow it to be sold or mortgaged until he had first been paid compensation for the slaves – hardly very brotherly conduct, but there it was! Nikostratos was now, he claimed, completely stuck. Could Apollodoros possibly come up with the balance of the ransom as well, just in the short term, and he, Nikostratos would do his level best to raise it somehow,[36] offering himself as collateral? If he failed to come up with it, he would simply enslave himself to his good friend Apollodoros.

This story, one would think, was by now beginning to smell to high heaven, but Apollodoros, on his own testimony, as yet suspected nothing. He responded nobly once again (s. 12):

> When I heard these words of Nikostratos, having no idea that he was lying, I answered, as was natural for a young man who was an intimate friend, and who was far from thinking that he would be defrauded, 'Nikostratos, in time past I was a true friend to you, and now in your misfortunes I have helped you to the full extent of my power. But since at the moment you are unable to find the whole amount due, I indeed have no funds on hand, but I grant you a loan of whatever part of my property you choose, for you to mortgage for the balance of your debt, and to use the money without interest for a year, and to pay off the foreigners. When you have made the collection from your friends, pay off my mortgage, as you yourself propose.'

Once again, Nikostratos thanks him most heartily, but urges him to act without delay. So the poor innocent Apollodoros mortgages a lodging-house (*synoikia*) in his possession for sixteen minae to a person produced by Nikostratos, a certain Arkesas of Pambotadai, who lent him the money at an interest rate of sixteen per cent.

But now things began to turn nasty, and the beautiful friendship to fall into ruins. If, as we may, I think, assume, there never was a kidnap, nor yet a ransom demand, the money presumably was swallowed up by the three brothers, acting in collusion. But Nikostratos had now to take steps to ensure that he never had to pay any of this money back.

---

[36] He proposes, in fact, an *eranos*, which was a whip-round of one's friends.

The best way to do that was to somehow contrive that Apollodoros be deprived of his civil rights (suffer *atimia*), and thus be debarred from taking actions in the courts, on the head of some trumped-up charge. One convenient way to bring this about was to have him convicted as an undischarged state debtor (normally a consequence of failure to pay a fine imposed by the state for some offence or delinquency).

This aim was pursued by a device that is left somewhat obscure in Apollodoros' narrative (ss. 14–15) – either because he does not wish to dwell on it too closely, or because he expects it to be obvious enough to the jury. The brothers contrived that a miller called Lykidas take a case against Apollodoros concerning some disputed property, which was of a type that did not involve a summons (a *dikê aprosklêtos*) – presumably it was merely posted in some public place, such as the Stoa of the Eponymous Heroes, and the defendant was expected to take due note of it. Apollodoros, we must presume, failed to take note of, and therefore to respond to, this case in time, Arethousios testified falsely on behalf of Lykidas,[37] and a judgement of 610 drachmae was secured against him, payable to the public treasury. Apollodoros thus became a state debtor, and as such debarred from civic activities. Further to this, in pursuit of the claim for the 610 drachmae, the brothers descended on Apollodoros' town house and removed furniture to the value (he claims) of more than 20 minae (i.e. 2,000 drachmae).

But now at last Apollodoros struck back. He paid off the fine, freeing himself from his debt to the Treasury, and thus his *atimia*, and instituted a suit against Arethousios for false witness (*pseudoklêteia*). But in the interval before the law-case came on, things got very nasty indeed (ss. 15–16). The brothers resorted to various forms of sabotage and intimidation:

> Arethousios came to my farm at night, cut off all the choice fruit-grafts that were there, and the tree-vines [*anadendrades*] as well,[38] and broke down the nursery-beds of olive trees set in rows round about, doing more damage than enemies in war would have done.[39] And over and above this, as they were neighbours and my farm adjoined

---

[37] More exactly, he subscribed his name dishonestly to the citation, the crime of *pseudoklêteia*, for which Apollodoros duly prosecutes him.

[38] That is, vines trained to grow up trees. Apollodoros, as we observe, was quite a progressive agriculturalist.

[39] It is indeed true that in general Greeks at war did not cut down one another's olive trees, recognising how long they took to come to maturity.

theirs, they sent into it in the daytime a young boy who was an Athenian, and put him up to plucking off the flowers from my rose-bed, in order that, if I caught him and in a fit of anger tied him up or struck him, they might bring against me an indictment for assault [*hybris*].[40]

Apollodoros sidestepped this trap, but there was worse to come (ss. 16–17). When the *anakrisis*, or preliminary examination, of the charge against Arethousios had already taken place, and the case was just about to come to court, Apollodoros was journeying up late in the day on foot from the Piraeus to Athens, and was just passing the stone-quarries,[41] when Nikostratos, who had been lying in wait for him, sprang upon him, beating him with his fists, and then seized him round the waist and tried to throw him into the quarry. Fortunately, there were passers-by who heard his shouts, and he was rescued.

This is, admittedly, a slightly odd story. If it were true, then it constituted a serious premeditated assault, such as would even attract the death penalty (as we shall see from the first case looked at in the next chapter). One would expect Apollodoros to sue, but we have no record that he did so. It sounds rather like one of those wild allegations so often fired off at the latter end of an Athenian forensic speech, which seem simply to serve as a kind of dramatic backdrop to the main charge. But on the other hand, it is fairly circumstantially described, so one cannot be sure.

At any rate, Apollodoros was not swayed from his purpose, and he secured a satisfactory conviction against Arethousios. Remarkably, he claims that the jury favoured imposing the death penalty, but he himself went along with the defence in accepting a fine of one talent (admittedly, a very considerable sum). His stated reason for this is rather nicely put: 'This was not because I wished to save Arethousios from the death penalty (for he deserved death on account of the wrongs which he had committed against me), but that I, as a son of Pasion, and a citizen only by decree of the people, might not be said to have caused the death of any Athenian.'

But of course, as we know, securing a judgement in an Athenian court is only an advance to square one: one has still to recover the money; and this is in fact what the present case is all about.

---

[40] Such a charge could also be made an occasion for disfranchisement.

[41] Into which criminals were sometimes tossed, dead or alive. Plainly, a nasty drop was involved. This, we may recall, was where the notorious Leontios, son of Aglaion, is mentioned in Plato's *Republic* (IV 439E) as pausing to gawk at the dead bodies of executed criminals – thus giving Plato an excuse for postulating a tripartite soul!

Arethousios, having been passably prosperous before, straightway became, to all appearances, penniless.[42] Specifically, two quite useful slaves, Kerdon and Manes, whom Apollodoros proposed to seize in at least part-payment of the judgement, are now claimed by Nikostratos (reversing the putative situation earlier in the story, where Arethousios claimed that the runaway slaves were really his, and thus prevented a mortgage on Nikostratos' farm!). However, Apollodoros is able to produce witnesses to attest that Arethousios is in fact the beneficial owner of both slaves, so he doubtless won this case also. But it remains a sad end to a beautiful friendship!

Our brief survey, then, has indicated to what an extent enmities were a driving force in Athenian life, prompting as they do the majority of cases in the courts brought on some other overt pretext, such as a concern for ritual purity, or for the integrity of the family or the citizen body. Again and again, when some high-minded reason for prosecution is presented in an Athenian court, we are well advised to look for some personal or political motive, or both.

---

[42] As Apollodoros remarks (s. 28), 'Before Arethousios became a debtor to the state, he was admitted to be the richest of the brothers, but since the laws declare his property to be yours, Arethousios is made out to be a poor man. His mother lays claim to one part of his property, his brothers to another.'

CHAPTER FIVE

A Peculiar Institution: The Etiquette
of Homosexual Relationships

THEORY

A notable feature of ancient Greek society, in contradistinction to that of later, Christian-dominated periods up to the present day, was the relative degree of tolerance of homosexual relationships, and in particular of pederasty. It is not that these things were a matter of indifference; it is just that the popular attitude to them was not (in general)[1] burdened by preoccupations with the *unnaturalness* of homosexual relationships, and the offence to the divinity consequent on that. In Greek mythology, indeed, none of the major gods was in much of a position to take offence at human homosexual relationships. The issue, for the average Athenian, was rather what behaviour was consistent with *manliness*, and with the much-vaunted ideal of 'moderation in all things'. In a society where respectable young ladies were fairly strictly confined to the home, and where there was really no possibility of forming romantic or, *a fortiori*, intellectual attachments with members of the opposite sex of one's own social status, while older and younger males were much thrown together in school and in the gymnasium, it was more or less inevitable that a degree of institutional homosexuality would be the order of the day – together, of course, with resort to prostitutes or *hetairai*, such as we have met a selection of in Chapter 2. There were probably no more 'true' homosexuals in Classical Athens than there are in modern society, but there was, at least in the upper echelons of society, such as we are inevitably mainly confronted with, widespread practice, and tolerance, of homoerotic relationships, at least between young men and boys of a certain age-group, broadly between the ages of fifteen and twenty-five (with a little leeway at either end).

What we are primarily concerned with in the present context are the 'moral' attitudes surrounding this phenomenon, and, as we shall

---

[1] Plato, in particular in the *Laws* (VIII 836Bff.), being a notable exception. Indeed, such a passage as this serves as something of a foundational text for the later concept of the unnaturalness of homosexuality.

observe, they are of some complexity. I will start with some 'theoretical' discussions, drawn from that great theorist of homoerotic love, Plato, and then turn to some examples – amusing, I hope, as well as enlightening – of how things worked out in practice.

In his delightful dialogue, the *Symposium*, Plato chooses to lead up to his properly philosophical revelation, presented by Socrates himself (sheltering behind the persona of the wise woman Diotima), by allowing a series of more conventionally minded Athenian gentlemen to air their views on the subject of love.[2] It is the first two speeches, those of Phaedrus and Pausanias, which are of most interest for our purpose. In both cases there is observable a considerable degree of idealisation of the realities of pederastic relationships, but we need not assume, on the other hand, that they are totally divorced from reality. In more traditional societies – notably, in modern times, in many Polynesian societies, but also, among the ancient Greeks, particularly in Crete[3] – there is to be found, in the area of 'rites of passage', a tradition of institutionalised homosexual rape, whereby a boy is 'kidnapped' by a older youth or man, led off into the wilderness, and sexually assaulted, but then adopted by his abductor and initiated into the traditions of adulthood. In Crete, such a 'rape' was something of an honour, and normally led to lasting friendship. The Cretans were admittedly regarded as somewhat peculiar, in respect of this practice, by the rest of Greece, but they do in fact seem to have preserved here a genuinely primitive tradition. It is traces of this more primitive notion of initiation into manhood through pederasty that we can see preserved in the high-minded sentiments expressed here by Phaedrus and Pausanias.

Let us first consider the speech of Phaedrus. After a brief mythological exordium, he gets straight to his main point (178Cff.). As we may note, he assumes without hesitation that what is under discussion is pederastic love (though heterosexual love does get a look in later, with the example of the faithful Alcestis):[4]

---

[2] We may recall that the work takes the form of a series of after-dinner speeches on a chosen theme, which is the praise of Eros, or Love (both as a god and as a passion), of a convivially competitive nature, each later speech having somehow to 'cap' the previous one.

[3] Cf. (on Polynesians) F. E. Williams, *Papuans of the Trans-Fly*, 2nd edn, Oxford, 1969; (on Cretans and Dorians in general) R. Bethe, 'Die dorische Knabenliebe, Ihre Ethik und ihre Idee', *Rheinisches Museum* 62 (1907), 438–75; Jan Bremmer, 'An Enigmatic Indo-European Rite: Pederasty', *Arethusa* 13 (1980), 279–95. There is a remarkable account of Cretan customs in this respect in Strabo, *Geogr.* 10. 4, 21, taken from the fourth-century historian Ephorus.

[4] I borrow the Penguin translation of Walter Hamilton.

Now, as Love is the oldest of the gods, so also he confers on us the greatest benefits, for I would maintain that there can be no greater benefit for a boy than to have a worthy lover from his earliest youth, nor for a lover than to have a worthy object for his affection. The principle which ought to guide the whole life of those who intend to live nobly cannot be implanted either by family or by position or by wealth or by anything else so effectively as by love. 'What principle?', you ask. I mean the principle which inspires shame at what is disgraceful and ambition for what is noble; without these feelings neither a state nor an individual can accomplish anything great or fine.

Suppose a lover to be detected in the performance of some dishonourable action or failing through cowardice to defend himself when dishonour is inflicted upon him by another; I assert that there is no one, neither his father nor his friends nor anyone else, whose observation would cause him so much pain in such circumstances as his beloved's. And conversely we see with regard to the beloved that he is peculiarly sensitive to dishonour in the presence of his lovers. If, then, one could contrive that a state or an army should entirely consist of lovers and loved,[5] it would be impossible for it to have a better organization than that which it would then enjoy through their avoidance of all dishonour and their mutual emulation; moreover, a handful of such men, fighting side by side, would defeat practically the whole world. A lover would rather be seen by all his comrades deserting his post or throwing away his arms than by his beloved; rather than that, he would prefer a thousand times to die. And if it were a question of deserting his beloved or not standing by him in danger, no one is so base as not to be inspired on such an occasion by Love himself with a spirit which would make him the equal of men with the best natural endowment of courage. In short, when Homer spoke of God 'breathing might' into some of the heroes, he described exactly the effect which Love, of his very nature, produces in men who are in love.

Phaedrus now adduces two examples from Greek mythology: first, Admetus' wife Alcestis, who was prepared to die for her husband, when none of his other relations were willing to do so, and was on

---

[5] Since, by the way, this was in fact the composition of the so-called 'Sacred Band', an elite corps of the Theban army, which was put together by the Theban general Epaminondas in the early 370s, impressing itself on the general public consciousness only at the battle of Leuctra in 371 BC (in which the Thebans for the first time beat the Spartans), and such an arrangement is not attested for any other military formation, this allusion is plausibly proposed as an indication of the date of composition of the *Symposium*; but that is not our concern at present.

the head of that sent back to life by the gods after her death; and then Achilles, in his determination to avenge the death of his friend Patroclus, even though it betokened his own death, following on his slaying of Hector. This latter example, though, Phaedrus finds the more significant, on the grounds that Achilles, as he argues, was not the lover, but the *beloved*, of Patroclus (being, as he was, the younger and more beautiful of the two):

> The truth is that, while the gods greatly honour the courage of a lover, they admire even more and reward more richly affection shown towards a lover by the beloved, because a lover is possessed and thus comes nearer than the beloved to being divine. That is why they honoured Achilles more highly than Alcestis and sent him to the Isles of the Blessed (180AB).[6]

Phaedrus' speech is followed by that of Pausanias. Pausanias would actually seem to have been in a 'serious' homosexual relationship, being notoriously the lover of Agathon, who is a grown man (and a successful playwright), and the host at this party. His views in favour of the superiority of homosexual love might thus be expected to be somewhat more pronounced than most, but we need not suppose them to be entirely out of line with those of the average Athenian gentleman. He proposes (180DE) to make a distinction between two kinds of Eros, each dependent on a distinct variety of Aphrodite, the 'vulgar'(*Aphroditê pandêmos*) and the 'heavenly' (*Aphroditê ourania*).[7] He distinguishes between them as follows:

> There can be no doubt of the vulgar nature of the Love which goes with the Vulgar Aphrodite; it is quite random in the effects it produces, and it is this love which the baser sort of men feel. Its marks are, first, that it is directed towards women quite as much as young men; second, that in either case it is concerned with their bodies

---

[6] This is an odd remark, as it assumes Alcestis to be the lover rather than the beloved, as she ought surely to have been, but there it is. It was axiomatic, in homosexual relations, that the beloved boy was not meant to take pleasure in the physical aspect of the relationship, so that affection shown by him would be that much more creditable. See on this the remarks of Sir Kenneth Dover, *Greek Homosexuality*, pp. 81–109.

[7] There is a nice irony here in Pausanias' choice of titles, which we are doubtless meant to enjoy. *Pandemos* was the title of Aphrodite as worshipped in the city of Athens, as Aphrodite 'of all the people'. Her sanctuary was below and south of the Athena Nikê temple on the Acropolis. There was nothing particularly 'vulgar' about her worship, except that it was open to the whole people. *Aphrodite Ourania*, on the other hand, was a much more exotic lady. She was the Cypriote Aphrodite, a Hellenised version of the Middle Eastern goddess of love Ashtaroth, whose temple in Corinth was notoriously a centre for ritual prostitution.

rather than with their souls; third, that it prefers that its objects should be as unintelligent as possible, because its only aim is the satisfaction of its desires, and it takes no account of the manner in which this is achieved. That is why its effect is purely a matter of chance, and quite as often bad as good. In all this it partakes of the nature of its corresponding goddess, who is far younger than her heavenly counterpart, and who owes her birth to the conjunction of male and female.[8]

But the Heavenly Aphrodite, to whom the other Love belongs, for one thing has no female strain in her, but springs entirely from the male, and for another is older and consequently free from wantonness. Hence those who are inspired by this Love are attracted towards the male sex, and value it as being naturally the stronger and more intelligent. Besides, even among the lovers of their own sex one can distinguish those whose motives are entirely dictated by this second Love; they do not fall in love with mere boys, but wait until they reach the age at which they begin to show some intelligence, that is to say, until they are growing a beard. By choosing that moment in the life of their favourite to fall in love, they show, if I am not mistaken, that their intention is to form a lasting attachment and a partnership for life; they are not the kind to take advantage of the ignorance of a boy to deceive him, and then are off with a jeer in pursuit of some fresh darling.

Pausanias continues on this theme for some while longer, actually proposing that pederasty, or the pursuit of young boys, should be outlawed. He then (182Aff.) turns to mocking the Dorians on the one hand, and the Ionians of Asia Minor on the other – the former, for laying down absolutely, because of their relative inarticulateness and ignorance of the powers of persuasion, that 'it is good to gratify a lover'; the latter, because of their slavishness (owing to their domination by the Persians), for banning homosexual relations altogether. The Athenians, predictably, have got it just right (182D):

Our institutions are far nobler than these, but, as I have said, they are not so easily grasped. On the one hand, a love which is open is reckoned among us nobler than a love which shuns observation, and the love of those who are most eminent by birth or merit, even though they may be inferior in looks, is held in the highest esteem. Besides this, the remarkable degree of encouragement which a lover

---

[8] Pausanias is getting mileage out of the confusion in the mythological accounts of the origins of Aphrodite, identifying Pandemos as the daughter of Zeus and Dione, and Ourania as the daughter of Kronos, without a mother (180D).

receives from all and sundry is evidence that no shame attaches to him; success in a love-affair is glorious, and it is only failure that is disgraceful, and we do not merely tolerate, we even praise the most extraordinary behaviour in a lover in pursuit of his beloved, behaviour which would meet with the severest condemnation if it were practised for any other end.

If a man, for example, with the object of obtaining a present of money or public office or some other position of power, brought himself to behave as a lover behaves towards his favourite, begging and praying for the fulfilment of his requests, making solemn promises, camping on doorsteps,[9] and voluntarily submitting to a slavery such as no slave ever knew, he would be restrained from such conduct by enemies and friends alike; the former would abuse him for his servility and lack of spirit, and the latter would direct exhortations at him and blush for him.

We must bear in mind here that the speeches of the *Symposium* are part of an after-dinner entertainment, and are of a distinctly playful nature, but still Pausanias must be reckoned to be presenting a picture, even if a slightly hyperbolic one, of social reality. For our purposes it is enough to recognise that, at least for younger men, below the age, perhaps, of thirty (though Pausanias introduces no such age restriction here), the pursuit of boys was a perfectly respectable and well-tolerated outlet for one's sexual impulses. If one looks attentively at what sort of conduct one might be teased or reproached for, either on the comic stage or in a court of law, one will find that it involves either effeminacy on the part of a grown man,[10] or *excessive* enthusiasm for love affairs (this latter being a breach of moderation, or *sophrosyne*), particularly beyond a certain age.[11] We shall observe a certain sensitivity to this criticism being evinced by the defendant in the first of our case-histories below, modifying the blanket approval which Pausanias is claiming for such behaviour

---

[9] This may seem particularly excessive, but the fact that there exists a whole sub-genre of love poetry, the *paraklausithyron*, or 'lament at the door', would seem to attest to the acceptance of the practice, at least by young men of a certain age – though surviving poems concern heartless mistresses, rather than boys.

[10] One may instance Aristophanes' merciless mockery of Agathon (his host at this party!) in the *Thesmophoriazusae* (ll. 101–276).

[11] If we turn back to the opening scene of Plato's *Lysis*, dealt with in the last chapter, we find Hippothales' friends teasing him good humouredly for his excessive devotion to young Lysis, manifesting itself in the composition of encomia in both poetry and prose, which he inflicts on all who will listen (204CD). As we shall see below, Aeschines has to defend himself from similar jibes from the supporters of Timarchos (probably including Demosthenes).

here. But, as I say, this is a far from serious discourse.

What is quite lacking here, however, is any preoccupation with the 'unnaturalness' of these practices, or the possible harm they might do to the psyches of the boys involved – any more than anyone would be concerned with the psychological welfare of courtesans. Pausanias' condemnation of the pursuit of young boys, as a manifestation of the 'vulgar' Eros, does not really stem from any concern about the welfare the boys involved, but rather with the state of mind of the men concerned in such relationships. The only relevant concerns are with issues of manhood and of moderation. And here, as in the case of heterosexual relations even today, there is very much of a double standard. Let us return to Pausanias (183C):

> So we see that according to our way of thinking a lover is allowed the utmost licence by both God and man, and the natural solution would be that in this country it is a very fine thing both to be in love and to show complaisance towards one's lovers. But when we reflect that the boys who inspire this passion are placed by their fathers in the charge of tutors, with injunctions not to allow them to hold any communication with their lovers, and that a boy who is involved in such communication is teased[12] by his contemporaries and friends, and that their elders make no attempt to stop such teasing and do not condemn it, we are led to the opposite conclusion, and infer that such love is reckoned amongst us to be highly disgraceful.

And so, as we see, there is some ambivalence, and something of a double standard. Pausanias' rather bland solution to the conundrum is to assert that there is no absolute right and wrong in this area, but all depends on the circumstances. The case-history of Timarchos, to which we shall come shortly, will flesh this out considerably.

Pausanias ends by asserting (184DE), with admirable high-mindedness, that the only real justification for a boy 'gratifying' his lover (which certainly involved submitting to acts of sex, though there is quite an amount of learned discussion as to exactly what sort of acts)[13] is the pursuit of virtue (*aretê*). Only in this case, the desire to become a better person under the guidance of one's lover, is there, he declares, no disgrace in being deceived. It was not, certainly, felt to be likely, or proper, for a boy to return the love of his lover, or be too demonstrative in his affection for him, but Plato in a notable passage

---

[12] Or 'reproached': *oneidizô* is something between 'tease' and 'reproach'; it can certainly imply serious disapproval.
[13] See, for example, Dover, *Greek Homosexuality*, pp. 91–100.

of the *Phaedrus* (255A–E) does advance the theory of what he terms *anterôs* on the part of the beloved, as follows:[14]

> Thus the loved one receives all manner of service, as if he were a god, from a lover who is not pretending but loves in all sincerity; of his own nature, too, he is kindly disposed to him who pays him such service. Now it may be that in time past he has been misled by his schoolfellows or others, who told him that it is shameful to associate[15] with a lover, and by reason of this he may repel his advances. Nevertheless, as time goes on, ripening age and the ordinance of destiny [*to khreôn*][16] together lead him to welcome the other's society, for assuredly fate does not allow one evil man to be friend to another, nor yet for one good man to lack the friendship of another.
>
> And now that he has come to welcome his lover and to take pleasure in his company, it comes home to him what a depth of kindliness he has found, and he is filled with amazement, for he perceives that all his other friends and kinsmen have nothing to offer in comparison with this friend in whom there dwells a god [*entheos philos*]. So as he continues in this association and society, and comes into contact with his lover in the gymnasium[17] and elsewhere, that flowing stream which Zeus, as the lover of Ganymede, called 'the flood of passion' [*himeros*], pours in upon the lover. And part of it is absorbed within him, but when he can contain no more the rest flows away outside him, and as a breath of wind or an echo, rebounding from a smooth, hard surface, goes back to its place of origin, even so the stream of beauty turns back and re-enters the eyes of the fair beloved. And so by the natural channel it reaches his soul and gives its fresh vigour, watering the roots of the wings and stimulating them to growth,[18] whereby the soul of the beloved, in its turn, is filled with love. So he loves, yet knows not what he loves; he does not understand, he cannot tell what has come upon him; like one that has caught a disease of the eye from another, he cannot account for it, not

---

[14] I borrow the translation of R. Hackforth, with minor variations.

[15] The verb used is *plêsiazein*, which can, but need not, have a sexual connotation.

[16] Why 'destiny', one might ask? This probably has something to do with Plato's theory of 'elective affinities' (to borrow a term of Goethe's). In a case of 'higher', or philosophic love, lover and beloved are in the train of the same god, and come to recognise a spiritual affinity.

[17] Where they would find themselves, in the normal course of events, wrestling naked together, for example.

[18] A reference to the fanciful notion advanced somewhat earlier (246B–D; 251B–D), that the soul is a naturally winged thing, which loses its wings on descending into incarnation, but may cause them to sprout again by the contemplation of embodied beauty.

realising that his lover is as it were a mirror in which he beholds himself. And when the other is beside him, he shares his relief from anguish; when he is absent, he likewise shares his longing and being longed for, since he possesses that counter-love [*anterôs*] which is the image of love, though he supposes it to be friendship [*philia*] rather than love. He feels a desire – like the lover's, yet not so strong – to see, to touch, to kiss him, to lie down with him, and now before long the desire, as one might suppose, leads to the act.

The theory being propounded in this remarkable passage – a passage, one would think, that could only have been penned by a man profoundly susceptible to these passions himself – is the following, and it is in accord with the norms of Athenian propriety, so far as we can observe them. It was not considered proper for a boy or youth to be too demonstrative in response to a lover – in particular, he was not meant to take any obvious pleasure in sexual contacts – but it was also a fact of life, presumably, that a 'noble' lover, such as is envisaged in this passage (and by Pausanias, in his speech in the *Symposium*)[19] would stimulate feelings of affection and gratitude in his beloved, which would lead to the granting of 'favours'. This state of mind is characterised here as *anteros*, a term surely coined by Plato, in at least this sense,[20] on this occasion.

Plato goes on (256AB), rather coyly, to recognise that, in the course of nature (perhaps after a few drinks, or a vigorous work-out together in the gymnasium), the lovers might be led to indulge in some form of sexual intercourse (though in that case they would forfeit the highest rewards, in the afterlife, of 'philosophic' love). He does not commend this, but he is not too disturbed by the possibility of it either – certainly not to the extent that he came to be in his old age, when composing the *Laws*[21] – and in this he is quite in accord with at least upper-class Athenian sentiment in general.

A rather nice portrayal of a 'noble' love of this sort in action is portrayed by Xenophon in his *Symposium*, which is the record of a dinner party[22] given by the millionaire aristocrat Kallias, son of Hipponikos, in honour of his favourite, the boy Autolykos, who has

---

[19] And also by Socrates, in his speech in Xenophon's *Symposium* (ch. 8), discussed below.
[20] This is the earliest attested use of the word, but there is some indication that it was in wider use, with the more straightforward meaning of 'requited love'.
[21] As mentioned above, n. 1.
[22] It is plain, in fact, that Xenophon has Plato's *Symposium* in mind, though his allusions to it are rather devious (e.g. 8, 9; 31–2).

just won the *pankration* at the Greater Panathenaia of 422 BC. Among the guests are the boy's father, Lykon,[23] as well as Socrates and a group of his followers. What is interesting for our purposes is that there is no hint of reticence or concealment in Kallias' infatuation with young Autolykos, while more or less everyone else at the party is avowedly in love with someone as well (8, 1–3) – Socrates, for example, (among others) with young Kritoboulos (son of his old friend Kriton, whom we have met before); and Kritoboulos in turn, by his own account (4, 10–15), with the young Kleinias, son of Axiochos, and cousin of Alkibiades; Charmides is also both beloved of many, and a lover himself.[24] All the guests, however, are declared to be overwhelmed by the beauty of young Autolykos, to the extent that the party starts off quite subdued, as if in awe at the presence of a divinity (1, 9–10):[25]

> An observer of the scene would at once have reflected that beauty has something naturally regal about it, especially if it is combined with modesty and self-discipline in the possessor, as it was then in Autolykos. In the first place, his good looks drew everyone's attention to him, as surely as a light draws all eyes towards it in the dark; and secondly, there was not a man there whose feelings were not moved at the sight of him. Some became more silent, and the behaviour of others underwent a sort of transformation. Possession by a god always seems to have a remarkable effect. Those who are influenced by other gods tend to become more intimidating in their appearance, more truculent in their speech, and more aggressive in their conduct; but those who are inspired by discreet love wear a kindlier expression, speak in a gentler tone, and behave in a way more befitting a free man. Such was the effect that love had upon Kallias on this occasion, as was duly noted by those who were initiates of this god. So they proceeded to dine in silence, as if they had been ordered by some superior to do so.

Things do lighten up in due course, but the whole work is suffused with an atmosphere of high-minded pederasty, culminating in a

---

[23] Probably not the same Lykon as was one of Socrates' accusers much later, in 399 – though it would be a nice irony on Xenophon's part if this were so; Lykon is made to commend Socrates as he is leaving, after Socrates' speech, as an 'excellent fellow' (*kalos k' agathos*, 9, 1).

[24] Charmides, Plato's uncle, is portrayed by him in the dialogue called after him as being a youth of quite outstanding beauty ten years before this, in 432. His beauty, indeed, quite bowls Socrates over when he comes upon him, and especially when he gets a chance to peek down his cloak (*Charm.* 155CD).

[25] I borrow here the Penguin translation of Hugh Tredennick.

discourse by Socrates, in chapter 8, on the distinction between the higher and lower sorts of love, and an encomium of the former – and of Kallias for practising it, in relation to Autolykos. Xenophon here (8, 9–10) borrows the distinction between the 'heavenly' and the 'vulgar' Aphrodite, propounded by Pausanias in his speech in Plato's *Symposium* (180DE),[26] and in other ways (as mentioned above) betrays the fact that he has perused that work, but what is significant is that Xenophon, as a relatively straight-thinking Athenian gentleman, should find this distinction useful for his purposes. This is not, then, a distinction dreamed up by Plato, but one which corresponds well to the ideology of pederasty entertained by at least some of the Athenian upper classes, which seeks to distinguish between 'noble' and 'self-restrained' relationships between man and boy, which have an educational and socialising character, and 'vulgar' carnal desire, which brings disgrace on both parties (8, 19–21). We shall see the orator Aeschines propounding a similar distinction in his speech *Against Timarchos* (below, p. 123). Xenophon advances the theory – a version of the *anterôs* described, as we have seen, by Plato in the *Phaedrus* (255A–E) – that the boy loved by a noble lover will return affection for the love bestowed upon him (8, 17–18):

> In the first place, who could hate a person by whom, he knows, he is considered truly good, and secondly who, he can see, is more concerned about what is good for his beloved boy than what is pleasant for himself, and moreover whose affection, he trusts, could not be diminished even by the calamity of a disfiguring disease? Must not those whose affection is mutual look at each other with pleasure and converse in friendship; must they not trust and be trusted, be considerate to each other, share pleasure in their successes and sorrow if anything goes wrong; must they not continue in happiness so long as they are together, and, if either falls ill, must not the other keep him company much more constantly; and must they not care for each other even more in their absence than in their presence? Aren't all these characteristics filled with Aphrodite's charm? It's this sort of conduct that maintains people's mutual devotion to their friendship and their enjoyment of it even into old age.

Kallias himself is presented by Xenophon as a paragon of this sort of love, and contrasted starkly with the rather seedy Syracusan entrepreneur whom he has hired to provide the after-dinner entertainment,

---

[26] Cf. above, p. 104.

consisting of a boy and girl (presumably slaves) who do tricks and then act out an erotic pageant together, who freely admits to having his will with his boy all night and every night (4, 54) – though it cannot be said that Xenophon exhibits any radical disapproval of this behaviour.[27] It is simply behaviour proper to the lower classes, or to foreigners, and with slaves.

PRACTICE

About a boy

But enough now of theorising, and of high-mindedness. Let us turn to look at a few examples of how things worked out in practice, at the more disreputable end of the spectrum of society.

First we may adduce a rather comical affray which reached the Athenian law-courts some time early in the fourth century, for which Lysias composed a speech.[28] What had happened was this. Our speaker (whose name, as is not infrequently the case in forensic situations, is not mentioned) and his opponent, whose name is Simon, became involved in conflict over a boy, Theodotos, with whom both had fallen in love. Our protagonist, however, he would have us believe, approached the boy with respect and gentility, and thus diverted him away from his rival Simon, who was treating him roughly (rather as the boorish Phrynion is portrayed by Apollodoros as treating Neaira).[29] What emerges in the course of the narrative (s. 22) is that young Theodotos was, not to beat about the bush, a 'rent-boy'.[30] Simon claims to have hired him (presumably for a period of time, such as a year) for 300 drachmae (s. 22) – very much in the same way that

---

[27] Albeit he does allow Socrates some mild irony at the Syracusan's expense, 4, 54.

[28] Oration III, *Against Simon*. The mention of the battles of Corinth and Coronea as recent events (in which the speaker's antagonist Simon had disgraced himself) would seem to place the date of the trial as not much later than 394 BC.

[29] Above, p. 30.

[30] Theodotos is described (s. 5) as a 'Plataean lad' (*Plataikon meirakion*), an appellation that has caused some confusion. What seems most likely, however, is that he was not a citizen of the small Boeotian border-town of Plataea (whose people had been granted Athenian citizenship, with some restrictions, back near the beginning of the Peloponnesian War in 427 BC), but rather the offspring of one of the slaves who had been granted citizenship, with 'Plataean' status, as a consequence of enlisting in the Athenian navy in the last years of the War. Theodotos should therefore be a free person, but, strangely, there is some talk (s. 33) of his being subject to giving evidence only under torture, which would imply servile status. It is hard to know what to make of this, but Theodotos may have been in a sort of 'twilight zone' between freedom and slavery, rather as was the case with Neaira, and generally in the case of those of ex-servile status; it was quite possible for them to be re-enslaved, if they stepped out of line in any respect.

hetairai would hire themselves out to a patron for a period of time – and therefore to have constructive ownership of him. Our friend disputes this (ss. 24–6), but in the process reveals the sort of relationship that we are dealing with here. He is also studiously vague as to how he came to seduce Theodotos from Simon, but, if we allow our cynicism free play, we may reconstruct a scenario (to some extent resembling that involving Phrynion, Neaira and Stephanos) where our man first comes upon Theodotos at a dinner party or symposium given by his erstwhile friend Simon, chats him up, discerns him to be dissatisfied with his lot, and proposes that he throw Simon over, and come to live with him. Theodotos decamps, and then the fur begins to fly.

The first incident that we are allowed to know of (ss. 5–8) involves Simon coming round drunk, with some cronies, to our friend's house, having heard that Theodotos is with him, and demanding to get him back. He manages to force his way into the house, and finds himself in the women's quarters. Here we learn something of our friend's situation. He is not himself a married man (perhaps not being that way inclined), but he is presiding over a household of ladies, comprising his widowed sister and a number of nieces, whom he describes as 'having been brought up so modestly that they are ashamed to be seen even by their kinsmen'. Having Theodotos on the premises, then, our friend does not regard as a possible occasion of scandal!

At any rate, Simon is ejected from the house, but he does not give up. It would seem that our friend was not dining at home, but at a neighbour's (with Theodotos). Simon finds out where this is, appears outside, and challenges him to come out. When our friend comes out, Simon straightway attacks him. He defends himself, and then Simon withdraws to a distance, and begins to pelt him with stones – missing him, but hitting a friend of his own. The incident seems to have ended there, but it left our friend in serious embarrassment, as he tells us. Normally, a suit for assault and battery (*hybris*) would have ensued, but considerations of propriety stood in the way. He is most unwilling to 'get down in the gutter' with Simon, and expose himself to derisive and disapproving comment from society in general. Here our friend makes a number of remarks pertinent to our theme, which is how such behaviour would have been viewed by the public at large. Straight away in the exordium, our friend spells out his problem (ss. 3–4):[31]

---

[31] I borrow the Loeb translation of W. R. M. Lamb, with minor alterations.

What especially bothers me, gentlemen of the Council,[32] is that I shall be compelled to speak to you about the facts of this case; for it was my feeling of shame at the mere thought that many would know of my troubles that made me put up with my wrongs. But since Simon has placed me in such a necessity,[33] I will relate to you the whole of the facts without the slightest reserve.[34] If I am guilty, gentlemen, I expect to get no indulgence; but if I prove my innocence as regards the counts of Simon's affidavit, while for the rest you consider my attitude towards the boy *too senseless for a man of my age*, I ask you not to think the worse of me for that, since you know that all mankind are liable to desire, but that he may be the best and most temperate who is able to bear its misfortune in the most orderly spirit.

There is much of significance here, particularly in the phrase which I have italicised. We are not dealing here with activity which is *morally* reprehensible – at least in a modern, or Judaeo-Christian sense – but rather with a type of carry-on which is unworthy of a man of his age and station. It is a breach of *sôphrosynê*, and thus liable to be adversely commented upon. Our friend also seeks to make the point, a popular one in Greek love-poetry, and by implication also in popular belief, that the passion of love is something that simply falls upon one from without, and must be endured as best one can. It was not his fault, he would like to claim, that he fell in love with Theodotos. He should be judged, rather, on how prudently he managed this affliction.

He returns to this theme in s. 9, by way of explaining his response to Simon's assault on him:

So I, gentlemen, feeling myself grossly ill-used, but ashamed – as I have already told you – at my misfortune [*symphora*], put up with it, and preferred to go without satisfaction for these offences rather than be thought lacking in sense by the citizens: for I knew that, while his actions would be found appropriate to his wickedness, I should be derided for the treatment I received by a number of people who are in the habit of resenting any ambition that one may show for a good standing [*khrêstos einai*] in the city.

So there it is: our friend, who is plainly well-to-do,[35] and of a

---

[32] The case he is now involved in, as we shall see, is a serious one, of wounding with intent to kill, and as such it was heard before the Council of the Areopagus.

[33] Sc., by initiating a suit against him, as mentioned in the previous note.

[34] This is of course somewhat disingenuous. There are many details we would like to know more of, as I have already suggested.

[35] There are various indications of this, as we shall see: not only the fact that he can take off on a cruise around the Aegean (s. 10), but also the fact that he was the subject of an *antidosis* (s. 20).

certain age (one may assume, I think, well over thirty, which was the approximate age below which such goings-on as this would be regarded with a certain tolerance), has ambitions to be regarded as *khrêstos* in the city – he may even have had political ambitions – and this would be a topic for his enemies to seize on.

He decides, therefore, he tells us (s. 10), to give the affair a chance to blow over by retiring for a while from Athens, and he takes off, with Theodotos, on some kind of protracted cruise. He is rather vague about this – as about so much else. Was it a business trip, or just a pleasure cruise? Did they go to a particular place (Cyprus, for instance), or did they just travel around? And how long did this strategic retreat last? He is not going to tell us. All he will say is: 'So I took the boy (since the whole truth must be told), and left the city. When I thought it was time enough for Simon to have forgotten the young fellow, and also to have repented of his former offences, I came back again.'

No such luck. He returned, in due course, and landed with Theodotos in the Piraeus; but Simon, far from having forgotten all about it, is waiting for him, and the sorry tale is about to come to its climax. Once again, though, the narrative is made somewhat obscure by reason of certain explanatory details being omitted. It would seem that our friend himself remained initially in the Piraeus, but sent Theodotos on ahead to the city, where he was lodged with a certain Lysimachos, presumably a friend of our man (s. 11). Lysimachos' house, however, it would seem, happened to be more or less next door to one which was being rented by Simon. Once again, one must suspect that there is a certain amount that we are not being told. Why on earth is Theodotos sent up to the city, to lodge with Lysimachos? And is it pure chance that Simon is renting a house in the immediate vicinity? Let our hero tell the story in his own words:

> I lodged myself in the Piraeus; but this man [sc. Simon], observing immediately that Theodotos had arrived and was staying with Lysimachos – who lived just beside the house which this man had rented – invited some of his friends to join him.[36] They were at lunch, and were drinking, and posted watchers on the roof so that, when the boy should come out, they might seize him. At this juncture I arrived

---

[36] Simon obviously feels (unless – as our friend would like the Areopagus to believe – he is a complete lunatic) that he has some claim on the boy; that is why he has invited his friends over as witnesses, as well as to assist in the kidnapping. This action, once again, bears a certain analogy to that of Phrynion when Neaira returns with Stephanos to Athens from Megara (above, p. 33).

from the Piraeus, and in passing I turned into Lysimachos' house.[37]
After spending some little time there, we came out. Then those people,
already drunk, sprang out at us; some of his party refused to join in his
criminal action, but Simon here, and Theophilos, Protarchos and
Autokles began dragging the boy away. He, however, flung off his
cloak and ran.

There ensues a mad chase through the streets of Athens. Our friend is
careful to specify that he himself turned aside and went off by another
route, feeling confident, he tells us, that young Theodotos would get
away from his pursuers, albeit without his cloak.[38]

This, alas, did not happen. Theodotos, rather rashly, after running
a few blocks, took refuge in a shop belonging to one Molon the fuller,
where Simon and his henchmen, being no respecters of persons,
pursued him. They beat up Molon, who tried to protect him, and
started to drag Theodotos off with them. At this point, our friend, on
his own account, happens once more upon the scene (ss. 17–18):

> They had already got as far as Lampon's house when I, walking by
> myself, met up with them; and considering it a monstrous and
> shameful thing to stand by and see the young fellow subjected to such
> lawless and violent outrage, I seized hold of him.

The result of this intervention was a general melée, in which, he
admits (s. 18), everyone got their heads broken. Now this in turn
should have resulted in litigation, but it would seem that Simon,
despite the outrageous colours in which he is painted by our friend,
was just as reticent about taking to the law as he himself was, because
no indictment ensued – at least for the present. Who ended up with
Theodotos we are not told, but we must presume that he returned to
the bosom of our friend.

Even this, however, was not the end of the story. After an interval
of fully four years (s. 20), Simon, learning that our friend had had a bit
of 'bad luck', having been on the receiving end of an *antidosis* suit,
which it would seem that he lost,[39] decided to kick him when he was

[37] Our hero is above all concerned, even at the risk of absurdity, to suggest that there was
absolutely no premeditation on his part in the melée that followed. But what are we to
make of *trepomai pariôn*? It is made to sound as if he simply dropped in to Lysimachos'
on an impulse, since he happened to be passing!
[38] He is also still concerned to avert any suggestion of premeditation on his part, of
course.
[39] This would simply mean that he had to perform the *leitourgia* in question, rather than
go through a full exchange of properties; but still a serious embarrassment, both
socially and financially.

down, so to speak, and revive his grievance – there being no statute of limitations on enmity in Athenian society. The suit that he initiated was a serious one, alleging assault with intent to kill (*dikê traumatos ek pronoias*), which was tried before the Areopagus, the most august court in the land, and carried a penalty of exile, disfranchisement, and confiscation of property. After this long interval, Simon now has the nerve to claim that our friend set him up and tried to kill him, in the battle that took place after the return from the Aegean cruise. It is hardly likely that he got very far with this claim, but he did put our friend to considerable trouble, expense, and embarrassment, and in the process, through the efforts of Lysias, has immortalised their little tiff.

The sins of Timarchos

A much more serious tiff is the subject of our other case-history, that of the Athenian orator Aeschines with a certain Timarchos of Sphettos, whom Aeschines is indicting in 345 BC for the heinous crime of engaging in politics after having prostituted himself when he was a boy.[40] There was indeed a law on the subject (attributed, as was conventional, to Solon), which Aeschines is able to adduce, to the following effect (*In Tim.* 21):[41]

> If any Athenian shall have prostituted his person [*hetairêsêi*], he shall not be permitted to become one of the nine archons, nor to discharge the office of priest, nor to act as an advocate [*syndikêsai*] for the state, nor shall he hold any office at home or abroad, whether filled by lot or by election; he shall not be sent as a herald; he shall not take part in debate, nor be present at the public sacrifices; when the citizens are wearing garlands, he shall wear none; and he shall not enter within the limits of the place that has been purified for the assembling of the people. If any man who has been convicted of prostitution act contrary to these prohibitions, he shall be put to death.[42]

---

[40] There is now an excellent translation of this work, with introduction and commentary, by Nick Fisher, *Aeschines, Against Timarchos*, to which I am much indebted.

[41] I borrow in what follows the Loeb translation of Charles Darwin Adams, with minor variations.

[42] The status of laws and testimonies included in the texts of Greek orations is always suspect, but the great majority of this is actually quoted by Aeschines in the text, so we cannot go far wrong here in adopting it. We may also note a number of other stern 'Solonic' regulations for the supervision of gymnasia and schools (ss. 9–12), prohibiting, for instance, any adult other than a member of a relevant family from hanging about either type of establishment. I will return to these a little later.

This is pretty stern stuff. As so often, however, when issues of morality or of religious observance are raised in Athenian courts, and high-minded sentiments are uttered, it is prudent to look beyond immediate appearances – *cherchez la politique*, in fact, or at least *l'inimitié*. And such is indeed the case here. In order to understand why this case was brought, we must indulge in a brief survey of the political background.

For a number of years before the date of this trial, King Philip of Macedon had been a major threat to Athens' interests, particularly in Northern Greece. In 349 he moved against Olynthos, the chief city of Chalkidike, which had been playing a devious game for some time in setting off Philip against Athens for its own aggrandisement, but was now allied to Athens. Urged on by Demosthenes, who had been fulminating against Philip for some years previously (his so-called 'First Philippic' was delivered in early 351), the Athenians prepared to send troops to Chalkidike to defend Olynthos. Philip, however, cleverly created a diversion by provoking a revolt on the Athenian doorstep, in Euboia, with the consequence that troops were tied up there (against the advice of Demosthenes, who wanted all energies directed to Chalkidike) until it was too late to save Olynthos, which accordingly fell in the summer of 348.[43] In the aftermath of this, and after a futile effort to rouse up a Panhellenic alliance to oppose Philip, it was resolved, on the initiative of the statesman Euboulos, whose influence was still superior to that of Demosthenes, to make peace, and accordingly an embassy was sent to Philip, led by one Philokrates, a supporter of Euboulos, and including Aeschines, who was also a supporter of Euboulos, and Demosthenes, who was emphatically not.

A peace was in fact arranged, in the summer of 346, but from this a major quarrel arose between Aeschines and Demosthenes, of which this trial is a spin-off. The terms of the treaty were that each side should retain what it held at the time of the signing of the treaty, but Philip engaged in some sharp practice between the Athenian taking of the oath and his own, by using the time to conquer the Thracian Chersonese, which he had long had his eye on. The peace held, but in the aftermath Demosthenes launched a series of attacks on partisans of Euboulos, notably Philokrates and Aeschines, whom he accused of traitorous pandering to Philip. Timarchos, a sidekick of Demosthenes,

---

[43] It is in this context that the quarrel of Demosthenes with Meidias is to be placed (above, p. 90). Meidias, it will be recalled, was a supporter of Euboulos, and had served on the Euboian expedition (with results satirised by Demosthenes). Euboia was actually lost as well, despite the expedition, adding to Athens' discomfiture.

was put up to bring a charge of 'corruption on an embassy' (*para-presbeia*) against Aeschines. It is against this threat that the present prosecution is a counterblast.

With that off our chest, we may proceed. Aeschines' strategy, in dealing with the threat of Timarchos, was to launch a counter-attack. It would seem to have been the case (Aeschines makes much play, during his speech, of the facts being 'widely known')[44] that Timarchos had enjoyed a somewhat wild and dissipated youth, drinking, dicing and whoring – and, we are invited to believe, submitting to sexual indignities himself. It is on the latter point that Aeschines seeks to nail him.

However, even indulgence in passive homosexual relations, of itself, would not constitute a very serious allegation in classical Athens; at best it would constitute a basis for ridicule. If Aeschines is to land a serious blow on Timarchos – and indeed put him out of business as a politician and potential prosecutor, which is his intention – he must prove that Timarchos actually hired himself out as a prostitute, or *hetairos*[45] (*hetairêsis*), in order to bring him under the severe provisions of the law quoted above. To do this, it appears to the attentive modern reader, he had to bend the facts, and even the probabilities, considerably.[46]

His account of Timarchos' early career is as follows. At around the age of fifteen,[47] following on the death of his father, Arizelos, Timarchos is alleged to have attached himself to a doctor in the Peiraeus called Euthydikos,[48] presumably with the overt aim of qualifying as a doctor himself, but really, as Aeschines maintains, to use Euthydikos' surgery as a good base for picking up customers for himself. This is indeed what happened, before very long. There chanced along to the surgery a certain Misgolas, a man about town.[49] Aeschines, who is

---

44 E.g. ss. 44–5, 70, 77–8, 86–93 – this despite the fact that many of the events described or alluded to occurred up to twenty-five years earlier.

45 Fisher chooses to translate this 'escort', a decision which he defends with some plausibility (Intro. pp. 41–2), but the term still sounds odd; as the masculine equivalent of *hetaira*, it is perhaps best left untranslated.

46 He would seem to have satisfied the jury at the time, though, since he won the case.

47 Aeschines is a little vague here, but his phrase *epeidê apêllagê ek paidôn*, 'when he had just passed from boyhood', should denote an age of fifteen or even younger.

48 We know of this man from one other text, the speech of Demosthenes, *Against Boiôtos* II, (XL, 33), where he is reported as being suborned to manufacture and then testify to a false head-wound for a litigant in a law-case, but then confessing the truth about it. This would have occurred about 350 BC. How exactly one qualified as a doctor in fourth-century Athens we have little idea, but probably it was just a matter of apprenticeship.

49 Misgolas is a curious name for an Athenian, but there is no question but that he was a citizen. A man of the same name who may well be his grandfather occurs on an inscription of 403/2, as secretary to the treasurers of Athena and the other gods (*SEG* 23. 81. 5).

plainly anxious not to antagonise this man any more than he has to, gives a rather quaint description of him (s. 41):

> There is one Misgolas, men of Athens, son of Naukrates, of the deme of Kollytos, in all other respects an excellent person [*kalos k' agathos*], such as one would not in any way find fault with, except that he is remarkably devoted to this pursuit [sc. pederasty], and is accustomed always to have in his company singers or lyre-players [*kitharoidoi ê kitharistai*].[50]

Aeschines' allegation is that Misgolas actually paid Timarchos to come and live with him:

> Now this Misgolas, observing Timarchos' reason for staying in the house of the doctor, *paid him a sum of money in advance* to change his lodgings, and got him into his own home; for Timarchos was well-developed, young, and immoral – just the person for the thing that Misgolas wanted to do, and Timarchos was willing to submit to.

We may note here that the key element in the indictment is the paying of money. If Timarchos had simply agreed to come and live with Misgolas, the charge would have been less serious (and indeed Aeschines is unable to produce any proof that money changed hands), but even so, as Aeschines insists a little later (s. 51), Timarchos would be open to a charge of *hetairêsis*, being a 'kept man', since he was living in Misgolas' house at Misgolas' expense.

One problem, indeed, that Aeschines has to face (and tries to make the best of) is the fact that Timarchos, though an orphan, had been left quite a respectable fortune by his father (s. 42), which would on the face of it make prostitution seem improbable.[51] Aeschines' way of getting round this is to assert both that Timarchos did what he did out of a natural lewdness, and that his expensive habits caused him to run through his fortune rather quickly. Aeschines finds his case strengthened, however, by the fact that Misgolas was only the first of a succession of Timarchos' patrons (s. 53):

> So then, when Misgolas found him too expensive and let him go, next Antikles, son of Kallias, of the deme Euonymon, took him up.

---

[50] We must assume that these occupations carried a corresponding stigma to that of female flute-girls, who performed (not just on the flute) at symposia.

[51] We are actually given a detailed account of his father's wealth later in the speech, (ss. 97–105), with the rhetorical purpose of showing how improvident Timarchos was, and how heartless to his immediate relations, such as his widowed mother and his invalid uncle Arignotos.

Antikles, however, is absent in Samos as a member of the new colony,[52] so I will pass on to the next incident. For after this man Timarchos had left Misgolas and Antikles, he did not repent or reform his way of life, but spent his days in the gambling-place, where the gaming-table is set, and cock-fighting and dicing are the regular occupations. I imagine that some of you have seen the place – at least you will have heard of it.

The individual Timarchos next took up with was a phenomenon indeed. He was a public slave (*dêmosios*) by the name of Pittalakos. We will return to this man in connection with our discussion of slavery,[53] but we may note certain details here. Pittalakos, of course, serves very well Aeschines' purpose in linking Timarchos with the underworld of Athens, and in the humiliating role of a 'rent-boy' to boot (s. 55):

> Now the sins of Pittalakos against the person of Timarchos, and his outrages committed upon him, as they have come to my ears, are such that, by Olympian Zeus, I should not dare to repeat them to you. For the things that he was not ashamed to do in deed, I had rather die than describe to you in words.

With this masterly *praeteritio*, covering what was probably Aeschines' total ignorance of what went on with Pittalakos, he passes on to Timarchos' next patron, the prominent Athenian politician Hegesandros, son of Hegesias, of Sounion, and his equally prominent brother, Hegesippos, who were political associates of Timarchos, and thus of Demosthenes.[54] Aeschines spins a most lively tale, involving rivalry between Pittalakos and Hegesandros for the 'favours' of Timarchos, leading to the disgraceful beating up of Pittalakos and the trashing of his gaming establishment (ss. 58–61), but here chronology

---

[52] And so can't be called to testify (Aeschines has just extracted an unwilling testimony from Misgolas himself, at least to the fact that Timarchos lived with him, s. 50). Antikles would seem to have been a reasonably prominent member of society. His father Kallias is recorded as a *hellenotamias*, a high imperial financial official, in the year 410/9. The cleruchy, or settlement, of Samos referred to is doubtless the new settlement sent out in 352/1.

[53] Below, p. 140. The account here actually constitutes very interesting evidence of the status and life-style of 'public slaves', a class of person about whom we know all too little. It is very possible, however, despite Aeschines' description, that Pittalakos is actually a 'retired' public slave, i.e. had bought his freedom. Otherwise, his affluence and apparently liberated life-style is well-nigh incomprehensible.

[54] Hegesandros had been a Treasurer of Athena in 362/1, before going to Thrace in 361/0 as financial aide (*tamias*) to the general Timomachos of Acharnai. At the time of this trial, he and his brother were closely allied with Demosthenes in efforts to undermine the Peace of Philokrates.

comes against him. The association of Hegesandros with Timarchos is described as following Hegesandros' return from a military campaign in Thrace in 361/0. But we know that Timarchos served as a member of the Council for 361/0, so that he must have been at least already thirty years of age, and far from being a 'rent-boy', even if he kept low company.

From this point on, Aeschines' case, to a modern, analytical eye (though not, evidently, to the jury), begins to unravel somewhat, despite much colourful and entertaining detail with which he regales us as to Timarchos' more recent goings-on. What concerns us rather more in the present context, however, is his rather charming revelations as to his own attitude to pederasty, which he proposes to set against the attitude, and behaviour, that he attributes to Timarchos. The occasion for this remarkable apologia seems to have been that Timarchos, or rather a supporting speaker (*synêgoros*) of his (s. 132), had directed[55] something of a *tu quoque* at him, alleging that he himself was well known to be susceptible to the charms of young lads, and was known to have composed execrable verses to his favourites, and even to have been involved in fights. His reply is worth quoting at some length (ss. 135–7):

> And just here I understand that he is going to carry the war into my own territory, and ask me if I am not ashamed, on my own part, after having made a nuisance of myself in the gymnasia and having been many times a lover, now to be bringing the practice into reproach and danger. And finally – so I am told – in an attempt to raise a laugh and start silly talk among you, he says he is going to give a recitation of all the erotic poems I have ever addressed to one person or another, and he promises to call witnesses to certain quarrels and fisticuffs in which I have been involved in consequence of this habit.

Now, in view of what has gone before, we might expect Aeschines indignantly to deny these scurrilous imputations; but not so. Instead, what we get is a most interesting defence of 'honourable' pederasty, such as might have come from the mouth of Socrates himself:

---

[55] Passages of this sort in the published versions of forensic speeches are generally taken to be editorial additions based on subsequent knowledge of the content of one's opponent's reply, but it is also possible that Aeschines got wind of Timarchos' response through a form of 'industrial espionage'. However that may be, he speaks specifically of 'one of the generals', who will get up to support Timarchos, and he shows quite detailed knowledge of this man's argument.

Now as for me, I neither find fault with love that is honourable, nor do I say that those who are outstanding in beauty are prostitutes [peporneusthai]. I do not deny that I myself have been a lover [erôtikos] and am a lover to this day, nor do I deny that the jealousies and quarrels that commonly arise from the practice have happened in my case. As to the poems which they say I have composed, some I acknowledge, but as to others I deny that they are of the character that these people will impute to them, for they will tamper with them.

This, one might say, is a rather unexpected turn. Aeschines, the stern moralist and scourge of lechery, at the mature age of forty-five or so, is admitting still to being a lover, hanging about gymnasia and penning verses to his favourites – verses, indeed, which are such as to have various constructions put upon them! He is, however – unlike our friend, the opponent of Simon, in the previous case – quite unashamed. It is all a question of *how* you love:

> The distinction which I draw is this: to be in love with those who are beautiful and chaste is the experience of a kindhearted and generous soul; but to hire someone for money and to indulge in licentiousness with him is the act of a man who is boorish [hybristês] and ill-bred. And whereas it is an honour to be the object of a pure love, I declare that he who has prostituted himself for monetary gain is disgraced.

That, then, is the sticking-point: the giving of presents is quite acceptable (puppies, fighting-cocks, even perhaps a horse), but once money changes hands, or one goes to live with one's lover, the line of respectability has been crossed, and one becomes a *hetairos*, or even a *pornos*.

Aeschines now launches into a remarkable disquisition, in response to allusions by 'the 'general' to famous noble lovers in history and myth, such as Harmodios and Aristogeiton, or Achilles and Patroklos. After first quoting an old law (presumably of Solon), forbidding slaves 'to exercise in the gymnasium, or *to be the lover of a free boy*', he draws the remarkable conclusion that, by forbidding these activities to slaves, the legislator was commending them to free men.[56]

---

[56] One wonders how Aeschines felt such a law squared with those that he has quoted at the outset of the speech (ss. 9–12), forbidding the presence of adults, other than family members, from consorting with boys in gymnasia or schools. One can only assume that such laws were honoured rather in the breach than the observance; otherwise, many of the activities of Socrates (cf. the settings of such dialogues as the *Charmides* or the *Lysis*), not to mention those of Aeschines himself, would have become indictable offences.

He follows this with an extended disquisition on Homer's treatment of the relation between Achilles and Patroklos (ss. 141–50), culminating in some general moral reflections, and then turns to a consideration of contemporary Athenian society. In what must seem to modern sensibilities a quite extraordinary passage, he runs through a number of well-known members of society who have been, or even still are, the objects of 'noble' love, followed by a selection of characters who more resemble Timarchos. The individuals concerned are mostly otherwise quite unknown to us, but the passage seems to deserve quotation nonetheless, for the light it throws upon contemporary attitudes – assuming, of course, that Aeschines is interpreting them correctly (ss. 155–9):[57]

> But not to dwell too long on the poets, I will recite to you the names of older and well-known men, and of youths and boys, some of whom have had many lovers because of their beauty,[58] and some of whom, still in their prime, have lovers today, but not one of whom ever came under the same accusation as Timarchos. Again, I will tell over to you in contrast men who have prostituted themselves shamefully and notoriously, in order that by calling these to mind you may place Timarchos where he belongs.
>
> First I will name those who have lived the life of free and honourable men. You know, fellow-citizens, Kriton, son of Astyochos, Perikleides of Perithoidai, Polemagenes, Pantaleon, son of Kleagoras, and Timesitheos the runner,[59] men who were the most beautiful, not only among their fellow-citizens, but in all Hellas, men who counted many a man of eminent self-control[60] as lover; yet no man ever censured them.
>
> And again, among the youths and those who are still boys, first, you

---

[57] He did, after all, win his case!

[58] As Nick Fisher acutely remarks, *Against Timarchos*, p. 298, it is not quite clear how one can manage *chastely* to have *many* lovers – consecutively, or simultaneously? This is very much what Timarchos is being accused of earlier. But we must assume that there is a chaste way of doing everything.

[59] Of these men, only the first, Kriton, shows up on an inscription (as contributing money for the outfitting of triremes in 340 BC, and thus pretty rich). As for Timesitheos, he is probably a member of a wealthy family, of whom we have a number of inscriptional records throughout the fourth century (the name is an unusual one), but none of the attested holders of the name seems quite to fit chronologically. See Fisher, ibid., p. 298.

[60] One might speculate as to exactly what 'self-control' (*sôphrosynê*) might connote in such a context; not necessarily, I think, 'chastity' in the Judaeo-Christian sense (as the word is translated, rather misleadingly, by Adams). One may perhaps think back to Plato's eloquent passage of the *Phaedrus* 255A–E (quoted above, p. 108).

know the nephew of Iphikrates,[61] the son of Teisias of Rhamnous, of the same name as the defendant. He, beautiful as he is to look upon, is so far from reproach that the other day at the Rural Dionysia, when the comedies were being played in Kollytos,[62] and when Parmenon the comic actor addressed an anapaestic verse to the chorus, in which certain persons were referred to as 'big Timarchian whores', nobody thought of it as being aimed at this youth, but, one and all, as meant for you, so unquestioned is your title to the practice.

He goes on to mention two more beautiful youths (one of whom, Antikles the *stadion*-runner, went on to win the Olympic title in 340), and then turns to the 'bad boys', of Timarchos' type:

But as to those men who are kindred spirits with Timarchos, for fear of arousing their enmity I will mention only those towards whom I am utterly indifferent. Who of you does not know Diophantos, called 'the orphan',[63] who hauled [*apêgagen*] the foreigner before the Archon, whose associate on the bench [*paredros*] was Aristophon of Azenia?[64] For Diophantos accused the foreigner of having cheated him out of four drachmae in connection with this practice [sc. male prostitution], and he cited the laws that command the Archon to protect orphans, when he himself had violated the laws that enjoin chastity.

Or what Athenian was not indignant at Kephisodoros, the so-called [*kaloumenos*] 'son of Molon',[65] for having ruined his surpassing

---

[61] The well-known general (c. 415–353 BC). he had actually started from humble beginnings, but had become rich by reason of his military successes, as had his brother Teisias. This Timarchos is otherwise unrecorded, but his brother Timotheos turns up on an inscription, dedicating an altar to Herakles in the Agora.

[62] The Rural Dionysia were held, with a procession and carnival, at mid-winter throughout the demes of Attica, and in some demes, at least, re-runs of the tragedies and comedies of the previous year were staged. Kollytos is actually a suburban, rather than a rural deme, situated not far south-west of the Agora. Many of the audience could thus have attended such a performance.

[63] The jury well may, but we, alas, do not. It is quite a common name.

[64] This is a rather obscure reference to us, though no doubt perspicuous to the jury. We do not otherwise know that the rather extreme procedure of *apagôgê* (a form of summary arrest) was employable for offences against orphans, but Aeschines must know what he is talking about. The point of mentioning Aristophon is that he was a very senior politician, which made the situation that much more outrageous. Diophantos' action almost deserves to be added to the definitions of *chutzpah*, alongside Leo Rosten's: 'killing one's father and mother, and then pleading for mercy on the ground that one is an orphan'. Other confusing aspects of the case are what age we must suppose Diophantos to have been (he must have been over eighteen to have taken a case on his own); and what the four drachmae was payment for – a one-night stand, or a more protracted arrangement. Aeschines is being distinctly elliptical.

[65] A slightly mysterious reference also: if he was 'called' the son of Molon, he was presumably not really the son of Molon. Perhaps Molon was his lover.

beauty by a most infamous life? Or Mnesitheos, known as the cook's son?[66] Or many others, whose names I am willing to forget?

Once again, Aeschines exercises the art of *praeteritio*. This litany leads to a rather effective appeal to the jury, to tell him to which class of person they feel that Timarchos belongs (s. 159). They plainly give him a satisfactory answer, and his case is essentially won.

As I suggested at the outset, all this high-minded indignation is really provoked by political exigencies, not by a crusading evangelical urge to clean up Athenian society. Nevertheless, in the process of seeking to destroy Timarchos, Aeschines has plainly said a mouthful, giving vent to a wide range of issues concerning that very Athenian institution, the practice of pederasty, and for that we must be grateful to him. If we reflect on this practice from a modern perspective, one thing we seem entirely to miss is any suggestion that pederasty as such was *bad*, either mentally or physically, for the boys concerned. It was all a matter of how the relationship was entered into. As Aeschines – and Pausanias in Plato's *Symposium* – would maintain, an honourable love, entered into by the boy for purposes of self-improvement, is a thoroughly noble thing; it is only when motives of greed enter into it that it becomes disgraceful. Either, I think, we must conclude that Athenian adult males were quite oblivious to the harm that they were doing to the psyches of the young (and of course to the harm that had previously been done to them), or that in fact, in a society where such practices were accepted, no significant harm was done.

---

[66] Once again, a nickname. A cook (*mageiros*) would normally have been a slave, or at least a freedman.

CHAPTER SIX

Slaves and Slave-Masters

GREEK SLAVERY: THEORY AND PRACTICE

There are a number of unsatisfactory human relationships comprised under the heading of slavery, and the Greek world was acquainted with most of them. I do not propose to enter here upon a comprehensive survey of the many possible varieties of slavery. That has been very well done repeatedly elsewhere.[1] However, some terminological distinctions do need to be established at the outset.

A broad distinction may be made, first of all, between serfdom and what is generally termed 'chattel slavery'. Serfs are peasants who are tied to the land they occupy, under the control of a landlord, either of the same race or of another, dominant race. The most notable examples of this relationship in the Greek world were the Helots of Laconia, subject to their Spartiate lords, and the Penestae of Thessaly, subject to their local aristocracy. The relationship of serfdom was not, however, something that manifested itself in Classical Athens, so we need not concern ourselves with it further. What we must focus on is chattel slavery.

Already in the Homeric poems we find chattel slavery a common and accepted feature of life. A natural result of defeat in any of the Greeks' interminable wars was enslavement, primarily of the women and children (if the adult males were slaughtered – as in the sack of Troy), but not infrequently of adult males as well. One could also fall victim to the depredations of Phoenician or other pirates, who would carry off unwary citizens of cities that they visited, and sell them into slavery elsewhere. This is what had happened to Odysseus' faithful swineherd Eumaios (*Od.* 14. 403ff.) – he was of noble family, but was kidnapped by Phoenician traders, through the connivance of his nurse, who was herself a Phoenician, but enslaved to his father; and

---

[1] I have derived most benefit in this connection from such works as Moses Finley (ed.), *Slavery in Classical Antiquity* and *Ancient Slavery and Modern Ideology*; and Yvon Garlan, *Slavery in Ancient Greece*.

so Eumaios came to be sold to Odysseus' father, Laertes.[2] The same was the case with Odysseus' old nurse, Eurykleia (*Od.* I. 430ff.). She is named as the daughter of Ops, son of Peisenor (and thus, by implication, of respectable ancestry – Homer being a bit of a snob in these matters), but Laertes bought her (in circumstances not specified) for twenty oxen; he did not, however, as might normally have been the case, take her to his bed, out of respect for his wife!

Both Eumaios and Eurykleia, we may note, are *Greek*, though from other tribes. Homer does not betray any feeling that enslavement, whether of Greeks or foreigners, is unnatural or improper, though he is prepared to recognise it as a great misfortune.[3] However, a negative attitude towards enslaving fellow-Greeks certainly manifested itself in classical times, and indeed intensifies from the fifth to the fourth centuries.[4] It can be attributed partly to a feeling of discomfort at putting compatriots in this position, and partly to a more practical concern for security: it was felt to be much safer to have a thoroughly heterogeneous slave population, so that they would have much less impetus to combine against their masters (and indeed there is nothing resembling a slave revolt recorded for the whole classical period in Athens). Plato, in the course of legislating for his ideal state in the *Laws* (V, 777B–778A), actually expresses rather well what must have been the standard attitude of the Athenian gentleman towards slaves. It is worth, I think, quoting at length:[5]

> The slave is a difficult sort of possession to handle. The frequent and repeated revolts in Messenia,[6] and in the states where people possess a lot of slaves who all speak the same language, have shown the evils of the system often enough; and we can also point to the various crimes and adventures of the robbers who plague Italy, the 'Rangers' [*Peridinoi*], as they're called. In view of all this, you may well be puzzled to know what your general policy ought to be. In fact, there are just two ways of dealing with the problem open to us: first, if the

---

[2] In connection with Eumaios we may note something relevant to the situation of slaves much later, in Classical Athens, that he actually lives on his own, managing an establishment (pig production) that involves having four other slaves under him. We shall note various parallels with this situation presently, from the classical period.

[3] At *Odyssey* XVII 322–3, he allows Eumaios to make the remark that 'Zeus takes away half the *aretê* of a man, when the day of slavery comes upon him.'

[4] The high-minded attitude is well expressed by Plato in Book V of the *Republic* (471A), where he makes Socrates argue that wars between Greeks should really be regarded as 'civil strife', and thus that enslavement of a beaten enemy should be excluded. More practical considerations are adduced at *Laws* Book V, 777CD (quoted below).

[5] I borrow here the Penguin translation of Trevor Saunders, slightly altered.

[6] These, of course, involved indigenous serfs, rather than chattel slaves.

slaves are to submit to their condition without giving trouble, they should not all come from the same country or speak the same tongue, as far as that can be arranged; and secondly, we ought to train them properly, not only for their sakes, but above all for our own.

The best way to train slaves is to refrain from arrogantly ill-treating them, and to harm them even less, if that's possible, than you would your equals. You see, when a man can hurt someone as often as he likes, he'll soon show whether or not his respect for justice is natural and un-feigned and springs from a genuine hatred of injustice.[7] If his attitude to his slaves and his conduct towards them are free of any taint of impiety and injustice, he'll be splendidly effective at sowing the seeds of virtue …

Even so, we should certainly punish slaves if they deserve it, and not spoil them by simply admonishing them, as one would free men. Virtually everything you say to a slave should be in the form of an order, and you should never become at all familiar with them – neither the women nor the men.[8] This is how, it must be said, a lot of foolish people do treat their slaves, and usually only succeed in spoiling them, and in making life more difficult – more difficult, I mean, for the slaves to take orders and for themselves to maintain their authority.[9]

One would normally hesitate to adduce Plato as evidence for normal Athenian moral or social attitudes, but on the subject of slavery here he seems very much in tune with the majority of 'right-thinking' folk. It must certainly have been a problem for basically decent, good-hearted citizens to avoid getting too familiar with the servants, especially if they had grown up together with them in the household. As we have already seen exemplified in the *Odyssey*, and as we shall see again from such fourth-century sources as Menandrian comedy and forensic speeches, it is difficult indeed to maintain the proper degree of aloofness from such figures as one's old nurse or tutor (*paidagôgos*), or from a trusted steward of one's property or manager of one's factory, or yet from one's personal servant (the frequently-featured 'clever slave' of New Comedy), who might have grown up in the household along with you, and was only too well aware of all your weaknesses and foibles.[10]

---

[7] A nice commentary on this point is provided by an anecdote told of Plato (e.g. by Plutarch, *De Lib. Educ.* 10D, and *Adv. Col.* 1108A), that he became angry with one of his slaves and, precisely because he was angry, asked his nephew Speusippos to beat the slave for him.

[8] Including, of course, sexual familiarity, with either women or boys.

[9] This is a feature of the Boorish Man (*agroikos*), as satirised by Theophrastus in *Characters* 4: he chats with his slaves about matters of the greatest importance.

[10] All these relationships could easily be paralleled from literary and other sources about the ante-bellum South in the United States, for example.

Aristotle, in his turn, makes a valiant effort to come up with a theory of slavery, or of the Natural Slave – not covering himself with glory in the process. In Book I, chapters 4–5 of the *Politics*, he first characterises the slave as an 'animate instrument', in an effort to dehumanise the slave *qua* slave, and then goes on to enquire whether there is such a thing as a natural slave. He starts (1254a13–17) by offering a definition of the slave:[11]

> From these considerations we can see clearly what is the nature of the slave and what is his capacity. We attain these definitions – first, that 'anyone who by his nature is not his own man but another's, is by his nature a slave'; secondly, that 'anybody who, being a man, is an article of property [*ktêma*], is another's man'; and thirdly, that 'an article of property is an instrument [*organon*] intended for the purpose of action and separated from its possessor'.

From this he moves on, at the beginning of chapter 5, to raise the question whether there are any persons who are *by nature* such as are here defined – 'whether, in other words, there are persons for whom slavery is the better and just condition, or whether the reverse is the case, and all slavery is contrary to nature'.

Aristotle has little patience with this latter view, which he is aware has been advanced in the past by certain troublesome sophists.[12] However, in order to establish his own preferred view, he has to advance some controversial postulates. Having assumed that we agree (1254b2ff.) that, 'in animate beings, there is an element that rules (i.e. the soul), and an element that is ruled (i.e. the body), and the soul rules the body with the authority of a master; and it is clearly natural and beneficial to the body that it should be ruled by the soul', he goes on to advance this thought:

> We may thus conclude that all men who differ from others as much as the body differs from the soul, or an animal from a man (and this is the case with all those whose function is bodily service, and who produce their best when they supply such service) – all such are by nature slaves, and it is better for them, on the very same principle as in the other cases just mentioned, to be ruled by a master. A man is thus by nature a slave if he is capable of becoming (and this is the reason why he also actually becomes) the property of another, and if he participates

[11] I borrow here the translation of Sir Ernest Barker, *The Politics of Aristotle*, pp. 11–12.

[12] Elsewhere, in the *Rhetoric* (I 13, 1373b17–18, he mentions the sophist Alcidamas, a pupil of Gorgias, who declared 'God has left all men free, and nature has made no man a slave.'

in reason to the extent of apprehending it in another, though destitute of it himself. Herein he differs from animals, which do not apprehend reason, but simply obey their instincts. But the use which is made of the slave diverges only minimally from the use made of tame animals; both he and they supply their owner with bodily help in meeting his daily requirements.

Aristotle's whole strategy is to assimilate the slave as closely as possible both to animals and to implements. It is doubtful that many ordinary Athenians had thought out so coherent a rationale of slavery as presented by Aristotle here, though doubtless they would have nodded approval had they had a chance to read his work – as did many a plantation owner in the Deep South some two millennia later. He goes on (1254b27ff.), even more remarkably, to argue that 'it is Nature's intention also to erect a physical difference between the body of the free man and that of the slave, giving the latter strength for the menial duties of life, but making the former upright in carriage and, though useless for physical labour, useful for the various purposes of civic life.'

This suggestion that the bodies of free men are actually useless (*akhrêsta*) for bodily labour verges on the fantastic.[13] A ray of realism breaks in just below, however, where he admits that 'the contrary of nature's intention often happens: there are some slaves who have the bodies of free men – as there are others who have a free man's soul.' Such aberrations, though, do not bother him greatly. He concludes, slightly wistfully (1254b34ff.):

> But if Nature's intention were realised – if men differed from one another in bodily form as much as the statues of gods [sc. differ from the bodies of men] – it is obvious that we should all agree that the inferior class ought to be the slaves of the superior.[14] And if this prin-ciple is true when the difference is one of body, it may be affirmed with still greater justice when the difference is one of soul (though it is not as easy to see the beauty of the soul as it is to see that of the body).
>
> It is thus clear that, just as some are by nature free, so others are by nature slaves, and for these latter the condition of slavery is both beneficial and just.

[13] Unless perhaps we can interpret the Greek term *akhrêstos* here as meaning merely 'ill-adapted', which seems possible.

[14] The ideal, of course, of theorists of eugenics – who are beginning to raise their ugly heads again these days, with the advent of the possibilities deriving from cloning. Aristotle, and Plato before him, I fear, would have been quite happy with the development of selective breeding techniques.

As I say, it is doubtful that any ordinary Athenian gentleman had worked out a theory of 'natural' slavery that was at all comparable in precision to that of Aristotle, but there was a widespread belief, probably originating in the years following on the defeat of the Persian expeditionary force in the years 480–479, that Asiatic races in particular (but also more northerly peoples such as the Thracians and the Scythians) were intellectually and morally inferior to Greeks, and ideally suited to slavery. There is a remarkable passage in the Hippocratic treatise *Airs, Waters, Places* (of uncertain date and authorship, but probably to be dated to the mid-fifth century) which provides a 'scientific' underpinning to Greek intuitions of racial superiority (s. 16):

> So much for the differences of constitution between the inhabitants of Asia and of Europe.[15] The small variations of climate to which the Asiatics are subject, extremes both of heat and cold being avoided, account for the mental flabbiness and cowardice as well. They are less warlike than Europeans and tamer of spirit, for they are not subject to those physical changes and the mental stimulation which sharpens tempers and induces recklessness and hotheadedness. Instead they live under unvarying conditions. Where there are always changes, men's minds are roused so that they cannot stagnate. Such things appear to me to be the cause of the feebleness of the Asiatic race, but a contributory cause lies in the customs; for the greater part is under monarchical rule.[16]

– but of course, for our author, monarchical or tyrannical rule is itself only a natural result of the general spinelessness of Asiatics.

This, however, only justifies the suitability for enslavement of one major source of slaves; for Thracians, Celts, and Scythians our author has the converse argument (ss. 19; 23) that their climate is *too* extreme, and induces 'recklessness and hotheadedness' without any compensating quotient of rationality, such as is characteristic of Greeks. These races are therefore also suitable for enslavement, though needing a certain amount of 'breaking in' first. Dotty chauvinistic theorising of this sort, at any rate, did help to assuage whatever slight feelings of discomfort may have been felt by intellectual or

---

[15] The author has just been contrasting the two continents in respect of climate, the following remark encapsulating his views: 'Everything grows much bigger and finer in Asia, and the nature of the land is tamer, while the character of the inhabitants is milder and less passionate.' The blissful ignorance and inconsequentiality on which these conclusions are based are quite breathtaking, but this does not detract from the importance of the text as an underpinning for racial prejudice.

[16] Trans. Chadwick and Mann, in the most useful Penguin collection of texts, *Hippocratic Writings* (Harmondsworth, 1978), edited by Geoffrey Lloyd.

morally sensitive Athenians at the enslavement of at least non-Greeks.

We may turn now to some practical considerations.[17] A major subject of controversy, as regards Classical Athens, is the question of the level of the slave population at any given time, and the extent of slave ownership among the population at large. As we have seen in other connections, the Athenians were remarkably haphazard, by modern standards, about the compiling and keeping of statistics on matters dear to the hearts of modern economists and social scientists, but not of vital interest to ancient states. The only comprehensive estimate that we have of the slave population of Attica is one that relates to the very end of our chosen period, and provides a total that is so improbably large that virtually nobody, including myself, is prepared to believe it, while having no very convincing explanation as to how it arose. In 317–316, during his brief period of rule in Athens, the Macedonian-backed dynast Demetrius of Phaleron took a census, which revealed just 21,000 adult male citizens (and therefore, let us say, a citizen population of about 100,000, including women and children), 10,000 resident aliens, or *metoikoi*, and 400,000 slaves – a quite astonishing number.[18] More moderate calculations, based on our admittedly meagre data for yearly consumption of corn at various times in the fourth century, would indicate a maximum of 150,000 slaves, over and above the presumed number of citizens and metics.[19] This is supported by another snippet of information, dating from 338, occurring in a fragment of a speech by the Athenian politician Hyperides,[20] who is defending himself for a proposal, in the aftermath of the defeat of Athens by Philip at Chaeronea, to free the slaves of Attica on condition that they were prepared to fight for the state. He mentions a figure of 'more than one hundred and fifty thousand, both from the silver mines [sc. in Laureion] and up and down the country'. This number again is doubtless a guess, but probably a reasonably realistic one.

[17] I provide these merely as background. It is no part of my purpose to enter into any detailed discussion of these very knotty questions.

[18] This datum is relayed to us by Athenaeus in the *Deipnosophistai* (the latter part of Book 6 of which is devoted to topics related to slavery), on the authority of a certain Ctesicles (a late Hellenistic authority), in Book 3 of his *Chronicles*. The truth may be that nobody had any accurate idea of slave populations at this or any other time (except perhaps for such enterprises as the Laureion silver-mines), since there was no pressing reason to count them, and wildly inflated guesses were made, but this enormous figure (as with those of 460,000 for Corinth, and 470,000 for the rather small island of Aegina, reported in the same passage) remains disturbing.

[19] Cf. e.g., A. W. Gomme, 'The Slave Population of Athens', *Journal of Hellenic Studies* 66 (1946), 127–9.

[20] *Against Aristogiton*, Fr. 3.

We may therefore reckon, I think, that there were in Attica as a whole – including the mines, which absorbed perhaps up to 25,000 when being worked to full capacity – somewhat more slaves than freemen in the Classical period. The next question is: how were they distributed? Again, in the absence of reliable data, there is a wide variety of views. The most reasonable position seems to be this. At the bottom end of society, we have some indication that, at least in and around 403, just after the end of the War, up to 5,000 citizens could be identified as owning no land (and thus being liable to disenfranchisement, on the proposal of a reactionary by the name of Phormisios).[21] Such citizens could hardly be expected to own slaves to any extent, which leaves a total of approximately 20,000 potential slave-owners.[22] Of these, the majority would be of fairly modest means, just the top 6,000 (those liable to the property tax, or *eisphora*) being reasonably well-off, while the next 9,000 or so, forming the 'hoplite class' (i.e. those who could afford to provide their own armour for battle), would constitute something approximating to a 'middle class'.

It is widely agreed that all landowners of any substance owned at least one or two slaves. Since quite a number of people seem to have possessed a number of allotments of land around Attica, as well as a town-house of some sort, we might suppose that they would need at least one slave to work each allotment (which they themselves would need to call in on regularly, in rotation), as well as a few to run the town-house. People who owned factories, like the fathers of Demosthenes and of Timarchos, for instance, would own groups of from half a dozen to twenty or more slaves, mostly living on their own, under the supervision of a manager (himself either a slave or freedman), to run those enterprises; while other citizens again owned bands of slaves whom they hired out to others on a contract basis. At the top end of this scale one hears of magnates like Nikias in the late fifth century hiring a thousand slaves to a concessionary at the silver mines at Laureion,[23]

---

[21] Attacked by Lysias in a speech (XXXIV) of which only a fragment survives.

[22] The total of adult male citizens at this stage will have declined considerably from the maximum of 30,000 at the beginning of the Peloponnesian War. The proportion of landless may also now have been comparatively high, but a figure of 15–20 per cent landless during the period as a whole does not seem unrealistic.

[23] Xenophon, *Ways and Means*, 4. 14. This concessionary, one Sosias the Thracian, may even be identical with a slave that Nikias is reported, also by Xenophon (*Mem.* 2. 5, 2), to have purchased for fully one talent 'to be his manager at the silver mine'. We would have to suppose that Nikias subsequently freed Sosias (as, later, did his employers the banker Pasion, or Demosthenes Sr. his manager Milyas), but there would be nothing extraordinary in that, after all.

but in many cases it would just be a matter of hiring out a few slaves to help with the harvest or the vintage.[24]

Instead of generalising in a void, however, it might be best to cast our minds back over the previous chapters, and see how many slaves manifest themselves in the employ of the various characters we have met there, since between them they provide a fair cross-section of at least the top half of Athenian society.

To begin, then, with Euphiletos, in Chapter 1, we can see that he has a modest establishment in town, but also a farm in the country. In town, we have evidence only of his wife's maid and a serving-girl (whom his wife pretends to tease him about), who is presumably a different person, though it would be strange if he did not have a general male factotum as well. He will also probably have had a slave resident in his farm, to help him with his labours as well as minding the place in his absence, and this slave could well be married (to another slave). I would postulate, then, for Euphiletos – a man of modest means and pretensions, but able to engage Lysias as a speech-writer! – a total of four slaves, while recognising that we have evidence of only two.

Ischomachos' establishment, on the other hand, is a very different matter. It is plain that he is a member of the richest class in the state, master of an extensive household and a large estate (or estates).[25] From his conversation with Socrates in Xenophon's *Oeconomicus*, we derive the impression of a large and fairly specialised household. At

[24] An interesting remark, in this connection, is made by a defendant in Lysias' speech *On the Olive Stump* (VII), which we will be considering in Ch. 7 below, in relation to the topic of piety and impiety (ss. 34–5); 'If one of the gods were to take a man who owned fifty or more slaves and were to transport him and his wife and children to a deserted place, along with the rest of his property and his slaves, where no free man were likely to come to his aid, what and how great would be his fear, do you think, that he, his children and wife would all be killed by their slaves?' This is part of an argument in support of the proposition that slaves have no love for their masters, but it seems incidentally to give an insight into what a prosperous citizen (such as this man is) would think of as a reasonable average amount of slaves for one man to own.

[25] We know from Lysias (*Speech* XIX 46) that he left on his death an estate of 'less than ten talents' to be divided between his two sons, a very respectable amount – though he was rumoured during his lifetime to be worth more than seventy talents (which is the point of relaying this information). The speaker is trying to minimise things, so we may speculate that the truth, for Ischomachos' lifetime, lies somewhere in between these two figures. As for his estates, in Xenophon's *Oeconomicus* (XX 22–5), he is made to speak of his father's policy of buying up lands which were undercultivated, and developing them, as a good mode of investment. This would imply a number of separate plots, apart from his main estate, but when he is describing his daily routine (XI 14–18), only one estate (within walking distance of the city) seems to be in prospect. In any case, he is a pretty large-scale landowner.

any rate, when Ischomachos is instructing his wife in management of
the household, we find the following (IX 5):

> Then I pointed out to her the women's quarters, separated from the
> men's by a bolted door, so that nothing may be taken out that
> shouldn't be, and so that the slaves [*oiketai*] may not breed without
> our approval. For the good ones are generally more loyal if they have
> children, while if wicked ones pair off, they simply become more
> resourceful in devising mischief.

– and a little further down (IX 9) mention is made of indicating to the
relevant slaves 'the various utensils that they would need for baking,
cooking, woolworking, and so on'. All the indications are of a large
and highly structured household, rather on the scale of a noble
establishment of the Victorian era, or an ante-bellum estate in the
Deep South – we might conjecture something like eight or ten slaves
in the house, and another dozen or so assigned to farm work.

Emphasis is placed, in this connection, on the importance of
selecting a good housekeeper (*tamia*, IX 11), as it is, a little later on
(XII 3ff.), on the choice and training of a good steward (*epitropos*), for
the field slaves. In the description of these privileged and trusted
figures, we seem to gain an insight into the various layers of privilege
that could be enjoyed by people who were still officially mere chattels,
on the legal level totally within the power of their masters. Xenophon (through his mouthpiece Ischomachos) fully recognises that
slaves are capable of a high degree of moral excellence, since he demands
such from his overseers, both male and female, and that even basic
slaves respond satisfactorily to humane treatment, and various sorts of
incentive. The following passage is significant (XIII 6–12):

> 'Other living things, Socrates', he said, 'learn to obey in these two
> ways: by being punished when they try to disobey, and by being well
> treated when they serve with enthusiasm … [9] As for human beings,
> one can make them more obedient by the application of reason [*logos*]
> as well, by making clear to them how advantageous it is for them to
> obey; and yet for slaves the education that seems fit only for beasts is
> effective also in teaching them to obey, for in gratifying their bellies
> to the extent they desire, you can achieve a good deal with them. But
> the ambitious amongst them are spurred by praise as well; for some
> natures are as hungry for praise as others are for food and drink.
>
> [10] These things, then, that I do in the expectation of having more
> obedient human beings for my use, I teach to those that I want to

appoint as stewards, and I support them also in the following ways: I make sure that the clothing and the shoes I must supply to the workers are not all alike, but rather some are worse and some are better, so that I may be able to honour the stronger with the better items, and give the worse to the worse. [11] For it seems to me, Socrates', he said, 'that it is a great discouragement to the good when they see that the work is done by themselves and yet that they receive the same as those who aren't willing to toil or risk danger when there is need of it. [12] I myself, therefore, do not at all consider that the better and the worse deserve to receive equal treatment, and when I see that my stewards[26] have given the best things to those who are worth the most, I praise them, but if I see someone being honoured over others by reason of flattery or some other favour that benefits no one, I do not ignore that, Socrates, but rather reprimand the steward concerned and try to teach him that what he is doing is not to his own advantage.'

There is quite a lot to be learned from this work of Xenophon's, both about the structure of a large Athenian household and about attitudes to slaves. Ischomachos, as we have seen earlier, is very much of a Xenophontic ideal Athenian gentleman, but his expressed attitudes are for all that probably not far removed from the norm for the right-minded prosperous citizen.

If we move on, now, to our third exemplar from Chapter 1, the misanthropic small farmer, Knemon, we find what may be regarded as the low point of slave ownership in Athenian society: Knemon runs his household, consisting of himself and his daughter, with the help of just one old slave-woman. As it ultimately turns out, in fact, he is owner of a property worth two talents, such as would have enabled him to own at least one other slave to help him on the farm; it is simply his meanness that stands in the way.[27] As a small farmer, with a property of perhaps ten to fifteen hectares, we could expect him, I think, to have a minimum of a serving-maid in the house, and a 'boy' to help him in the fields (even his penniless step-son, Gorgias, after all, has one slave, Daos).

As for the family of young Sostratos, they are plainly well-to-do, with a country estate in Phyle as well as an establishment in town.

---

[26] This plural would indicate that Ischomachos has a multiplicity of stewards – one, presumably, running each of his estates. But in that case we must raise the overall total of field slaves, perhaps into the twenties.

[27] Cf. Gorgias' remarks, ll. 326–32: 'This property of his is worth about two talents, and he farms it still all by himself, without a man to help – no family slave, no hired hand from the area, no neighbour – it's all done by him, and him alone.'

We meet only two slaves, Sostratos' personal attendant, Pyrrhias, and Getas, an older family retainer, but these are doubtless only the tip of a rather large iceberg. The sort of picnic that Sostatros' mother is engaged upon would require the services of about half-a-dozen man- and maid-servants, of whom we catch glimpses,[28] as well as of the cook Sikon, whose status is somewhat unclear, but who is probably a freedman, and now his own master. In New Comedy, as far as one can see, cooks are normally boastful, self-important figures,[29] to an extent inconsistent with current servile status, but in real life they were just as likely to be slaves rented out by their masters (as is the flute-girl Parthenis, ll. 432–3), and perhaps even living on their own. About slaves of this category we will have more to say below.

There is not much evidence to be derived on slave ownership from the case-histories of Chapter 2, though we may note with interest that Neaira, herself only a step out of slavery, is nonetheless the owner of two slave-girls as personal attendants; but there is more to be gleaned from Chapter 3. Here we find, for instance, Demosthenes' father owning two slave-run factories, a sword-making establishment employing 'thirty-two or thirty-three slaves, worth five to six minae each, and none worth less than three minae', and a sofa factory employing twenty.[30] We must also, I feel, assume something like a dozen more to run the Demosthenes household (which we are told in the same passage was estimated to be worth half a talent – 3,000 drachmae – and was thus a considerable establishment). In connection with Demosthenes Sr., we may note also the foreman (epitropos) of his shield factory, Milyas, who had been his slave, but had been freed, probably in Demosthenes' will, but possibly even before that.[31]

The accounts of the estates of Kiron and of Diodotos, in the same chapter, do not, unfortunately, reveal numbers of slaves, but since they were comparable in prosperity with that of Demosthenes, we may assume similar numbers, at least in the household. In the case of Diodotos, on the analogy of a situation to be examined below (n. 32), we may, I think, assume a number of trusted slaves acting as his

---

[28] E.g. Getas blames 'the women' for loading him with burdens, ll. 403–5; and Sostratos' mother gives orders to her maidservants at ll. 439–40.

[29] Cf. ll. 644–5: 'No one gets away unscathed with maltreating a cook!'

[30] Demosthenes, Against Aphobos I (XXVII), 9.

[31] Demosthenes is somewhat vague on this point (XXVII 19; XXIX 5), doubtless because Aphobos is trying to demand Milyas to be handed over to give evidence under torture, as a slave. But at least it is clear that Milyas continued to administer the factory as a freedman for many years after Demosthenes' father's death.

shipping agents in various parts of the Greek world, but we are given no evidence on that.[32]

If we turn to Chapter 4, the only situation in which slaves figure is in the contretemps of Apollodoros with his erstwhile 'friend', where it is an expedition allegedly in pursuit of three runaway slaves that leads to the 'friend', Nikostratos, being captured by pirates and having to be ransomed. It is certain that Apollodoros had quite a household of slaves, a number of whom would have been working on his farm (two of these had actually been given by him, he says, to Nikostratos, and it was they who had run away, along with one of Nikostratos'), but we lack any further details of these.

If we turn now to Chapter 5, the case of Timarchos grants us various insights. First of all, we have an account of the property of Timarchos' father (*Against Timarchos*, 97), which includes 'nine or ten slaves who were skilled shoemakers, each of whom paid him a fee of two obols a day, and the manager of the workshop, who paid him three obols, and a woman skilled in flax-working, who produced fine goods for the market, and a man skilled in embroidery'. This gives us a total of perhaps a dozen slaves engaged in commercial activity, to which we must certainly add half a dozen or so domestic slaves at least (the family, after all, had a town house, a suburban estate in the deme of Sphettos, and another farm in Alopeke, all of which needed to be looked after).

In connection with the slaves in the shoe factory, we may note something that is a prominent feature of the slave economy, the phenomenon of slaves living on their own (*khôris oikountes*), often (if involved in a factory or workshop) under the control of a manager, himself a slave or a freedman, and paying to their master a daily tax (the *apophora*). If we can take it that a tax of two obols a day is not totally exorbitant (there is no point, after all, in making the slave's life impossible), then I think that we must assume that such slaves could earn more or less what was the normal wage of a skilled free workman, approximately a drachma (six obols) a day, and a manager perhaps a drachma and a half, or even two. Two obols a day, after all,

---

[32] We do, however, gain a remarkable insight into the degree of independence that could be enjoyed by such a slave from a speech in the Demosthenic corpus, *Against Phormio* (XXXIV), where the slave agent of a pair of metic businessmen in Athens, one Lampis, is entrusted with their affairs in the Crimean Bosporos (and indeed woefully betrays their trust). But Lampis is plainly in control of large sums of money, and has to take important business decisions. If all had gone well, one feels, he could well have been freed, and invited to take over the business on the retirement of his former owners, even as was Pasion in the banking area.

is a sum generally reckoned to have been sufficient to keep oneself alive in Classical Athens. One can see from this that a frugal and industrious slave 'living apart' could accumulate capital with which to buy his freedom, and in fact quite a bit of this went on.

The second feature of interest to us in the story of Timarchos is the situation of Pittalakos. Pittalakos, as we have seen, is described as a 'public slave' (dêmosios), and is indeed treated with the contempt proper to a slave later in the story by the seedy politician Hegesandros and by Timarchos himself, when they break into his house, smash up his gaming properties, kill his fighting quails and cocks, and then tie him up and give him a thrashing (ss. 58–9). And Pittalakos then, in trying to obtain redress, behaves like a slave by taking a seat as a suppliant at the Altar of the Mother of the Gods in the market-place (from which they then, by unseemly cajoling, manage to persuade him to remove himself).

On the other hand, though, Aeschines tells us (s. 62) that Pittalakos, when he obtains no redress, proceeds to go to law with them. This presents us with a quandary, since no slave, whether private or public, could initiate legal proceedings at Athens. Either Pittalakos is in a fact a freedman, and has retired from the public service (he does, after all, run a considerable gambling establishment, which must, one would think, have interfered significantly with the day job), and Aeschines is obscuring this fact for rhetorical effect; or he is operating with the help of a sponsor – a prostatês (which he would have had to do, after all, even if he were a freedman). Certainly, when Hegesandros, by way of intimidation, threatens to re-enslave him,[33] he does find refuge with a prostatês, one Glaukon of Cholargos (even as Neaira did with Stephanos), and Glaukon takes the case to arbitration (where, in fact, it is allowed to run into the sand, when Hegesandros becomes rather more influential in politics, and thus more dangerous to tangle with). Pittalakos, then, remains something of a mystery, but full of interest, nonetheless.[34]

We can see from even this small sample of texts how integral slave-ownership was to Athenian society, and something of the size of slave

---

[33] Here Aeschines seems to reveal his hand, as he is forced to claim, quite implausibly, that Hegesandros attempted to appropriate a slave belonging to the city, by alleging that he himself was his owner – something, one would think, he could never have got away with. Hegesandros' ploy would be made much more plausible if Pittalakos were in fact now a freedman.

[34] From the fact that, at s. 65, when Aeschines is summoning Glaukon to testify, he describes him as 'restoring Pittalakos to freedom' (aphelomenos eis eleutherian), one might assume that Pittalakos had in fact attained freedman status.

holdings in a variety of Athenian households. Let us now turn to consider the portrayal of slaves, first, in some texts of Old and New Comedy, and then in just one forensic speech in which a slave, or at least ex-slave, figures in the action, in the hope of advancing somewhat our insight into how the Athenians viewed their slaves.

SLAVES IN COMEDY

Aristophanes, The Knights

At various points in the plays of the only surviving playwright of Old Comedy, Aristophanes, we find slaves figuring in the action, but in just three, *The Knights* (424 BC), *The Frogs* (405 BC), and *Wealth* (388 BC) do they play a sufficiently substantial part to throw much light on Athenian attitudes to slavery. The first two plays in particular, however, if approached with discernment, can yield some insights. From Aristophanes, as a comic playwright, one cannot expect any great degree of sympathy for the plight of slaves, but he does show a certain *empathy*, enabling us to derive some dim view of how the world appears from the slaves' point of view – or rather, how an Athenian audience might expect it to appear.

The plot of *The Knights*, briefly, is as follows. The household of Demos, a cranky and suspicious, but also rather deaf, old gentleman (whose name also means 'People'),[35] has been thrown into confusion by the purchase of a new slave, a Paphlagonian.[36] It is not stated that this new slave has been brought in as an overseer (*epitropos*). On the face of it, he is just a slick operator, and a bully, and is causing trouble all through the household in that capacity, by worming his way into the good graces of his owner. The two slaves whom we meet, who

---

[35] In fact, its ordinary meaning is 'the people', or 'deme', but we know from other evidence (e.g. Demos, son of Pyrilampes, identified by Socrates as the beloved of Kallikles in Plato's *Gorgias* 481D) that it was a recognised proper name as well. Demos also gets a mention in Aristophanes' *The Wasps* (l. 98), where his beauty is attested to.

[36] This character represents the Athenian demagogue Kleon, who was dominant in politics from the death of Pericles in 429 until his own death in battle, at Amphipolis, in 422. This would have been made clear by his mask, which will have been a portrait mask, as will have been those of the two other slaves, who represent the generals Nikias and Demosthenes, two other prominent, but more conservative politicians of the time. None of the 'real' names of any of these slaves is used at any stage. 'Paphlagon' is not Kleon's name, but refers to his country of origin, a region on the northern, Black Sea coast of Asia Minor, from which many slaves derived – though Aristophanes has chosen it for the pun on *paphlazein*, 'to bubble' (of boiling water), or 'bluster'. We are not concerned in the present context, however, with the real identities of the slaves – except to note the delightful nature of Aristophanes' role reversal, the representation of the three chief political figures of contemporary Athens as slaves.

are nameless, but identifiable (as suggested above, n. 36) through portrait masks as the eminently respectable Athenian generals Nikias and Demosthenes, are lamenting their fate under this new regime, and considering their options (ll. 1–39). These comprise running away and seeking sanctuary in a temple, this latter being a recognised resource for a slave claiming undue oppression from his or her master.[37] In conjunction with these subversive deliberations, Aristophanes manages to work in two other basic 'slave jokes', masturbation – more or less the only form of sexual satisfaction available to most slaves most of the time (ll. 26–9) – and filching the wine (ll. 85–100). Copious reference is also made to flogging, which is the proximate cause of the desire of these two to run away (until they get a better idea, which does not concern us in the present context). 'Demosthenes' sums up the predicament of the household in the following explanatory narrative (ll. 40 –72):[38]

> All right, here goes. Our master is a real case. He's a country bumpkin [agroikos] and bad-tempered to match, he's got a morbid craving for beans,[39] and he flies into a rage at the drop of a hat – Demos of the Pnyx,[40] a dyspeptic little old fellow, and rather deaf. Well, the first of last month[41] he went out and bought a new slave, a tanner[42] from Paphlagonia, and a greater swine of a stool-pigeon never walked this earth. This tanner fellow soon got to know Master's ways, and then he fell at his feet, licked his boots, wheedled, flattered, sucked up, everything to take him in, with all the trimmings – in real leather! 'Demos', he'd say, 'why don't you try just one case today and then have a good bath and get stuck into a slap-up supper on your three obols?[43] Shall I serve the first course now?' Why, only the other day I'd baked a lovely Spartan cake down in Pylos,[44] and round he sneaks

[37] This, even if successful (it was up to the archon to judge), only gave the slave the right to be sold to another master, so it was not much of a relief.

[38] Certain details are plainly contrived to suit the joke that 'Demos' is the Athenian People, and the Paphlagonian the demagogue Kleon, but the overall picture portrays a possible situation in a medium-sized Athenian household. I borrow the lively translation of Alan Sommerstein in the Penguin Classics translation, with some modifications.

[39] That is to say, a lover of casting votes, which were cast in the form of beans (kyamoi).

[40] Under the guise of giving Demos' demotic, Aristophanes names the Pnyx, where the Assembly sat.

[41] Slave auctions were normally held at the noumenia, the beginning of the lunar month.

[42] Kleon ran a family hide-tanning business. It was actually possible, as we have seen earlier, for a slave to be in the tanning business, but in that case he would be far more likely to be 'living apart' than as part of a household, so this is just a gibe at Kleon.

[43] Three obols was the daily honorarium for attending the lawcourts as a juror.

[44] This is a reference to a significant incident in the war in the previous summer (425) to the production of the play. Demosthenes, as general, had captured Pylos on the west

and grabs it and serves up *my* cake as if it was all his work! And he won't let anyone but himself wait on Master. If we try, he chases us away. All through dinner he stands behind Master with his fly-whisk (also real leather), and flicks away the – politicians …[45] He spews out lies about all and sundry, so as to get us all flogged. And then he makes the round of the whole household, taking bribes, blackmailing people, and putting the wind up us with this sort of talk: 'Look at Hylas! Master gave him the works yesterday – all my doing. Be sure you stay on the right side of me, or it'll be your turn tomorrow.' And we pay up.[46] If we don't, we'll only find ourselves eight times deeper in the shit when dumped on by Master.

They then manage to steal some wine from the pantry to help them in their deliberations as to a way out of their troubles. Fantasy though this is, there is a certain amount to be derived from it about the realities of an Athenian household. It is not quite clear from this portrayal, it must be said, exactly what rank in society Demos occupies. On the one hand, he is described as *agroikos*, which is a term denoting boorish, countrified habits, and he is also represented as serving as a juryman, and valuing the three obols that he gets from that, which would place him, in modern terms, somewhere in the 'lower middle class'. On the other hand, though, he plainly runs an establishment of at least four slaves and probably more. Of course, the standard hero of Old Comedy – men like Dikaiopolis of *The Acharnians*, Strepsiades of *The Clouds*, or Philokleon of *The Wasps* – are of very much this class, but all seem well enough supplied with the accoutrements of a good life, including a plurality of slaves. Taking one thing with another, though, it seems reasonable to conclude that even quite modest households in Athens might include four to six slaves.

What is more relevant to our present purpose, though, is the remarkable callousness, from our point of view, which characterises

---

coast of the Peloponnese, and had penned up on the island of Sphakteria a Spartan force which had come to dislodge him. The Spartans sued for peace, but Kleon persuaded the Athenians to reject their overtures, and, taunting Nikias, who was also a general, with cowardice for not being willing to lead a force to the scene, led an expedition against Sphakteria himself, with a corps of light-armed infantry, and captured 300 Spartans. Kleon thus became the man of the moment for 425/4, and it is at just this juncture that Aristophanes decides to pillory him.

[45] I omit here a little passage of pure fantasy.

[46] How, one might ask, could slaves 'pay up'? Perhaps with some of their accumulated savings (such as they were generally able to earn, for extra-good behaviour or special services); or else just payment in kind of some sort.

the portrayal of slave existence and the slave mentality in Greek comedy.[47] We can hardly, as remarked above, expect a high degree of sensitivity or sympathy from Old Comedy in particular, but the overall impression one derives is that Athenian audiences were prepared to laugh heartily at the spectacle of slaves clutching their sides and lamenting their latest beating, while entertaining the direst suspicions as to what the rascals were up to when they themselves were not around to supervise them.

Aristophanes, The Frogs

For the rest of *The Knights*, Aristophanes allows the slave motif to slip into the background, as he pursues richer fantasies. We may turn, therefore, to his much later play, *The Frogs*, composed just in the last months of the War, when Athens' fate was already sealed. Here we are presented with a relationship between a rather Wodehousian young man about town – actually the god Dionysos himself – and his personal servant, Xanthias. Xanthias is no Jeeves (indeed, he resembles rather, if anything, Baldrick of the *Blackadder* TV series), but he is in an interesting way a predecessor of that stock figure of New Comedy, the Clever Slave. It is always dangerous, of course, to extrapolate from comedy to real life, but it does seem reasonable to suppose that (as in the American South, after all) relationships of some intimacy and frankness could arise between young masters and slave-boys who had, perhaps, grown up with them in the household, or who had been bought specially to look after them.[48]

The play begins with a comic routine in which Dionysos and his personal servant are journeying across the stage, with Xanthias, on the one hand, riding on the single donkey, but on the other hand carrying all the baggage, and complaining about that loudly. He answers his master back freely, and plainly has very little respect for his competence, valour, or intelligence. This banter continues, with Xanthias giving as good as he gets, through a visit to Dionysos' cousin Herakles (as whom, with vast implausibility, he is proposing to

---

[47] Aristophanes actually alludes to various stock slave jokes and routines, which he claims to have transcended (though he is perfectly prepared to use them himself on other occasions), at *Peace* 742–7 and *The Frogs* 1–18.

[48] Similar relationships, though rather more moralising and censorious, can be assumed to arise between a young master and his old nurse or tutor (*paidagôgos*) – once again, as in the American South – and these are also portrayed in New Comedy (and in the case of an old nurse, rather charmingly, as we shall see below, in a speech in the Demosthenic corpus, 47, ss. 52–73).

disguise himself on his visit to Hades), and down as far as the Lake of Acheron, where Charon is plying his trade as ferryman of the dead.

Here there is occasion for a little joke about the status of slaves: as a slave, Xanthias is not allowed into Charon's boat (ll. 190–1), but has to walk round the lake, still carrying the baggage.[49] Further badinage ensues on the other side of the lake, but the next significant remark does not occur until the pair reach Pluto's palace, and Dionysos discovers, to his great alarm, that Herakles had left a very bad reputation, not to mention sundry debts to landladies, behind him, for all of which he, disguised as he is in Herakles-costume, is being held liable. So he gets Xanthias to change costumes with him – and then to change back, when the prospect suddenly improves, with an invitation to dinner from Persephone – and then back again, when the indignant landladies appear, demanding satisfaction. Finally, in response to the bewilderment of the doorman Aiakos, Xanthias (who is currently being Herakles) grandly offers his 'slave' (Dionysos) for torture, to testify to the truth of his claims (ll. 612ff.):[50]

> XANTHIAS: I swear by Zeus, I've never even been here before, and I've not stolen so much as a hair's worth of stuff belonging to you, strike me dead if I have. I'll tell you what I'll do. I'll let you torture this slave of mine. And if I'm proved guilty, you can take me off and kill me.
>
> AIAKOS (interested): Aha! And what kind of tortures may I use?
>
> XANTHIAS: Oh, give him the whole works – string him up on the frame,[51] flog him with the cat o'nine tails,[52] flay him, stretch him on the rack! And you could pour vinegar up his nostrils, load him with bricks – anything you like, really, only don't hit him with a leek or a fresh spring onion. I won't have that!
>
> AIAKOS: Fair enough. But if I injure this boy of yours in the process, I suppose you'll be wanting compensation?
>
> XANTHIAS: No, no! No problem there. You just take him off and torture him.

This little exchange, which is no doubt meant to be highly amusing, manages to cast a lurid light on what must be regarded as one of

---

[49] This embodies a reference to the fact that slaves had recently been offered, and granted, their freedom for volunteering to serve as rowers in the fleet at the battle of Arginusai in 406 (Xanthias excuses himself for not volunteering by reason of bad eyesight!).

[50] I base myself once again on the lively Penguin translation of David Barrett.

[51] The *klimax*, lit. 'ladder', but here a kind of frame on which victims could be tied.

[52] *Hystrix*, lit. 'porcupine', but plainly here a nasty sort of barbed whip.

the darker aspects of the Athenian legal system, which we have already had occasion to advert to,[53] namely the convention that the evidence of slaves could be taken only under torture. The rack would seem to have been the normal instrument used (and one would like to think that its use may have been something of a formality), but we cannot be sure that the other tortures mentioned here are mere Aristophanic fantasies. They sound realistic enough. The stipulation about compensation to the master in case of permanent injury to the slave (grandly waived here by Xanthias) is also a well-attested provision of the system. That an Athenian audience could be expected to laugh uproariously at all this (and the flogging scene which follows is indeed most amusing) is fairly indicative of the popular attitude to the miseries of a slave's existence.

One more passage of the play reveals rather nicely something of the beliefs held by Athenians as to what their slaves got up to behind their backs. It comes after the *parabasis*, when Dionysos is safely ensconced in Pluto's palace, enjoying his dinner, and Xanthias and an elderly slave of Pluto's[54] are found gossiping outside the doors (ll. 738–53):

SLAVE: Oh, 'e's a real gen'leman, your master is! I can tell that.

XANTHIAS: Yes, you can always tell. There are only two things a real gentleman understands: boozing and fucking.[55]

SLAVE: No, but I mean, fancy 'im not beating you for making out that you were the master and 'im the slave!

XANTHIAS (*with a lordly wave*): He'd have been sorry if he'd tried!

SLAVE: Ah, that's the way I like to hear a slave talking. He, he, he! I love that!

XANTHIAS: Love it, eh?

SLAVE: Why, there's nothing I like better 'n cursin' Master behind 'is back!

XANTHIAS: Ah, you sly old beggar! I bet you mutter a few things under your breath when he's given you a beating, eh?

SLAVE: Mutterin'? He, he, he! Yeah, I like a bit o' mutterin'.

XANTHIAS: And what about prying into his private affairs?

SLAVE: Pryin'? He, he, he! Yes, I like a bit o' pryin'.

---

[53] Pp. 23, 66.

[54] This may or may not be intended to be Aiakos; editors differ on this, and it matters little for our purpose.

[55] Aristophanes here indulges in a spot of word-play: *pinein kai binein*, which David Barrett renders, nicely, but a little obscurely, 'soaking and poking'. The implication is that both these activities would be available at a normally lively Athenian dinner party or symposium.

XANTHIAS: Ah, we're going to get along fine, you and me. Have you
    ever tried eavesdropping when he's got company?

SLAVE: Eavesdroppin'? Ah, that's real sport, that is!

XANTHIAS: And then you pass it on to all the neighbours, eh?

SLAVE: Well, that's where the fun comes in, ain't it? No end of a kick
    that gives me.

XANTHIAS: Put it there, grandpa! Give us a hug, that's right!

We seem here to have a glimpse of an 'upstairs-downstairs'
scenario, such as would be equally characteristic of any large household in Victorian Britain. Such activities, along with sneaking nips of
the wine and going to sleep on duty, would seem to be the characteristic sins of servants everywhere, and in all ages.

Menander, The Arbitration *and* The Shield

There are a number of other Aristophanic texts that one could have
adduced in this connection, notably *The Wasps*, where the two slaves,
Sosias and Xanthias, are strenuously engaged, on the orders of their
master, Bdelykleon, in trying to keep their master's old father, Philokleon, confined to the house, and away from the lawcourts; and his
last play, *Peace* (dating from 388, and already, in structure, a 'Middle',
rather than an 'Old' Comedy), where the hero Chremylos' old
servant, Karion, berates his master and answers him back very much
in the way that Xanthias does to Dionysos, but these to a large extent
duplicate the two domestic situations that we have already looked at,
so we may now turn instead to have a look at two representative
New Comedies, *The Arbitration*, and *The Shield*, of Menander.

    In the first of these, we find a situation where a young Athenian
gentleman, Charisios, has discovered, with shock and horror, that his
wife of five months has surreptitiously had a baby, and exposed it. In
consequence, he has left his house in protest, and is shacked up across
the way with a slave flute-girl (and courtesan) named Habrotonon,
whom he has hired from a brothel-keeper.[56] His personal servant,
Onesimos, whose officious tale-telling[57] has apprised him of this

---

[56] His cantankerous old father-in-law Smikrines alleges that he is paying twelve
drachmae a day for Habrotonon (ll. 10–11), which does seem excessive by any
reckoning. Smikrines himself calculates it as the equivalent of well over a month's
subsistence 'for a man' (presumably an unskilled labourer), at two obols a day – a
pretty miserly rate of pay, admittedly.

[57] Oddly, near the beginning of the play, in a fragmentary passage (Fr. 2), we find the
cook, Karion, complimenting Onesimos in much the same terms as, in *The Frogs*
passage above, Xanthias commends the slave of Pluto: 'I like you, Onesimos! You're a

situation, is now in a rather awkward position (which will shortly become more awkward still), commuting between the two households.

The two slaves who give the play its name, however, Daos and Syros, are in a rather different situation. They are both 'living on their own' (*khôris oikountes*), but in a rural setting, rather than an urban industrial one. They are both slaves on the country estate of Charisios' friend and neighbour Chairestratos, Daos as a shepherd, Syros as a charcoal burner, and they have come into town to pay their 'rent', or *apophora*. They have also, however, come in for another purpose. Daos has found the baby which Charisios' wife Pamphile has exposed, but, being a bachelor, is in a bit of quandary about keeping it, so his friend Syros has successfully begged it off him, to give to his wife, who has just lost a baby (we note that there is no impossibility about slaves living on their own, at least in the country, having a wife). However, Syros then learns from a third party that some trinkets came with the baby, and he is now demanding that Daos hand these over as well, for the baby's sake.

This Daos indignantly refuses to do, and, as they happen to bump into old Smikrines leaving the scene as they enter it, they appeal to him to act as arbitrator between them.[58] Smikrines grumbles and abuses them, but he does agree to arbitrate, and in fact awards the trinkets to Syros, to the great indignation of Daos, which he does not mind expressing (ll. 359ff.).[59] Syros and Daos, then, are little different from serfs, or peasants on a large Victorian country estate, except as to their origins (presumably purchased from abroad, though possibly born and raised in the household) and the ultimately absolute power which their master would have over them. Their loyalty to their master, however, is portrayed as unquestioning.

---

busybody [*periergos*], like myself ... There's nothing pleasanter than knowing everything that goes on!'

[58] This is probably, though not certainly, a Menandrian spoof, as it seems unlikely that slaves could go to arbitration in any formal way at Athens, any more than they could go to law. However, arbitration (though it had formal rules) was basically an informal procedure, so it is possible that slaves could in some circumstances resort to it. Pittalakos, we may note, does so, in Aeschines' narrative (*Against Timarchus* 63), but, as I have said above, I feel that there is something about Pittalakos' situation which Aeschines is not making clear to us.

[59] Syros, we may note, makes a most eloquent plea (ll. 310–53), replete with references to Greek mythology, even as Onesimos, at the end of the play, both indulges in philosophical speculation (ll. 1087–99) and makes a reference to Euripides' *Auge* (ll. 1123–6). This is doubtless Menandrian foolery; but more intriguing is the fact that at l. 390 Syros is portrayed as being able to read an inscription on a ring. What can we conclude from this about literacy rates among rural slaves?

Rather different is the status of Onesimos, Charisios' personal servant. Onesimos should be, in New Comedy terms, a 'clever slave', but as it turns out he is being less than clever. Loyalty to his master has induced to him to report that his master's new wife, Pamphile, has just had an illicit baby, and it is this revelation that has precipitated the crisis which constitutes the plot. Onesimos now finds himself, if anything, in the dog-house, as being the bearer of bad news. The cleverness necessary to resolve the plot is in fact supplied by the 'flute-girl' Habrotonon. Habrotonon is an example of that stock character of New Comedy, the courtesan with the heart of gold. Her status, we may note, is not unlike that of Neaira when she began her career. She is under the control of a 'manager', or pimp, who rents her out for various occasions. As it turns out, she had been engaged the previous year by a number of Athenian matrons who were administering the Tauropolia (a women's festival in honour of Artemis Tauropolos), this time actually to play the flute, and thereby hangs something essential to the plot – to wit, that she saw Pamphile on that occasion after she had been raped (by Charisios himself, as it happens), and will remember her again, when she sees her now. On this occasion she has been hired by Charisios to provide him with more earthy consolations (though, to her pique, he has declined, so far, to make any use of her, and is moping instead).

Habrotonon, like all comic (and no doubt most real-life) courtesans, has an eye for her own advancement in the world, but she is also genuinely concerned for Charisios and his happiness, and to that end concocts a scheme, using the ring of his (which, it seems, Pamphile had managed to pull off during the rape) that has been recovered from among the trinkets of the exposed infant, to draw him out into an admission of what happened, and ultimately to reunion with his wife. What she herself may hope for, if all goes well, is pointed out to her, rather enviously, by Onesimos (ll. 538–40): to gain her freedom – Charisios will buy her from the pimp, he predicts, and set her free. In the event, it would seem (the text unfortunately becomes fragmentary at this stage), she is set free by Charisios' bosom friend Chairestratos, who has fallen in love with her, and is therefore destined to set up house with him, very much in the manner of the 'girl from Samos', Chrysis, with Demeas, as we saw above in Chapter 2 – or indeed, Neaira with Stephanos. Indeed, Habrotonon's story belongs as much there as here, though she does illustrate one of the possible routes out of slavery, at least for beautiful and obliging female slaves. No such luck for Onesimos, this time around, despite his loyalty to his master.

One other slave character we may note from the play, though she appears as a mere mute figure, is Pamphile's old nurse, Sophrone, who accompanies Smikrines on his mission to claim back his daughter (and his dowry) in Act V, and who has plainly been remonstrating with him all the way on Pamphile's behalf. By the time they come onto the scene, Smikrines is giving her ferocious abuse, while she makes no reply, but it is plain that she has previously been giving him as good as she got, in defence of her former nurseling's happiness. We here seem to get a glimpse of the high degree of both loyalty and freedom of expression characteristic of slave nurses and tutors within an Athenian household.

Unquestioning loyalty, also, is the characteristic of a fine character that we meet in another Menandrian play, *The Shield*. Here the situation is that a young man of good family, Kleostratos, having gone on campaign in Lycia, in the service of some Hellenistic dynast or other, in one of the many raiding expeditions characteristic of the turn of the third century,[60] has been (apparently) killed in battle, after accumulating much booty, and his faithful slave, another Daos, has gathered up all of this, including a number of (other) slaves, and his master's shield, and has brought everything home to Athens. Daos is actually Kleostratos' old *paidagôgos*, not his 'gentleman's gentleman', which betokens an even greater degree of loyalty than would be expected in the latter case, together with a high moral tone (such as we may observe in the case of Lydos in the *Double Deceiver* = Plautus' *the Two Bacchises*, above, pp. 43–5). Daos is amusingly berated for his loyalty by another slave, a nameless cook's assistant, at the end of Act I (ll. 238ff) – Daos has just explained, presumably, in a passage now lost, how he comes to be here:[61]

> SLAVE: Then be damned to you, if that's what you did. You're mad! You had your hands on all that gold and slaves, and you brought it all back 'for Master'? Why didn't you run away? Where d'you come from, anyway?
>
> DAOS: I'm a Phrygian.
>
> SLAVE: Aha, that's it then. You're no good! You're just a poofter.

---

[60] We hear, for instance, of Eumenes enrolling mercenaries for an expedition into Lycia in 318 (Diodorus Siculus, 18. 61, 4) and of Ptolemy I of Egypt storming the Lycian capital, Xanthos, in 309. Of these, the expedition of Eumenes is more suitable as a model for Menander. We may note that defeat came at the hands of the native Lycians, not of another dynast.

[61] I borrow here the Penguin translation of Norma Miller, with some changes.

Only us Thracians are real men. Getans – God, what heroes! That's why the mills are full of us.[62]

Daos is indeed a figure of outstanding rectitude, but he is by no means blindly subservient to authority. When faced by the blatant greed and selfishness of Kleostratos' uncle and the head of the family, (another) Smikrines, who is scheming to lay claim to Kleostratos' sister, who would be the heir (*epiklêros*) to the booty (which Kleostratos, we are allowed to know, had actually gone off to win in order to provide her with a dowry), Daos permits himself a considerable degree of irony. Smikrines obviously respects his opinion, and is trying to get him on-side (we must bear in mind that Daos himself, if the plot worked, would end up as the property of Smikrines):

SMIKRINES: I'll take the advice of some of my friends, and marry the girl myself.[63] That's more or less, I think, Daos, what the law prescribes. So you should have been thinking too, how to do this properly. After all, you're involved.

DAOS: Smikrines, I think the old saying 'Know thyself' enshrines a profound truth. Let me stand by it. Anything that concerns an honest servant [*oiketês*], you can refer to me and question me about … But property, and marriage to an heiress, and family and differences of relationship – heavens, Smikrines, don't involve Daos in that. You're free men, you deal with that yourselves.

SMIKRINES: For heaven's sake! Do you think I'm doing anything wrong here?

DAOS: I come from Phrygia. Many things that you Athenians approve of seem shocking to me – and vice versa, no doubt. Why ask for my opinion? Yours is naturally superior to mine.

Menander makes use of Daos admirably here to comment on the moral quality of an Athenian practice which was enshrined in (at least customary) law, but could be followed, as here, for dastardly purposes. What is interesting for our purpose, however, is how much Smikrines is portrayed as valuing Daos' opinion and support. In the

---

[62] The mills, like the silver mines, were of course the accepted repository for recalcitrant slaves – a favourite subject of threats from exasperated masters in comedy.

[63] It must be borne in mind that Smikrines was the head of the family, and thus technically had the right to take in marriage any female member of the family who was an heiress, whether or not she was already happily betrothed to a suitable young man, as is the case here – she is in fact betrothed to Chaireas, the step-son of her uncle Chairestratos, who is acting as her guardian.

event, of course, Smikrines is given in his come-uppance by a masterly
stroke, in which Daos is fully implicated – indeed, he concocts the
whole scheme (ll. 320ff.), very much in the manner of a 'clever slave'.
The rumour is to be put about that Smikrines' younger brother,
Chairestratos (who is, by contrast, a good guy) has suddenly died, and
this will distract Smikrines into demanding the hand of Chairestratos'
daughter instead, who comes with a far larger fortune. And by the
time the deception is revealed, Kleostratos' sister will be safely married
to Chaireas. In fact, all this is supervened on, in the (very fragmentary) Act IV, by the arrival of Kleostratos himself, who had not
been killed after all (the mangled corpse whom Daos has come upon
on the battlefield was simply a friend of his, who happened to have
borrowed his shield); but the fact remains that Daos' scheme would
have carried the day. He no doubt was rewarded in Act V with his
freedom – which, being Daos, he might not have accepted! Certainly
he would have remained a faithful family retainer till his death.

SLAVES IN REAL LIFE: TRYING TO AVENGE NANNY

This brings us, in conclusion, to the sad, but edifying, little story of a
real-life faithful retainer, this time an old nurse. It is told in the course
of a rather complicated court case, preserved among the private
speeches of Demosthenes,[64] involving the non-return of tackle for a
trireme, the details of which, fortunately, do not concern us. The
incident with which I am concerned here arises from an unsatisfactory provision of Athenian law which we have had occasion to
notice before this, that one could get a judgement against an opponent in court, but the state provided no means of recovering one's
award; one therefore had to gather one's friends, and set off to try to
recover it oneself, either by laying hands on the goods in question, or
by distraining on the estimated equivalent from among the defendant's possessions. In this case, a certain Theophemos, the villain in this
story, having refused himself to hand over the ship's tackle that he
had just been using during his trierarchy, and having thus caused the
(unfortunately unnamed) prosecutor to mount a punitive expedition
against him, managed to turn the tables on our hero, obtained a
judgement against him while he was out of the country, and raided
his farm in turn, utilising a bunch of cronies led by his brother

---

[64] XLVII: *Against Euergos and Mnesiboulos*. It is generally agreed not to be composed by
Demosthenes himself, but that is immaterial to our purpose. It certainly presents a
genuine slice of fourth-century life.

Euergos and his brother-in-law, Mnesiboulos. They first of all seized a flock of sheep belonging to our friend, complete with shepherd, but not content with that, moved in on his farm, which was quite close to town (near the Hippodrome, we are told, s. 53). I allow our friend to take up the story in his own words (ss. 53–9):[65]

At first they made a rush to seize the household slaves,[66] but since these escaped them and got off, one here and one there, they headed for my house, and bursting open the gate which led into the garden, they entered into the presence of my wife and children,[67] and carried off all the furniture that was still left in the house ... More than this, gentlemen of the jury, my wife happened to be lunching with the children in the courtyard, and with her was an elderly woman who had been my nurse, who was devoted and faithful to us, and had been set free by my father.[68] After she had been given her freedom, she lived with her husband,[69] but after his death, when she herself was an old woman and there was nobody to care for her, she came back to me. I could not allow my old nurse to live in want, any more than I could my *paidagôgos*;[70] at the same time I was about to sail as trierarch, and it was my wife's wish that I should leave such a person to live in the house with her.

Anyhow, they were lunching in the courtyard when these men burst in and found them there, and began to seize the furniture. The rest of the female slaves (they were in a tower room, where they live), when they heard the uproar, closed the door leading to the tower, so the men did not get in there; but they carried off the furniture from the rest of the house, although my wife forbade them to touch it, and declared that it was her property, mortgaged to secure her dowry ... But although my wife said this to them, they not only did not desist, but when my nurse took the cup which was set beside her, and from which she had been drinking, and put it in her bosom to prevent these men from taking it, when she saw that they were in the house, Theophemos and Euergos, this brother of his here, observing her

---

[65] I borrow the Loeb translation of A. T. Murray, with some modifications. For Theophemos, see J. K. Davies, *Athenian Propertied Families, 600–300 BC*, no. 7094. He was plainly a man of substance.

[66] We derive the impression from this narrative of something like a dozen slaves, male and female, about the place.

[67] This, as we have seen from earlier evidence, constituted a serious outrage to decency.

[68] Probably in his will.

[69] Presumably another freed slave.

[70] It is not quite clear why his *paidagôgos* is mentioned here. Either he is also living with them, or the speaker's point is that anyone would agree that one should look after one's old *paidagôgos*, so why not one's nurse?

doing that, treated her so roughly in taking the cup from her that her arms and wrists were covered with blood, as they wrenched her arms and pulled her this way and that, and she had lacerations on her throat, where they throttled her, and her breast was black and blue. And they pushed their brutality to such extremes that they did not stop throttling and beating the old woman until they had taken their cup from her bosom.

In effect, Nanny died defending the cup. Our friend was already in the Piraeus, preparing to sail, when he heard what had happened, and he came hurrying back. He got in the family doctor for Nanny (s. 67), but he reported to him sadly that her condition was hopeless, and on the sixth day after the raid she died. Our friend now took thought as to how he could avenge her death (s. 68), but when he went to the *exêgêtai*[71] for advice as to how to proceed, he was told, to his great frustration, that, since he was not a blood relation of hers, he could not sue for murder on her behalf; and neither could he sue for damages, as she was no longer a slave of his. All he could do is what he is now doing, getting at Euergos and Mnesiboulos in any way he can, which in this case involves indicting them for false witness (*pseudomartyria*). We can only hope that he won.

This last story reminds us yet again how precarious was the life of a slave, and even that of a freed person, in ancient Athens, but it also gives us, I think, some insight into what close degrees of affection could arise between masters of even a basic quotient of decency and creatures with which, if one were to credit Aristotle, no relation of friendship could arise.

---

[71] An official body of experts on traditional and religious law, the mode of whose appointment is rather obscure, to whom one could appeal for judgements on legal and religious matters.

CHAPTER SEVEN

Dealing with the Gods:
Piety and Impiety

SOME GENERAL PRINCIPLES

Once again, as with slavery, pederasty, and the treatment of women, we are faced here with an aspect of Athenian life that is alien to us, but not in this case, I think, particularly repellent. Indeed, in the area of religion and attitudes to the divinity, the Greeks may seem in many respects more acceptable to present-day sensibilities than would the excesses of superstition, sectarianism and intolerance which marred the Christian past. They were not, however, free of oddities of their own, and some of these will be explored in this chapter.

First of all, it must be specified that the Athenians of the classical period were not much concerned with religious doctrine. There was indeed no body of priestly authorities in any of the Greek states who could pronounce on matters of faith and morals. The oracles of Delphi or Dodona gave responses to specific queries, public or private, many of which became famous, but such responses had no general application, and could not become a body of religious 'case-law', by which people could live their lives. In Athens, as we have had occasion to observe,[1] there was a board of *exêgêtai*,[2] exponents of religious law and custom, who also gave responses to individual queries, presumably on payment of a fee (though there is no mention of that). These, if anyone, one would think, held the possibility for becoming propounders of religious doctrine in the state, but it is most significant for the understanding of the religious situation in ancient Athens that there was no question of this. The role of the *exêgêtai* remained firmly

---

[1] We may recall the man who wanted to prosecute the murderers of his nanny, in Ch. 6, p. 154 above.

[2] It appears, in fact, that there were just two of them, both by law members of ancient noble clans (*Eupatridai*), one elected by the people, the other appointed by the Pythian Oracle (i.e. the priests at Delphi) – presumably from a panel of candidates submitted by Athens. The former dealt primarily with queries about correctness of sacrifices and performances of ancestral rites, the latter with means of purification, but they seem to have made joint responses. It is suggested that, once appointed, they held office for life, but all concerning them is shrouded in uncertainty. See J. H. Oliver, *The Athenian Expounders of the Sacred and Ancestral Law*, Baltimore, 1950.

confined to advice on the correct performance of *ritual*; they were
not concerned – any more than was any other official – with *belief*.

A rather fine statement of the Athenian's image of themselves in
relation to religious observance comes from the pen of the orator
Isocrates, in his *Address to the Areopagus* of 355 BC. In the course of a
commendation of the ancestral political constitution and ethos of the
Athenians (by contrast with the degenerate attitudes of the present
generation), he says the following (ss. 29–30):[3]

> First of all, as to their relations with the gods [*ta peri tous theous*] – for it
> is right to begin with them – they were not erratic or irregular in their
> worship of them or in the celebration of their rites; they did not, for
> example, drive three hundred oxen in procession to the altar, when it
> entered their heads to do so,[4] while omitting, at their whim, the
> sacrifices instituted by their ancestors; neither did they observe on a
> grand scale festivals imported from abroad, provided these involved a
> feast, while contracting with the lowest bidder for the sacrifices
> demanded by the holiest rites of their religion. For their sole concerns
> were, on the one hand, not to destroy any institution of their fathers,
> and on the other hand to introduce nothing which was not approved
> by custom, believing that piety [*eusebeia*] consists, not in extravagant
> expenditures, but in disturbing none of the rites which their ancestors
> had handed on to them. And so also the gifts of the gods were
> bestowed upon them not fitfully or capriciously, but seasonably both
> for ploughing of the land and for the ingathering of its fruits.

We may note here the lack of any mention of the preservation of
correctness of *belief*; the whole emphasis is on the maintenance of
traditional rituals in their proper form. And the recompense for this is
the due bestowal by the gods of such benefits as rain in season and
freedom from disease or blight. Disorder in ritual will provoke
irregularities in divine support for the natural order. There is no
mention of 'keeping the faith', in a Judaeo-Christian sense.

This is not to say that one could not annoy the Athenians, and
indeed get into bad trouble, for public expressions of disbelief in the
traditional gods, or of outright atheism, but this was primarily because
such an attitude – on the part of such a figure as Diagoras of Melos,

---

[3] I borrow here the Loeb translation of George Norlin, with minor alterations.
[4] He seems here to be referring to an immoderate celebration that had recently taken
place in Athens to celebrate the victory of the general Chares over the forces of the
King of Persia.

the 'atheist', for example, in the fifth century[5] – would be considered by the general public as attracting divine retribution, if tolerated (the gods did not appreciate being disbelieved in). In general, however, such trials for impiety as took place – including the famous trial of Socrates in 399 – can always be seen as having a political dimension. When the philosopher Anaxagoras was banished from Athens in the 430s, it was not solely because he had declared the sun and stars to be no more than lumps of fiery metal; it was also because he was well-known as a friend and protégé of Pericles, whom his enemies wished to snipe at. In Socrates' case, also, the matter of his religious beliefs would never have come up, had he not been closely associated in the public mind with such figures as Kritias, leader of the Spartan-sponsored puppet regime that ruled Athens briefly in the wake of their defeat in 404, the so-called 'Thirty Tyrants', and Alkibiades, the 'bad boy' of Athenian politics in the two decades before that.

The heads of the indictment of Socrates were on the face of it absurd, and have tended to cast Athenian democracy in a thoroughly unfavourable light, such as it does not entirely deserve. Apart from the charge of 'corrupting the youth', he was accused of 'disbelieving in the gods which the state worships, and introducing new deities of his own'. The latter charge seems to have arisen from his well-known, but at least partly ironic, reliance on a 'daemonic voice' (*daimonion*), which he claimed to guide him in his actions – but always negatively, by dissuading him from courses of action, or from associating with certain individuals, never by prompting him to any positive action. The former charge no doubt arises from his tendency, in argument, to question, not the *existence* of the traditional gods (though many advanced intellectuals of the fifth and fourth centuries, such as the playwright Euripides, would certainly have questioned that), but rather the beliefs about their behaviour, as portrayed in the myths, and popular assumptions as to how we should relate to them. For Socrates, as for Plato after him, God, or the gods, are good, and no jealousy or malice can be imputed to them; they do not quarrel amongst themselves, nor can they be swayed by the prayers or sacrifices of unjust individuals. All these principles run counter to the assumptions of Athenian popular religion.

---

[5] Diagoras was a lyric poet, of outspokenly atheistical views, who hung about Athens in the last third of the fifth century, and was plainly tolerated for quite a time. He is repeatedly satirised by Aristophanes in his comedies (*The Clouds* 830; *The Birds* 1073; *The Frogs* 320), but sometime around 415 he went too far, by mocking the Eleusinian Mysteries, and was brought to trial for impiety (*asebeia*) and banished. He became in later times the paradigm of the atheist.

TEASING EUTHYPHRON: A CRITIQUE OF ATHENIAN
TRADITIONAL BELIEFS

It is with Socrates, then, that we may start this examination of Athenian attitudes to piety and impiety, and specifically with the little dialogue, the dramatic date of which is set just before his trial, in which Plato portrays him in conversation with the rather preposterous religious 'expert' Euthyphron.[6]

Socrates meets up with Euthyphron outside the office of the King Archon in the Agora, before whom trials for impiety would normally be heard, and where, as it emerges, they both have business. Euthyphron first enquires, in some astonishment, what brings Socrates to this unexpected place, and Socrates tells him of his arraignment for impiety by a certain Meletos. He then asks Euthyphron what business brings *him* there (3E). Euthyphron tells him, with some complacency, that he is there to prosecute his own father for impiety, and indeed for murder. Socrates is duly astonished at this, reacting initially as would any normal Athenian at hearing such a statement:[7]

> SOCR: Heracles![8] Indeed, Euthyphron, how true it is that most people don't know where the right lies; for I think it is not just anyone who can rightly do what you are doing, but only one very far advanced in wisdom.
>
> EUTH: Very far indeed, Socrates, by Zeus!
>
> SOCR: Is the one killed by your father a relative? But of course he must have been; for you wouldn't bring a charge of murder against him on behalf of a stranger.
>
> EUTH: I am amused, Socrates, that you should think it matters whether the man who was killed was a stranger or a relative, and do not see that the only thing to consider is whether the action of the slayer was justified or not, and that if it was justified one ought to leave him be, but if not, one ought to proceed against him, even if he shares one's hearth or eats at one's table. For the pollution [*miasma*] is the same if you associate knowingly with such a man and do not purify yourself and him by proceeding against him.

---

[6] There is no serious reason, I think, to doubt that Euthyphron, like the generality of Socrates' interlocutors, is a real person. He is referred to also in the *Cratylus* (396D, etc.), and there given a demotic, 'of Prospaltê'. Nor yet need we doubt the basic historicity of the story now to be recounted; it may have been a notorious incident, which Plato uses as a suitable launching-pad for Socrates' enquiry into conventional beliefs.

[7] I borrow here the Loeb translation of H. N. Fowler, with minor alterations.

[8] This oath has more or less the connotation, 'Well, I'll be darned!'.

In this case, the man who was killed was a hired workman [*pelatês*][9] of mine, and when we were farming at Naxos, he was working there on our land.[10] Now he got drunk one day, lost his temper with one of our house-slaves, and slaughtered him. So my father bound him hand and foot, threw him into a ditch, and sent a man here to Athens to ask the *exêgêtês*[11] what he ought to do. In the meantime, he paid no attention to the man as he lay there bound, and neglected him, considering that he was a murderer and that it was no great matter if he were to die. And that is just what happened to him; he died of hunger and cold and his bonds before the messenger returned from the *exêgêtês*.

And now my father and the rest of my relatives are indignant with me because, for the sake of this murderer, I am prosecuting my father for murder. For they say he did not kill him, and even if he had killed him, yet since the dead man was a murderer, I ought not to trouble myself about such a fellow, because it is unholy [*anosion*] for a son to prosecute his father for murder – which shows, Socrates, how little they know what the divine law is as regards holiness and unholiness. (*Euth.* 4A–E)

The later (second century AD) Platonist Numenius is on record[12] as asserting that Plato intended through the figure of Euthyphron to satirise the Athenian public in general, but effectively concealed his intentions so as not to provoke them into treating him in the same way as they had his master Socrates. On the face of it, this might seem

---

[9] This person will have been a free man, but of low status (*pelatês* properly means 'protégé' or 'dependant'). He may or may not have been an Athenian citizen, but he appears to have no readily contactable kin.

[10] This detail is interesting, but somewhat mysterious. A cleruchy, or settlement of Athenian citizens, had been established on Naxos by Pericles back in 447 or so, and one might assume that Euthyphron's family had acquired their holding at that time, but by the period of this conversation, all Athenian cleruchs had been dispossessed and sent home by the Spartan commander Lysander, after the defeat of Athens in 404. Either, then, we must assume that Euthyphron's family had somehow slipped through the net, or that they were not in fact cleruchs, but had bought land in Naxos as a private transaction, and were thus not subject to dispossession.

[11] Note the use of *exêgêtês* in the singular; this will refer to the exegete appointed by Delphi, whose primary concern was queries to do with pollution. Why, though, one might well ask, go to the trouble of consulting an exegete at all – a process which, from Naxos, would have taken the best part of a week, at least? Euthyphron's father, after all, could simply have enslaved the hired hand, especially if he were not an Athenian, in compensation for the loss of his slave; or he could have prosecuted him for damages (though it is unlikely that the hired hand had much in the way of assets!). We must assume, I think, that the father (who may have had a personal affection for the slave) was concerned, like our friend in the last chapter, in relation to his old nurse, as to whether any pollution accrued to him from this event.

[12] In his treatise *On the Secret Doctrines of Plato*, Fr. 23 Des Places.

improbable, as Euthyphron's views on ritual pollution are plainly extreme, in comparison to those of the ordinary Athenian[13] – Plato presents him as admitting quite freely that his family are outraged by his behaviour (4D), and that the public in general regard him as something of a lunatic (3BC) – but one can also see him, as did Numenius, as representing, albeit in an extreme and absurd form, the logical consequences of Athenian popular belief, and it is in that capacity that he is useful to us in the present connection.

Euthyphron's dilemma arises, after all, from pursuing to its logical conclusion a contradiction between two basic principles of Greek popular morality. The first is that shedding blood, or more generally, causing the death of another human being, even if such a killing be justified, incurs some degree of pollution; and, in turn, failing to avenge the killing of a relative will cause the pollution to fall on anyone in whom this responsibility resides. There is a second principle, however, which would have equal, if not greater, force in the popular mind, and that is that 'blood is thicker than water'; that relatives should stick together and support one another, and, above all, that a child should not indulge in violence of any kind against, or even show disrespect to, a parent – and that would include going to law against them.[14] Euthyphron is caught between these two imperatives, and, for reasons that seem to him to be in accordance with divine law, he chooses the former; his father and family, as would any normal Athenian, give precedence to the latter.

However, Euthyphron's dilemma is really only introduced in order to launch Socrates onto an enquiry into the true nature of piety and impiety. His demands for a definition of piety, and his subtle distinctions between 'what is pious' and 'what is loved by the gods' are of great interest philosophically, but not so relevant to our present concerns. More to the point is his examination of the definition of piety that he extracts from Euthyphron at 12E, that it is 'service, or

---

[13] There is a most interesting discussion of Euthyphron's position by Charles Kahn, 'Was Euthyphro the author of the Derveni Papyrus?', in *Studies on the Derveni Papyrus*, ed. A. Laks and G. W. Most, Oxford, 1997, 55–63. Kahn does not necessarily wish to maintain that Euthyphro *was* the author of that intriguing document, but he does want to argue for his Orphic connections, and I think that he is probably right in this.
    On beliefs about pollution in general, see Robert Parker, *Miasma: Pollution and Purification in Early Greek Religion* – though Parker does not in fact have much to say about this incident (cf., however, p. 119, n. 63).

[14] An exception to this, perhaps, is the provision that one may bring a *dikê paranoias*, or charge of incompetence, against a parent who has lost his mind, and is thus incapable of administering his affairs; but here the overriding concern is the preservation of the *oikos* in general.

tendence [*therapeia*] of the gods.' This is a definition that would satisfy most ordinary Athenians as uncontroversial. Religion was seen as primarily a matter of giving the gods their due, in terms of sacrifices and salutations, and receiving benefits in return; it was, in fact, a form of barter.[15] Socrates, however, is intrigued by the implications of this. He first of all gets Euthyphron to accept that *therapeia*, in the case of horses or oxen or dogs, has as its purpose the benefit and improvement of the recipient. He then proceeds (13C):

> SOCR: Then holiness [*hosiotês*], since it is the art of attending [*therapeia*] to the gods, is a source of benefit to the gods, and makes them better? And you would agree that when you do a holy or pious act you are making one of the gods better?
>
> EUTH: No, by Zeus, I would not!
>
> SOCR: Nor do I, Euthyphron, think that that is what you meant. Far from it. But I asked what you meant by 'attention to the gods' just because I did not think that you meant anything like that.
>
> EUTH: You are right, Socrates: that is not what I mean.
>
> SOCR: Well then, what kind of attention to the gods is holiness?
>
> EUTH: The kind, Socrates, that servants pay their masters.
>
> SOCR: I understand. It is, you mean, a kind of service [*hypêretikê tis*] to the gods?
>
> EUTH: Exactly.

Once again, Euthyphron is quite in line with Athenian popular belief, but Socrates has further problems to raise. If every art of service has as its purpose the production of some good result (as medicine produces health, and ship-building a ship), what fine result is service of the gods meant to generate? Euthyphron states confidently (14B) that prayer and sacrifice, when properly undertaken, secure the preservation of both families and states, and the neglect of these brings about their destruction. So, Socrates concludes, religion is really a science (*epistêmê*) of giving and asking (14D), a conclusion to which Euthyphron readily assents. He is made a little uncomfortable, though, just after this (14E), by the suggestion that holiness, or religion, is really a form of trading (*emporikê tis*), though he cannot see his way round that. What the gods get from us can be specified as 'honour and praise', and this is pleasing to them.

Socrates' final undermining of this conclusion is somewhat dialectical, and need not concern us, though it sends Euthyphron scurrying

---

[15] This conclusion is presented by Socrates a little further along, at 14E, and agreed to by Euthyphron: 'Then holiness would be a certain sort of barter between gods and men'.

off to attend to an imaginary piece of urgent business. We need only note his criticism of Athenian popular religious belief as having no place for a concept of holiness independent of 'what is pleasing to the gods', which is what he is looking for. We may reasonably suspect that no ordinary Athenian, any more than Euthyphron, would have attached much meaning to this enquiry. It would have made perfectly good sense to them that one should give the gods what they want, irrespective of whether it accorded with any transcendent norm of moral excellence, and that that was what piety consisted in. Socrates' questioning of this would have seemed merely vexatious and subversive.

A STORY OF AN OLIVE STUMP

But let us turn from abstract principles to some slices of real life, to try to discern what sort of misdemeanours might be expected to prove offensive to Athenian religious sensibilities. As has been suggested above, we would not expect these to be in the area of unorthodox belief; what we must expect to find, rather, are problems relating to malfeasance or misfeasance in the area of religious *observance*.

In fact a rather nice case confronts us from the corpus of the speeches of Lysias.[16] At some time probably in the later 390s, a rich Athenian citizen, whose name (as so often in these circumstances) is unknown to us, is brought to trial – probably by his political enemies, with the help of a professional *sykophantês* (so, at any rate, he alleges) – concerning a heinous crime committed by him in or around 397 BC.

What was this awful crime? To understand the nature of it, we must fill in a bit of background. Once upon a time, way back at the dawn of history, Poseidon and Athena contested the honour of being the patron deity of Athens. They each produced what one might call their 'party piece'. Poseidon struck the rock of the Acropolis, and caused a salt spring to well up; but Athena in response to that caused an olive tree to sprout on the same site.[17] The electorate (whoever they were!)[18] voted for Athena (what practical use is a salt spring, after all?), and Poseidon went off in dudgeon and flooded the Thriasian

---

[16] *On the Olive Stump: a Speech before the Areopagus*, Lysias VII. I borrow the Loeb translation of W. R. M. Lamb, with minor alterations.

[17] Presumably coming to fruition instantaneously – there would be no time to wait for an olive tree to go through its normal growth cycle! But this is folktale, of course.

[18] Most credibly the gods, as proposed by Apollodorus in his *Library of Mythology*, III 177–9, but possibly 'the people', as assumed by Varro (ap. Augustine, *City of God* XVIII 9), though what people there were in this era is unclear.

Plain, whereat he had to be appeased by being accorded various honours. Both the olive tree (in a series of reincarnations) and the salt spring survived throughout antiquity – the olive tree despite being burned by the Persians when they captured Athens in 480 (the burned stump immediately sent out a new shoot!) – and throughout the land of Attica there arose a network of sacred olive trees, called *moria*, which were allegedly cuttings from the original tree on the Acropolis.[19] The olive oil from these trees was special (only it could be used as prizes in the Games, for instance),[20] and it was absolutely forbidden to disturb or uproot any sacred olive, even if it had died (notionally, the stump might sprout again, as had the original after the Persian sack). Indeed, there was a Board of Inspectors (*epignômones*)[21] who seem to have compiled a monthly inventory, and made a yearly tour of the countryside, to check on the sacred olives.

This prohibition on the uprooting even of dead trees, however, could constitute a great nuisance for a landowner with limited acreage, who would have to plough round this stump,[22] and in consequence there was a considerable temptation to make away with an old stump, if one thought one could do this unnoticed. The penalty for such a heinous crime, however, originally (under the laws of Draco) *death*, even in the period with which we are concerned involved exile and confiscation of property, which is an index of how seriously such an act was taken by the Athenian people. The nature of the case also, unfortunately, rendered this a fruitful field for sycophancy, and for the settling of scores by personal enemies, the unfortunate defendant in such a case being, after all, put in the position of having to prove a negativity.

Such is the situation of our friend in the present instance, at least as he would have us believe. Like many another rich man in an Athenian

---

[19] This is of course on one level an absurdity. If the truth of the story were accepted, then logically *all* olive trees would descend from the original on the Acropolis. But again, we are in the realm of folktale.

[20] We learn from this speech (s. 2), that there were designated purchasers of the produce of these trees, who presumably had a contract to produce the olive oil for the state; and from Aristotle, *Ath. Pol.* 60, 1–2, that there was a levy of three half-*kotylai* (about 3/4 of a pint) from each tree, which constituted a sort of tax on the owners. How the whole process worked is obscure.

[21] As we also learn from this speech, s. 25. This incidentally reveals an interesting degree of detailed record-keeping (albeit for this rather odd purpose), of which we have little other evidence from this period.

[22] Indeed, as we learn (s. 25), it was not permissible to cultivate the ground in the immediate vicinity of a sacred olive, though the necessary distance from it is not here specified. This is one of the matters that the Inspectors inspected, and breaches incurred a fine.

lawcourt,[23] he portrays himself as a harmless, self-effacing private individual, who is being preyed upon by an unscrupulous gold-digger, in the person of the prosecutor, Nikomachos.[24] He certainly, with Lysias' help, makes out a strong case in his defence, and he probably won (which is why we have the speech), but he makes a number of interesting remarks in the process, and it is on these that I wish to dwell.

First of all, a short history of the property (ss. 4–5):

> This property belonged to Peisandros; but when his possessions were confiscated,[25] Apollodoros of Megara received it as a gift of the people and cultivated it for some time, until, shortly before the Thirty,[26] Antikles bought it from him and rented it out. I bought it from Antikles when peace had been made.[27] So I consider, gentlemen of the Council,[28] that my task is to show that, when I acquired the property, there was neither olive-tree nor stump upon it.

He then makes the obvious point that he cannot be blamed for any destruction of sacred olives that may have taken place before he took over in 403, in the process making two intriguing remarks: the first (s. 6) is the reminder that, during the war, 'the outlying districts were ravaged by the Lacedaemonians,[29] while the nearer were plundered *by our friends* [*philoi*].' Who, one might wonder, could these latter be, especially as cutting down olive trees was always regarded as something approaching a war crime. Could it be a veiled reference to the

---

[23] He lets it be known (s. 24) that he owns various other properties around Attica, on which there are both sacred olive trees and stumps (which he has never been accused of molesting); and he assumes that the court recognises that he is a wealthy man, who would be a natural prey for *sykophantai* (s. 13).

[24] It is suggested at various points in the speech (ss. 1; 20) that Nikomachos is a *sykophantês* rather than a personal enemy, but this may be a rhetorical ploy. If we could assume that this Nikomachos is the same as the Nikomachos prosecuted in 399 (by a person unnamed, but possibly our friend) for malpractice while acting as a reviser of the laws (Lysias XXX), one could construct a pattern of enmity of which this suit would be an expression; but unfortunately there is nothing else to link the two Nikomachoi.

[25] Peisandros was an opportunistic politician, first a radical democrat, then a reactionary oligarch, and one of the leaders of the oligarchic coup of 411, which brought into power the so-called Four Hundred. When they were overthrown, he fled into exile and his property was confiscated, and presented to Apollodoros of Megara, who had helped to assassinate another of the leaders of the Four Hundred, Phrynichos (cf. Lysias, *Against Agoratus* [XIII], 71).

[26] Sc. at the defeat of Athens in 404.

[27] This is slightly ambiguous, but he must mean after the settlement of 403, following on the overthrow of the Thirty.

[28] This trial is taking place before the council of the Areopagus, as is proper for trials for sacrilege.

[29] Particularly after the Spartan occupation of Decelea in 413.

activities of the Athenian democrats under Thrasyboulos, based in Phyle during the winter and spring of 404/3, from which base they ravaged the countryside controlled by the Thirty? This would place our friend's sympathies as being (mildly) anti-democratic, a fact that he would not wish to emphasise, though unable to resist a dig against the insurgents.

The second confusing remark (s. 7) is to the effect that this property, 'having been confiscated during the war, was left unsold [*apraton*] for over three years.' But surely its ownership is accounted for fully just above, at least after its confiscation from Peisandros? There may in fact have been a gap before ownership of it was bestowed on Apollodoros. At any rate, we have, in respect of this property, a more detailed account of its ownership and patterns of occupation than we have for any other piece of Attic real estate in the Classical period – and all because of an olive stump.

The account continues, for the period after our friend takes up ownership of it in 403 (ss. 9–10):

> When I took over the property, before five days were out I let it to Kallistratos, in the archonship of Pythodoros [404/3]. He cultivated it for two years, and had taken over no olive-tree, either private or sacred, nor any olive-stump. In the third year it was worked by Demetrios here for a year; and in the fourth I let it to Alkias, a freedman of Antisthenes,[30] who is dead. After that Proteas too hired it in the same state for a period of three years. Since that time I have cultivated it myself.

This in effect brings us down to the year 397/6 (archonship of Souniades), in which Nikomachos alleges (s. 11) that an olive stump was uprooted on the property. The point of this litany of owners and renters in fact is that they may be called as witnesses, as they duly are, to testify that there was no sacred olive stump on the land during their tenure, so that none can suddenly have popped up when our friend took over the land himself. In fact, as he tells us earlier (s. 2), Nikomachos (and the shadowy group of 'enemies' who are alleged to be behind him) initially wanted to accuse him of cutting down a living tree, but could find no record with the collectors of sacred olive oil of any oil collected from this property, so they had to change their story! Even then, as our friend emphasises (ss. 20–1), they waited

---

[30] An interesting detail here, in relation to the potential fates of slaves after they had gained their freedom. Alkias had plainly saved up enough to rent a little farm for himself after his emancipation (though he, sadly, died soon after).

quite a time – not specified, but long enough (perhaps five years?) for certain witnesses to have died, and the business of proof to have been made more difficult – before bringing their vexatious charge. Nikomachos is apparently unable to produce any witnesses himself (alleging (s. 21) that they have all been intimidated by our friend's power and wealth!), but claims to have personally seen our friend supervising his slaves in the clearing away of the stump, in broad daylight, and on a part of the estate adjacent to a public road (s. 28).

Our friend rightly pours scorn on the utter improbability of this, and suggests that, if Nikomachos had actually witnessed such a scene, and were truly concerned for the public welfare, he could have run off and 'brought the nine Archons to the scene, or some other members of the Areopagus' (s. 22). That the nine Archons should have come running in response to such a summons may seem totally fantastic, but that our friend should even suggest such a possibility is some indication of how seriously such an act as the destruction of a sacred olive – alive or dead – was viewed.[31] That Nikomachos should have waited so long to bring this charge is certainly an indication of its trumped-up nature.

But our friend now produces his trump card: he offers his slaves for torture (ss. 34–5):

> And further, gentlemen, take note of this further aspect of the case. I went with witnesses to see him, and said that I still had the slaves that I owned when I took over the property, and was ready to deliver any that he wished to the torture, thinking that this would put his statements and my acts to a stronger test. But he declined, asserting that no credit could be given to slaves. But it seems to me remarkable that when put to the torture in relation to some crime they have committed, they will accuse themselves, in the certain knowledge that they will be executed, but when it is on account of their masters, towards whom they naturally have most animosity, they can choose rather to endure torture than to get release from their present ills by an incrimination.

This brings into focus once again this bizarre and unpleasant provision of Athenian law, noted already at various points during this work, the taking of evidence from slaves under torture, but also another oddity, that, in cases of sacrilege, as with high treason, slaves who testified against their masters were rewarded with their

---

[31] It also indicates, incidentally, that the property was fairly close to the city.

freedom.[32] This would seem to weight things dangerously in favour of miscarriages of justice, but, in the absence of anything like a police or security service, the Athenians plainly felt that the risk was worth it. The only danger for slaves in such a situation was, presumably, that their testimony might be controverted by that of free men, as would have been the case here, in which case they faced execution; but our friend, in spite of his views on the natural enmity of slaves towards their masters, does plainly feel that he can rely on their support in this instance.

This, then, is to all appearances a pretty threadbare case, brought for very questionable motives, and our friend probably won it comfortably, but it does serve to point up the aspects of religious practice that particularly concerned the Athenians.

A RARE OLD SCANDAL: PARODYING THE MYSTERIES AND MUTILATING THE HERMAE

We turn next from what may seem to us a relative triviality to an incident, or series of incidents, which are of unquestioned importance, and which, indeed, rocked the Athenian state, in the spring and summer of 415 BC, more or less to its foundations. To appreciate fully their enormity, we must recall briefly the political and military situation.

In the spring of 415, as Thucydides tells us in his narrative of the Peloponnesian War,[33] following a period of respite in the long war with the Spartans and their allies, the Athenians decided to conquer Sicily. Ostensibly, their purpose was somewhat more modest: the support of their allies in that area, notably Egesta, and the neutralising of Syracuse, the most powerful state in Sicily, so as to prevent it from joining in the war on the Peloponnesian side (Syracuse being Dorian, and a colony of Corinth); but the real purpose, being advocated strongly by the playboy-politician Alkibiades in particular, was the conquest of Sicily as a whole, and its inclusion in the Athenian Empire. This project attracted the opposition of the more cautious and conservative elements in the state, including the millionaire Nikias (who

---

[32] We will see this provision operating in a significant way in our next case-history below. Another troublesome provision, by the way, also alluded to here (s. 7) was that the prosecutor in such cases was exempted from the usual provision of a fine of 1,000 drachmae and disqualification from bringing further lawsuits if one failed to gain a fifth of the vote of the jury – thus making vexatious prosecution in this area that much the more attractive.

[33] *Hist*. VI 8–26.

was therefore, in recognition precisely of his well-known caution, elected one of the generals to lead the expedition, Alkibiades being another, and a fairly neutral soldierly figure, Lamachos, the third); but it also seems to have alarmed certain more shadowy forces much more sympathetic to Sparta and opposed to the democracy than Nikias, and that may be the key to the remarkable events that ensued – though the main affair, the mutilation of the Hermae, remains officially an unsolved mystery.

One night in late spring, about a fortnight before the great expedition was due to leave, the people of Athens woke up to discover to their horror that virtually all of the little stone statues of Hermes which stood both at crossroads throughout the city and in front of many private houses, had been vandalised during the night. These *hermai* were simple rectangular stone pillars, surmounted by a head of the god Hermes, and often adorned, to enhance their apotropaic power, with an erect phallus. They served the role of marking boundaries, indicating paths, and warding off evil from the households outside which they stood. Since Hermes was the god of travellers, there seemed an obvious connection between this outrage and the forthcoming expedition. What exactly was done to the hermae remains somewhat obscure, since Thucydides (who was not actually himself in Athens at the time, it must be remembered)[34] tells us that their *noses* were smashed, but it would seem far more to the point if it were their *phalluses* that were knocked off; it may be, however, that not all of them were adorned with a phallus, and in that case the nose would do.

At any rate, the city was thrown into a panic, as the first thing people thought of was some kind of oligarchic, pro-Spartan plot. An emergency session of the Assembly was called, and anyone who knew anything was invited to come forward, with the promise of immunity and a large reward – and, if one were a slave, of freedom.[35]

---

[34] He had gone into exile in the wake of his unsuccessful military command in Thrace in the winter of 424, and did not return to Athens until after the war.

[35] Of our two primary sources for these events, Thucydides in Book VI of the *Histories* and Andokides in his speech *On the Mysteries*, each, it should be said, has certain drawbacks, but for the chronology of events Thucydides must be regarded as the more reliable, since Andokides, who is after all speaking in his own defence, has strategic reasons, as we shall see, for introducing certain distortions into the record. As regards the order of events in the Assembly, Andokides is quite misleading, in presenting (at the outset of his narration, ss. 11ff.) Pythonikos as standing up quite unexpectedly, *à propos* of nothing, and denouncing Alkibiades and others for parodying the Eleusinian Mysteries in a private house, whereas in fact this denunciation only followed on the initial call for information in the wake of mutilation of the herms.

As Thucydides describes the situation (VI 27–8), initially no one could come up with information on the actual mutilation, but people began to come forward with information on other acts of sacrilege, both parodies of the Mysteries in private houses and other isolated acts of vandalism against statues committed by young men when drunk, and this served to increase the atmosphere of paranoia.

The first offer of information seems to have been that of a certain Pythonikos, who said that, if immunity was offered, he could produce a slave of Alkibiades', who would testify that Alkibiades and others had performed a parody of the Eleusinian Mysteries at the house of a certain Poulytion. This offer was accepted, and the slave Andromachos duly named ten people, one of whom was caught and executed, while the other nine fled into exile. All of these people about whom we know anything were of the richest stratum of society, and many of them were followers of the sophists, so we are dealing here with an aristocratic, intellectual elite, of which the people would naturally be suspicious in any case. Further, the suggestion is made by our third authority, Plutarch, in his *Life of Alcibiades* (ch. 19), who seems to have some sources of information independent of either Thucydides or Andokides, that a sworn enemy of Alkibiades, the demagogue Androkles, took the opportunity to turn the situation against his rival by implicating him in something, and the implication would be that he was behind this intervention by Pythonikos.

At any rate, this broadened the scope of the witch-hunt significantly. It seems beyond doubt that parodies of the Eleusinian Mysteries were something of a favourite after-dinner entertainment in this period among the elite of the city. Why this should have been so is far from clear. It may have been simply the fascination of the illegal.[36] There was no difficulty, after all, about being initiated into the Mysteries,[37] and all or most of the participants in these charades would have been initiates, but there was a strong taboo on discussing or representing any aspect of the ceremony outside the bounds of the

---

[36] Thucydides describes them (VI 28) as being performed *eph' hybrei*, which may perhaps be rendered 'for devilment'. *Hybris*, as we have seen, is a rather flexible Greek vice, denoting, broadly, behaviour stimulated by arrogance or excessive self-confidence. Since the Mysteries were a thoroughly popular cult, despite being secret, there may also have been a measure of aristocratic contempt for them being manifested here, which the people in turn might be alert to.

[37] We have seen the orator Lysias inviting up Madame Nikaretê from Corinth, along with her girl Metaneira, to be initiated (above, pp. 27–8), and there was no problem about that. It was notorious, indeed, that the lowest scoundrels could be initiated, which is the reason that Diogenes the Cynic gave for not being initiated himself (Diogenes Laertius, VI 39).

sanctuary, and it is this taboo that Alkibiades and his friends were plainly taking delight in breaking; there seems to have been no sinister political aspect to their activities, and thus they were strictly irrelevant to the mutilation of the herms – except that some of the same people appear to have been involved in both activities.

The next informant was a resident alien called Teukros, who had fled to Megara when the scandal broke, and now signalled his willingness to spill the beans on both outrages if granted immunity. Immunity was promptly granted, and Teukros duly denounced eleven people of having taken part in parodies of the Mysteries in which he himself had participated, and a further eighteen who had mutilated herms. All of these either fled or were executed. What is worrying to us, and should have been disturbing for the Council, was that there is virtually no overlap between Teukros' list and that of Andromachos.[38] It begins to look as if almost everyone above a certain social level was celebrating the Mysteries in their drawing-rooms.

But this was not by any means the end, and here the story begins to impinge upon Andokides and his family. It should be specified at this stage that Andokides was of very good family, one of the oldest aristocratic families of Athens. It was not only distinguished, tracing itself back to the god Hermes himself, and to the hero Odysseus, but had plainly been very wealthy for many generations. An ancestor had been Treasurer of Athena in the mid-sixth century, an office which was only open to members of the highest property class, and other ancestors had helped to expel the Peisistratids and restore the democracy in 511/10. More recently, his grandfather Andokides had been a general twice with Pericles in the 440s. His father, Leogoras, it must be said, had nothing much to show for himself in the way of public service, but lived a life of conspicuous luxury, which had attracted the notice of the comic poets – for instance, Aristophanes in *The Wasps* (1269), produced in 422, where there is mention of 'dining with Leogoras'. Such a family could expect to attract suspicion at such a juncture, and so indeed it did.

The next informant (s. 17) was another slave, Lydos, the servant of Pherekles of Themakos. He told of the Mysteries being parodied at the house of his master, and named a further series of people, including Andokides' father Leogoras – though he rather oddly described

---

[38] Only a certain Theodoros, whom Teukros identifies as having mutilated herms, is mentioned by Plutarch's source (*Vit. Alc.* 19. 1) as taking part with Poulytion and Alkibiades in a profanation of the Mysteries; and Pherekles, whom Teukros also claims as a mutilator, is identified by a later informant, Lydos, as hosting a Mysteries–parody (Andoc., *De Myst.* 17).

him as being 'present, but asleep, wrapped up in his cloak'. This was enough, though, for an enemy of his, Speusippos, to call for his prosecution, a move which Leogoras countered by indicting Speusippos for introducing an illegal proposal, and winning his case against him. How he pulled this off is not clear, but it effectively got him off the hook for the moment.

This, however, was but a brief respite. Much worse was to come. The most comprehensive denunciation of all came from a certain Diokleides, who had an extraordinary tale to tell. I will let Andokides tell it, at some length, as it illustrates very well the state of paranoia into which the Athenian people had slipped, and how this could be exploited by an unscrupulous *sykophantês* (ss. 37–42):[39]

> The general state of alarm encouraged Diokleides to bring an impeachment [*eisangelia*] before the Council. He claimed that he knew who had mutilated the Hermae, and gave their number at roughly three hundred. He then went on to explain how he had come to witness the event …
>
> Diokleides' tale was that he had a slave working at Laureion,[40] and he had gone to collect his rent [*apophora*]. He rose at an early hour, since he had mistaken the time, and set out on his journey by the light of a full moon. As he was passing the gateway of the theatre of Dionysos,[41] he noticed a large body of men coming down into the orchestra from the Odeion. In alarm, he withdrew into the shadow and crouched down between the column and the pedestal with the bronze statue of the general on it. He then saw some three hundred men standing about in groups of fifteen or, in some cases, twenty. He recognised the faces of the majority, as he could see them in the moonlight.

Andokides at this point interjects a comment, before going on with the narrative:

> Now first of all, gentlemen, Diokleides gave his story this particular form simply to be in a position to say of any citizen, according as he chose, that he was or was not one of the offenders – a monstrous device!

He then continues:

---

[39] I borrow here the Loeb translation of K. J. Maidment, with some minor alterations.
[40] That is to say, at the silver mines, probably as an overseer or contractor, not as an ordinary miner.
[41] That is, coming round the south of the Acropolis.

After seeing what he had seen, he said, he went on to Laureion, and
when he learned next day of the mutilation of Hermae, he knew at
once that it was the work of the men he had observed. On his return
to Athens, he found a commission already appointed to investigate,
and a reward of one hundred minae offered for information. So,
seeing Euphemos, the brother of Kallias, son of Telokles, sitting in his
smithy,[42] he led him up to the temple of Hephaistos, and told him
what I have told you, how he had seen us on the night in question.
He then said that he would rather take our money than the state's, so
as to keep us as his friends.[43]

Euphemos, Diokleides claimed (s. 41), thanked him for confiding
in him, and invited him to come round to Leogoras' house and talk
business with Andokides and the others. This he accordingly did,
claiming that he was welcomed by Leogoras, who invited him in, and
that the family then offered him a bribe of two talents, to overmatch
the hundred minae offered by the state, and the deal was confirmed
the next night at Kallias' house. Diokleides' story then was that the
family, having promised to deliver the money at the beginning of the
following month, reneged on their promise; and so he went to the
Council, and told them what he knew.

This story, with its superficially convincing corroborative detail,
proved a bombshell.[44] Diokleides produced a list of forty-two people,
including Andokides and ten other members of his family. All were
arrested and lodged in prison, and a national state of emergency was
declared, the citizens being required to muster at various key points
in the City, the Long Walls, and the Piraeus, and spend the night
under arms (s. 45). And now finally the chickens came home to roost
for Andokides. Faced with the prospect of imminent execution, he

---

[42] It may seem somewhat odd that a member of a respectable family (Kallias is
Andokides' brother-in-law) should be anything like a blacksmith, but Euphemos may
have been supervising a slave-run workshop that he owned. Sokrates' father,
Sophroniskos, after all, was a stone-mason, probably in the same sense, and Sokrates
moved in the best circles.

[43] A plausible consideration, as we have seen in previous chapters – though, of course, if
his accusation succeeded, all his victims would be destroyed, and he would not have to
worry about them. We must suppose, however, in view of what will emerge
presently, that this whole tale of the attempted blackmail is a malicious lie.

[44] The timescale involved here requires some thought. Diokleides' expedition to
Laureion, real or imaginary, should have taken place at the end of a lunar month, since
that is the time that one would collect an *apophora* from a slave (Plutarch actually
confirms this, *Vit. Alc.* 20. 5 – and thereby hangs a significant detail, to which we will
return), but he speaks of Andokides' family promising to pay up the bribe 'in the
coming month' and then not doing so. This seems to imply that he waited a whole
month and more before coming forward.

tells us that, in response to an appeal from his cousin Charmides, who had a pretty good idea that Andokides at least knew who *had* performed the mutilation, even if he was not directly involved himself, he resolved to shop his associates under the protection of immunity, and save the rest of his family and friends.

We now at last approach to something like the truth about this affair – though not, I fear, the whole truth. Andokides is very much concerned to minimise the political significance of the whole operation – he makes it sound as far as possible like a student prank that got rather out of hand – and of course to minimise his own part in it; but basically we may, I think, accept his story. It indicates that Diokleides, crook and blackmailer though he may have been, was not entirely wide of the mark in targeting him; nor, for that matter, was Teukros earlier, since he had in fact named the ringleader Euphiletos, and most of his associates.[45] This consideration weighs with Andokides, as he tells us, against his discomfort at betraying his friends (ss. 51–3).

What Andokides reveals to us is a culture of aristocratic men's clubs, or *hetaireiai*, where young bloods of Athens got together to drink, gamble, slag the democracy, and go off on *kômoi* round the town, gate-crashing parties, either of respectable acquaintances[46] or of some favourite courtesan, and generally causing mayhem. In this case, though, it would really seem as if something rather more serious was afoot, though Andokides is loath to admit this. This, at any rate, is his story (ss. 60–2):

> Taking all this[47] into consideration, gentlemen, I found that the least objectionable of the courses open to me was to tell the truth as quickly as possible, to prove that Diokleides had lied, and so to punish the scoundrel who was causing us to be put to death wrongfully and deceiving the state, while being hailed as its greatest benefactor and being rewarded for his services.[48] I therefore informed the Council that I knew the offenders, and revealed exactly what had occurred.

[45] In fact, as he assures us, only four of the group had escaped the notice of Teukros, and in the event they managed to flee into exile, following on his denunciation of them, as did many of those denounced by Teukros – and they are now (sc. 400 BC), he tells us (53), all back in town, and restored to their properties (presumably as a result of the amnesty of 403).

[46] As in the case of Alkibiades and his associates barging in towards the end of the tragic poet Agathon's drinking party, as depicted by Plato in the *Symposium*.

[47] Sc. that he was not really causing any great further harm to the people that he was denouncing, and that they were guilty anyway.

[48] In his (brief) moment of glory, Diokleides was garlanded, driven to the Prytaneion in an ox-cart, and entertained to dinner, much in the manner of an Olympic victor (s. 45).

The idea, I said, had been suggested by Euphiletos at a drinking-party; but I opposed it, and succeeded in preventing its execution for the time being. Later, however, I was thrown from a colt of mine in the Kynosarges.[49] I broke my collar-bone and cracked my skull, and had to be taken home on a litter. When Euphiletos saw my condition, he informed the others that I had consented to join them and had promised to mutilate the herm next to the shrine of Phorbas[50] as my share in the escapade. He told them this to fool them; and that is why the herm which you can all see standing close to the home of our family, that dedicated by the Aegeid tribe, was the only one in Athens left unmutilated, it being understood that I would attend to it as Euphiletos had promised.[51]

We might be forgiven here for wondering whether we are being told the whole truth. On the face of it, we are being asked to believe that, over the wine one evening at the club, Euphiletos comes out with something like the following: 'I say, chaps, I've just thought of a splendid wheeze! Why don't we go out one of these nights and knock the cocks [or just possibly, the noses] off all the herms in the city?' – at which Andokides, the voice of reason and moderation, remonstrates with him, ('Oh come off it, Euph! That's a real dog of an idea!'), and interposes his veto. But, it would seem, the idea has taken hold in Euphiletos' mind, and he comes back to it when our hero is temporarily out of the way.

This scenario, however, will not really stand up to much con-sideration. Euphiletos and his clubmates must surely have known, unless they were completely mindless hooligans (which they were surely not), that an outrage on such a scale as this would cause a major political upheaval, as indeed proved to be the case. It is hard to see, indeed, how they hoped to escape detection. But if Euphiletos and certain other club members (whatever about Andokides himself) were dedicated members of the pro-Spartan Far Right, what they could hope for – like certain types of Far Left urban terrorist in modern times, such as the Red Brigades in Italy, or the Baader-Meinhof gang in Germany – was that, in the course of such a political

---

[49] This was a park on the eastern outskirts of the city, where much sporting activity took place.

[50] This reminds us how many little local shrines there were dotted about Athens (and the Attic countryside). Phorbas was a local *hêrôs*; he had been the charioteer of the national hero Theseus.

[51] It was still there in Plutarch's day (c. 100 AD), as he testifies (*Vit. Alc.* 21. 2), and was known as the Herm of Andokides.

upheaval, an opportunity would arise to overthrow the democracy – such as in fact occurred four years later, in 411, with the setting up of the regime of the Four Hundred.[52] The fact that that did not happen does not mean that certain oligarchic elements may not have had it in mind. They were not necessarily trying to stop the expedition to Sicily in its tracks – this would hardly have been possible at this late stage of preparation – just to create political instability at home in its wake.

At any rate, as Andokides continues the story, things now begin to turn a little nasty (ss. 63–4):

> When the others learned the truth, they were furious to think that I was in the secret without having taken any active part; and the next day I received a visit from Meletos[53] and Euphiletos. 'We have managed it all right, Andokides', they told me. 'Now if you are prepared to keep quiet and say nothing, you will find us just as good friends as before. If you do not, you will find us much more troublesome enemies than any others will be friends to you because of betraying us.' I replied that I certainly thought Euphiletos a scoundrel for acting as he had, but that he and his companions had far less to fear from my being in the secret than from the mere fact that the deed was done.

And in fact he did keep the secret well enough, until the principals were on the run anyway, and his own life and those of his family were in imminent danger. Andokides may not have been as innocent and virtuous as he wishes to make out (even as his father may not have snoozed through the whole parody of the Mysteries at Pherekles' house), but he tells a good story, and he convinced the Council on the main points. Andokides himself offered a slave for examination under torture (s. 64), and the *prytaneis*[54] commandeered some serving girls from the house of Euphiletos, and the upshot was that Andokides was vindicated. The wretched Diokleides was hauled back in for cross-examination, whereat he confessed immediately that the whole story was a lie, and he had been put up to this by two supporters of Alkibiades, Alkibiades of Phegos (a cousin of the famous

---

[52] Of which, we may reflect, two of the most vocal protagonists of the current witch-hunt, Peisandros and Charikles (s. 36), emerged as leaders! Charikles even managed, after spending a period of time after that in exile, to return and become a member of the Thirty in 404 (Peisandros, as we recall from our previous case-history, fled into exile at the end of the rule of the Four Hundred, and did not return, cf. n. 25 above).

[53] Meletos, we may note, appears both on Andromachos' list as a profaner of the Mysteries, and on that of Teukros as a mutilator of the herms. He thus constitutes one of the links between the two scandals.

[54] The ruling segment of the Council for that month.

bearer of that name), and Amiantos of Aigina.[55] He was arrested and put to death, for deceiving the Athenian people.

However, Andokides' problems were not over, by any means. His enemies had a shot or two in their lockers. Officially, he was in the clear, beneficiary of a grant of immunity; but it could be argued that he was nonetheless a polluted person, because of his involvement in the plot. Before the end of 415, a certain Isotimides introduced a motion in the Assembly debarring all who had committed impiety and confessed to it from the temples and the market-place of Athens, thus effectively cutting off anyone in Andokides' position, irrespective of any immunity he may have been granted, from the totality of civic life. Indeed, this decree is generally felt by modern scholars to have been aimed directly at Andokides by his political enemies. At all events, he took the hint and retired into voluntary exile, going off to Cyprus, where the family probably had interests, and where he duly prospered, involving himself in the import/export trade.[56]

AFTERMATH OF SCANDAL: A MISPLACED OLIVE BRANCH

But the call of home was strong. Andokides made one attempt to return in 411, having made what he hoped would be well-received contributions to the Athenian fleet based in Samos. The contributions were doubtless well received in Samos, but when he arrived back in Athens he found to his horror that there had been an oligarchic coup, the regime of the 'Four Hundred', led by his old enemy Peisandros, and they were now at odds with the fleet in Samos and all who helped it, so Andokides was arrested and clapped in gaol.

He was presumably released on the fall of the Four Hundred in the summer of 410, but there was no disposition to repeal the decree of Isotimides, so he retired once more into exile. He tried again, however, at some time in the ensuing years, probably in 409/8, but was again rebuffed, despite making an eloquent address to the Assembly (which survives as his speech *On His Return*). We must presume that

---

[55] It is pointed out by Plutarch (cf. n. 44 above) that Diokleides must have been going off to collect his *apophora* at the end of the month – the new moon, not the full moon – so he could not have seen anything by the light of the moon; but Andokides makes nothing of this point, though it would have suited his case excellently.

[56] We learn for instance, from his speech *On his Return* (s. 11), that he was able to profit from his family's connections with the Macedonian royal house to trade in timber from that source; but he was also concerned with trade in corn (ibid. s. 20).

the people simply lacked much sympathy with the gilded young (or youngish)[57] aristocrat with a slightly murky past.

So he withdrew again to his comfortable retreat in Cyprus, until, in the wake of the defeat of Athens in 404, the brief rule of the Thirty, and the restoration of the democracy in 403, with its attendant amnesty, he was encouraged to try again. This time the climate was altogether more favourable. While it is by no means clear whether the various provisions for reprieves from exile and loss of civil rights which he lists so comprehensively (*De Myst.* 73–9) really related to his rather peculiar situation,[58] it seems to have been generally accepted that he was covered by the amnesty.

And so matters would doubtless have remained, had Andokides been content to live quietly, and attend to his estates and his business interests; but he was not – and here, as we have seen with other extensive case-histories (such as those of Neaira, Demosthenes or Timarchos), other motifs in which we have had an interest in this work enter into the picture, notably inheritance and *enmity*. Our friend managed, in fact, in quite a short time to antagonise at least three distinct people or groups of people, thus generating for himself the enmity equivalent of the Perfect Storm.

First of all, as he tells us with fine self-righteousness (*De Myst.* 133–6), he fell foul of a powerful syndicate of tax-farmers, led by the prominent democratic politician Agyrrhios, who had put together a cosy little cartel for the collection of the two per cent import-export tax.[59] Andokides discerned that they were making an undue profit on this, and, forming a consortium of his own, underbid them to the tune of six talents, and still came out with a tidy profit. This enraged them, and they also feared exposure at his hands, so they resolved to get him out of the way, one way or another.

Secondly, he seems to have gone out of his way to antagonise a certain Kephisios, who, either just before the defeat of Athens, or during the regime of the Thirty, had contracted for the collection of a tax on the farming community, and had then defaulted on his payment to the state (ss. 92–3). Despite the fact that such a peccadillo

---

[57] Andokides will by this time have been in his early thirties (his date of birth is estimated to have been about 440 BC).

[58] He was not actually exiled, it will be recalled, but simply barred, as polluted, from the Agora and all temples and places of worship.

[59] Athens, like many other pre-modern states, lacking an extensive civil service, had adopted the practice of farming out the collection of taxes. If interested parties agreed not to bid against each other, this could result in the state being seriously short-changed, to the great advantage of the tax consortium.

might be thought to be covered by the amnesty, Andokides was apparently threatening to bring it into the open.[60]

His final quarrel, however, brought everything together, and it here that a further accusation of sacrilege enters the picture. He fell out seriously with Kallias, son of Hipponikos, heir to one of the greatest fortunes in Athens (most of which he had in fact squandered),[61] who was a relation of his by marriage,[62] over the question of the marriage of an heiress (epiklēros), the daughter of one of Andokides' maternal uncles, Epilykos. I allow Andokides to take up the story (De Myst. 117–19):

> And now, gentlemen, you would perhaps like to know what motive Kallias had in putting the bough on the altar.[63] I will explain why he tried to trap me. Epilykos, son of Teisandros, was my uncle, my mother's brother. He died in Sicily[64] without male issue, but left two daughters, who became the responsibility of Leagros[65] and myself. His private affairs were in a bad state. The tangible property which he left did not amount to two talents, while his debts came to more than five. However, I arranged a meeting with Leagros in the presence of friends[66] and told him that this was the time for decent men to show their respect for family ties [oikeiotētes].
>
> 'We have no right to prefer a wealthy or successful alliance[67] and

[60] His other accusers, Meletos and Epichares, both had murky pasts, the one as an informer, the other as an office-holder (member of the Council) under the Thirty (94–5), but Andokides does not make clear precisely how he had offended them. This Meletos, we may note, is probably the same as the accuser of Socrates, also on a charge of impiety, shortly after this – but not the same as the man implicated in the mutilation of the herms (above, p. 175).

[61] His father Hipponikos, we are told in a speech of Lysias, On the Estate of Aristophanes (s. 48), of which we have made use already (pp. 68–73 above), was reputed to have died worth about 200 talents, but Kallias managed to reduce this to less than two talents. He was a great lover of sophists, for one thing (as illustrated, for instance, in Plato's Protagoras and Xenophon's Symposium), and they did not come cheap.

[62] Andokides' father Leogoras had married a daughter of one Teisandros, whose granddaughter had been the first wife of Kallias. The top families of Athens, if not at enmity, tended to be elaborately inter-married. Kallias' father-in-law, Glaukon, was Plato's uncle, and Kallias' eldest son Hipponikos was married to a daughter of Alkibiades.

[63] We will return shortly to this bough, which is integral to the 'impiety' aspect of the story.

[64] This can hardly have been in connection with the disastrous Sicilian expedition of 415–13; it must rather have occurred on a business trip in the aftermath of the war, since it is plain that the problem of the heiresses only arose recently.

[65] This Leagros must have been the son of Glaukon and the other daughter of Teisandros, and thus the brother-in-law of Kallias.

[66] We may note once again the importance of friends as witnesses in negotiations of this sort.

[67] That is to say, the two main purposes of marriage in Athenian society, the accumulation of wealth or of political and social connections.

look down on the daughters of Epilykos', I argued, 'for if Epilykos were alive, or had died a rich man, we should be claiming the girls as their next of kin.[68] We should have married them then, either because of Epilykos himself or because of his money; we will do the same now because we are men of honour. So you get a court order for one of them, and I'll do the same for the other.'

Leagros duly agreed, it seems, to this remarkably high-minded proposal; but then things began to come apart. First of all, the girl chosen by Andokides fell ill and died; so that only left one daughter, pledged to Leagros. But then something rather odd happened – odd, that is, if Andokides' account of Epilykos' finances is at all accurate. Kallias steps into the picture, and offers, in effect, to buy the remaining daughter from Leagros (who is, as we recall, his brother-in-law) – not for himself, but for his son.[69]

When he hears of this development, Andokides steps in and files a *parastasis* (s. 120), a sort of injunction, requiring Leagros either to marry the girl himself or to concede her to him. At this, Kallias lodges a counter-claim, on behalf of his son, and battle is joined. Now, we might well ask ourselves, why all this high-minded, selfless competition for a poor orphan girl, burdened with heavy paternal debt? Are we unjustified in wondering whether perhaps the financial facts were not quite as stated by Andokides? But then, one might reflect, neither of these gentlemen should be so strapped for cash as to go to war for an *epiklêros*, even if she were blessed with a large dowry. On the other hand, one might further reflect, rich people never feel that they are rich enough; and in any case, neither Kallias (after all his expenditures), nor Andokides (in the wake of his various adventures) may have felt particularly secure financially.

At any rate, go to war they did, and the battlefield chosen by Kallias was a religious one – hence the relevance to the present topic. It happened to be the season of the Eleusinian Mysteries,[70] of which Kallias was an official, the so-called Torch-Bearer (*daidouchos*), being a member of one of the hereditary clans who administered the Mysteries, the Heralds (*kerykes*). Kallias, it seems, got in touch with

---

[68] We may cast our minds back to the scenario in Menander's *The Shield*, p. 151 above.

[69] By this son there hangs quite a tale, told amusingly by Andokides (ss. 124–9), but not really germane to our purpose – except to say that this is not Hipponikos, but an unnamed son by Chrysilla, the former wife of the 'perfect husband' Ischomachos, whom we met in Chapter 1 – transformed now from a demure young wife into a rather randy widow.

[70] Held every year in the month Boedromion (September–October). This would then be the autumn of 400 BC.

Kephisios, whom he knew to be at odds with Andokides, and slipped him a thousand drachmae to bring a charge of sacrilege against Ando-kides for attending the Mysteries, though he was a polluted person, and still under the ban introduced by Isotimides back in 415.[71]

This Kephisios duly did, first lodging a complaint (*endeixis*) with the King Archon for the regular hearing before the *prytaneis* (the ruling board of the Council) that took place in the wake of every festival (s. 111).[72] The *prytaneis* judged that there was a case to be answered, and referred the matter to the full Council – meeting, for such a purpose, in the Eleusinion, the temple of Demeter and Korê in Athens. Andokides duly attended the hearing, and in the course of that Kallias made a dramatic intervention. Again, I yield the floor to Andokides (ss. 112, 115–16):

> When the Council had assembled, Kallias, son of Hipponikos, who was wearing his ceremonial robes [sc. as Torch-Bearer], rose and announced that a suppliant's bough had been placed on the altar [sc. of the Eleusinion]; and he showed the bough to the Council. Thereupon the Herald[73] called for the person responsible. There was no reply, although I was standing close by and in full view of Kephisios. When no one replied ...[74] Eukles informed the Council that there had been no response. But now Kallias rose once more and said that, under an ancient law, as officially interpreted on a former occasion by his father, Hipponikos, the penalty for placing a bough in the Eleusinion during the Mysteries was death; and he added that he had heard that it was I who had put it there.
>
> Thereupon Kephalos[75] here leapt to his feet and shouted, 'Kallias, you impious scoundrel, first you are giving interpretations,[76] when you have no right to do such a thing as a member of the Kerykes. Then you talk of an "ancient law", when the stone beside you lays down that the penalty for placing a bough in the Eleusinion shall be a

---

[71] Andokides claims to know this because Kallias had actually approached mutual friends, whom he names (and produces as witnesses), offering to call off Kephisios if Andokides would abandon his claim to the heiress – which Andokides resolutely refused to do.

[72] We have seen Demosthenes lodging a similar complaint against Meidias after the Dionysia, above, p. 91.

[73] A certain Eukles, mentioned just below.

[74] Andokides here interrupts his narrative, first to call Eukles to testify to the truth of this, and then to answer a point made in the speeches of the prosecution, to which we will return.

[75] A prominent democratic politician, named at the end of the speech as a supporter (*synêgoros*) of Andokides in this trial.

[76] That is to say, acting as an *exêgêtês*, which in respect of questions concerning the Mysteries, was the preserve of the clan of the Eumolpidai, not the Kerykes.

fine of a thousand drachmae. And lastly, who told you that Andokides had put the bough there? Summon this person before the Council, that we too may hear what he has to say.

The stone was read, and Kallias could not say who his informant was. It thus became clear to the Council that he had put the bough there himself.'

This dastardly attempt thus fails miserably, but what is interesting for our purposes is the bizarre provision of which Kallias is able to make use. On the face of it, it far exceeds in dottiness the prohibition on uprooting sacred olive stumps. The placing of a suppliant bough is the equivalent of lighting a candle, or making a similar offering, in a Christian church, in support of some petition, but what was the problem about the laying of such a bough during the festival? One can only conjecture that it must have been seen as a sort of violation of the festival itself, constituting a distraction such as would annoy the Two Goddesses.

The second question that must be asked is why on earth anyone would be moved to do such a thing, when discovery meant death – or at least a large fine. What the prosecution is driven to allege (ss. 113–14) is that Andokides is so hated by the gods that they sowed confusion into his mind, so that he simply forgot this provision, while at the same time his guilt drove him to supplicate the goddesses. Andokides feels the need to reply to this suggestion by remarking that if the goddesses really wished to destroy him, they would have provoked him to own up when the question was asked by the herald at the Council.[77]

In the event, Andokides won his case, and went on to another decade of active participation in Athenian social and political life, before finally falling foul of the Sovereign People in 392, on the matter of the wisdom or otherwise of making peace with Sparta, a mistake

---

[77] He also feels the need to answer another bizarre argument which we find advanced in a rather dismal document, which is nonetheless of some interest, the speech *Against Andocides*, included among the works of Lysias (as *Oration* VI), though certainly not by him, but by one or other of Andokides' accusers other than Kephisios (whom it mentions (s. 42)), and that is that the gods permitted Andokides to sail the seas for many years as a trader without destroying him in a storm, in order to preserve him to face trial in Athens! Andokides waxes satirical in reply to this suggestion (ss. 137–9), but it would probably have found favour in some Athenian minds. It itself, of course, would serve as a counter-argument to the more obvious argument that, if he were as polluted as is alleged, the gods should have destroyed him while they had him at their mercy. The actual charge to which Andokides is replying, it must be specified, is, of course, not the preliminary enquiry before the Council described above, but a subsequent charge of impiety brought by Kephisios, with the support of Agyrrhios, Meletos and Charikles.

which caused him to retire once more into exile, and this time to vanish from history; but not before, as we see, he had contributed substantially to our understanding of one of the more obscure and dramatic incidents in the history of the Peloponnesian War, as well as providing some lively insights into Athenian society in the years immediately following.

We see, then, from these instances of what passed for piety and impiety in the Athenian popular mind, what were the presuppositions on which Athenian religion was based. It was not of primary concern what one believed – unless one were a very vocal and contumacious atheist – but it did matter a great deal how one behaved in matters of ritual, because it was by the right performance of a wide range of time-honoured rituals that the gods of Greece were kept happy, and might be expected to confer their usual blessings.

It has not been my concern here to deal with Athenian religion as a whole, popular or otherwise, but rather, by the adducing of a number of salient examples, to point up aspects of it that might strike us as odd. In fact, of course, a great deal of Athenian religious practice, both as regards great public festivals and in the area of local and private cults, accords pretty well with that of Christianity, at least in centuries previous to this; but it still remains the fact that the Greeks were blessedly free of any preoccupation with doctrinal orthodoxy.

CHAPTER EIGHT

A Vision of the Past: The Role of the Anecdote in the Formation of the Athenian Self-Image

THEORETICAL PRELIMINARIES

It seems appropriate to round off this survey of Athenian *mores* by considering a feature of their intellectual life which, while still finding some echo in our own, was nevertheless a great deal more decisive then than now, and that is the importance of anecdotal discourse in the formation of the Athenian view of their own historical development, and thus of their image of themselves. After all, for the Athenians of the Classical Age, as is to some extent also the case today, success in politics, in the arts, or in society generally, rested to a large extent on lending oneself to anecdote – to being, as we would say, 'a bit of a character'. The stories which are somehow generated about such a figure then take on the status of facts about the popular belief-system of the Athenians – provided only that we can assure ourselves that they really arise from the oral tradition of the Athenian people, and not from the over-heated brain of some Alexandrian scholar or gossip-writer. Even then, of course, they would tell us something, but not anything that concerns us at present.[1]

I propose to proceed by, first, making some attempt to define an anecdote – no easy task, in fact, since it is a concept with very ragged edges; and then by considering briefly what role the anecdote plays in society – that is to say, in which circumstances such stories are told, and with what purposes. Following on this theoretical introduction, I will examine a series of anecdotes involving notable figures in Athenian history in the areas of politics, literature and philosophy, selecting just one character in each field, and trying to relate each of the anecdotes to the overall 'image' of the person concerned, and also to what they might tell us about the attitudes to life and assumptions of the purveyors and recipients of such anecdotes.

[1] For a sceptical evaluation of the value of ancient biographical information, particularly about the lives of poets, see Mary Lefkowitz, *The Lives of the Greek Poets*, London, 1981.

Firstly, then, what is an anecdote? If we turn to the *Oxford English Dictionary*, we find, as the original meaning, 'a secret, or hitherto unpublished narrative, or detail of history'. This is etymologically accurate, but not of much help for our purpose. More to the point is the *derived* meaning, 'the narrative of an interesting or striking incident or event (*at first*, an item of gossip)'. The *OED* definition is perfectly sound, so far as it goes, but I would like to venture a little farther. Can we make any progress towards delineating something like a morphology of the anecdote, or is it an irreducibly amorphous entity?

The etymological meaning is, as we have seen, not of much help, but it provides a starting point. Anecdotes – the word, it seems, tended in earlier times mainly to be used in the plural – were the sort of juicy details which one would not publish in an official history. The *OED* gives, as an example, the book-title *Anecdotes of Florence, or the Secret History of the House of the Medicis* – and indeed, to go back to the Byzantine period: Procopius' *Anecdota*, his 'Secret History', comprised all the things he did not venture to include in his official history of the Emperor Justinian.[2] One can derive from this definition at least the useful characteristic that anecdotes are not the sort of items which find their way into official histories, the reason being, not so much that they are often irreverent (as they often are), but rather that their provenance is in some way irregular; they are not securely documented, having started their careers as orally transmitted stories. They do not therefore attain the level of documentation required for inclusion in a 'serious' history or biography.[3]

The secondary definition advances us somewhat further: 'the narrative of an interesting or striking incident or event'. To this let us subjoin the corresponding definition from Webster's *Dictionary*: 'a usually short narrative of an interesting, amusing or biographical incident'. The disjunction 'interesting, amusing or biographical' is slightly peculiar, but otherwise it is rather more helpful than the *OED* one. Neither of these, however, seems to me to address the essence of the anecdote.

Now it may be that in seeking that I am asking too much. The *Faber Book of Anecdotes*, edited by Clifton Fadiman,[4] is full of amusing

---

[2] The actual word *anekdoton* is not in fact the ancient term for this sort of story, as we shall see below. It seems only to be used as an adjective, meaning 'unpublished'.

[3] This distinction, of course, is only valid for modern times. It would not be relevant to the procedure of an Herodotus or a Plutarch.

[4] London/Boston, 1985.

stories, but only a minority of these are such as I would characterise as anecdotes. In his introduction, Fadiman makes some attempt to distinguish anecdotes from other similar items, such as he describes, broadly, as 'episodes', but, as he admits himself, much of what he includes in his collection is of the latter variety. As he says (p. xvi): 'We prefer our anecdotes to be short, free-standing, with a nub or point or centre. This book, nevertheless, contains many of which this cannot be said.'

Is it possible to make any advance on this definition of Fadiman's? I think that perhaps it is. I agree with Fadiman that an anecdote should be short, and have a nub or point or centre. But I think that one can be more specific. There is a class of stories, it seems to me, which one can separate off from all others, which concern a famous personality, in conversation (or possibly other, non-verbal interaction) either with another famous personality or with a nonentity of some sort (who then serves as a foil). The nub (or point or centre) of the anecdote then turns on a point of language – either a fine riposte, capping an initially witty or otherwise provocative remark, or a short utterance casting a vivid light either on the character of the subject of the anecdote or on some aspect of the world in general. An anecdote, then, in the sense I want to claim for it, involves essentially a verbal (or in general an intellectual) clash between two figures, at least one of whom is of some distinction, issuing in a flash of wit, or wisdom, or both.

My efforts at definition are supported, I think, by such ancient evidence as there is. The Greeks did not, as I have said, use the word *anekdoton* to denote this sort of story, but the term *chreia* actually covers it pretty well. Properly, a *chreia* is just a witty saying, but many *chreiai* come with fleshed-out contexts attached, and at that point they become in effect anecdotes, even as a simple saying can be regarded as a sawn-off anecdote.

The word *chreia* itself is probably classical, but the earliest attestation of its use is in the collections of *chreiai* made by the founder of Stoicism, Zeno of Citium, in the early third century BC, and the comedy writer Machon towards the middle of it. The rhetorician Theon of Alexandria (first century BC), at the beginning of his *Progymnasmata* (p. 201, 17 Walz), gives a definition of a *chreia* which corresponds quite well to what we want as the definition of an anecdote: 'A *chreia* is a concise statement or action which is attributed with aptness to some specified character, or to something analogous

to a character.'[5] A more expanded form of a *chreia*, he notes just
below (p. 202, 12ff.) is the 'reminiscence' (*apomnêmoneuma*), but this
is more tied to a particular figure and circumstance (as being more
factual, presumably) than the *chreia*.[6]

A curious phrase in the definition is 'something *analogous* to a
character'. Theon does not explain himself, but he presumably wishes
to comprehend by this stories involving a generic, anonymous figure,
such as 'a Spartan', or 'a man of Syracuse'. We would be familiar,
similarly, with modern anecdotes told of 'a Scotsman' or 'a famous
conductor'.

Theon's definition, then, if understood of a *chreia* which is not *too*
concise, will do very well for our purposes. We may note that he
includes 'action' (*praxis*) as a proper alternative to 'statement', and
that is as it should be. He even recognises, as I would, a 'mixed' class,
involving statement *plus* action (p. 202, 20).

Having thus laid down our theoretical foundations, let us proceed to
the consideration of some anecdotes, to illustrate more clearly what I
have in mind. I will take my start from what I would consider a
paradigmatic anecdote, involving a paradigmatic subject of anecdote,
the Athenian statesman Themistokles. It goes as follows:[7]

> A man of Seriphos[8] once taunted the great Athenian general, saying:
> 'You would not have attained your present fame, if you had been
> born a Seriphian.' 'No doubt', replied Themistokles, 'but then nor
> would you have attained any fame, had you been born an Athenian'.

Here, I would maintain, we have a quintessentially well-turned
anecdote. Let us consider its various elements. First of all, it involves a
confrontation between a famous man and a nameless foil. The confrontation consists in a brief, pointed exchange, initiated by the foil,
whose sally is neatly capped by the protagonist. Then, the dialogue
involves a conceptual or verbal twist, analogous to the last line of a
limerick. It is my contention that this twist in the tail, in one form or
another, is a necessary component of a good anecdote. Lastly, the
exchange embodies or illustrates a generalisable moral, in this case – if

---

[5] Cf. *The Chreia in Ancient Rhetoric, Vol. I: The Progymnasmata*, ed. R. F. Hock and E. N.
O'Neil, Atlanta, 1986.

[6] Theon here seems to recognise something 'free-floating' and archetypal in the
concept of the *chreia*.

[7] The story is found in Plutarch, *Life of Themistocles*, 18. 5, but also in Plato, *Rep.* I 329E,
and Cicero, *De Senectute* 3. 8.

[8] A small and insignificant Aegean island not far from Attica.

one is to spell it out with tedious explicitness – that great distinction can be helped by, but is certainly not guaranteed by, fortunate accidents of birth.

This story is of particular interest, since we happen to be able to trace its ancestry, at least to some extent. We have a much more circumstantial version of it preserved in our primary source for the life of Themistokles, the *Histories* of his near-contemporary Herodotus. In Book 8. 125, we find the following version of the story, and in this form I should say that it has a fair claim to being considered authentic:

> When Themistokles returned from Sparta[9] to Athens, a certain Timodemos of Aphidna, who was one of Themistokles' enemies, but otherwise a person of no distinction, seething with jealousy, taunted Themistokles, bringing up the issue of his visit to Sparta, saying that it was due to Athens that he had received these honours, not to himself. Themistokles, since Timodemos was going on about this, replied: 'Just so; I would not have been honoured by the Spartans, if I had come from Belbina,[10] but then neither would you, my fine fellow, though you are an Athenian.'

In this form, the story almost certainly reflects a real exchange in the assembly, since it is just the sort of witty reply for which Themistokles was well known, and which the Athenian public loved to remember. The name of the antagonist, and the exact circumstances of the incident, seem to guarantee that. What has happened to it in its later manifestations is simply that the peripheral details have been rubbed off, as it were, while the essential point has been preserved, in a ground-down and smoothly-polished form – and even that can vary in the telling, since the island can change from Belbina to Seriphos and back.

Another character on the Athenian scene who attracted anecdotes as dogs do fleas was the Cynic philosopher Diogenes of Sinope. There are many stories involving him to illustrate both types of confrontation I have identified, that with another famous character, and that with an unknown foil. but perhaps the most famous Diogenes story is of the former variety, involving as it does Alexander the Great. When Diogenes was living in Corinth, Alexander visited the city, and found him inhabiting a large earthenware tub, in front of which he was

---

[9] Where he had just completed a triumphal tour.
[10] A *very* small and insignificant island off Attica.

sunning himself. Alexander asked if there was anything he could do for him. 'Yes', said Diogenes, 'you could step out of my light.'[11]

This story seems to possess all the requisites for a good anecdote. It involves a confrontation between two well-known figures, it is witty, and it embodies an issue of some substance, that is to say, the Cynic ideal of self-sufficiency. Alexander is a suitable foil, as representing the ultimate in worldly success and ambition. Details which might be of concern to historians, such as what exactly Diogenes was doing in Corinth,[12] are totally eliminated (we shall have occasion to return to this problem). It is worth noting that in some versions of the story[13] Alexander is actually given the last word. He caps Diogenes' sally by remarking to his attendants: 'If I were not Alexander, I would wish to be Diogenes.'

I will return to Diogenes in due course, but now I would like to turn to the study of a representative sequence of anecdotes, involving, in turn, a statesman, a poet, and a philosopher – to wit, Solon, Sophokles and Diogenes himself, each of them well-loved in their way by the Athenian people, and thus lending themselves to being celebrated through the medium of anecdote.

THE STATESMAN: SOLON

Let us turn, then, to our first case-study, the father of Athenian democracy, Solon, son of Exekestides (c. 639–559 BC).[14] Solon himself, as a law-giver and statesman, chose to behave in a manner conducive to anecdote, by adopting a distinctly dramatic mode of presentation, composing his precepts in verse for ease of memorisation, and indulging in various striking *démarches*, which in itself provided a considerable stimulus to the host of stories that later arose.

---

[11] There are numerous attestations of this story, but we may instance Diogenes Laertius 6. 38 (where the meeting is said to take place 'in the Kraneion', a suburb of Corinth); and Cicero, *Tusc. Disp.* 5. 92. This is only the most famous of a number of confrontations between Diogenes and Alexander. For others, cf. DL 6. 32, 60, 63, 68 (though indeed it is possible that they are all part of the same basic confrontation).

[12] Had he really been soldanto slavery, and bought by a Corinthian called Xeniades? And if so, what was he doing pursuing an independent existence in a barrel 'in the Kraneion'? The chronology is also rather troublesome. Cf. K. von Fritz, *Quellenuntersuchungen zum Leben und Philosophie des Diogenes von Sinope*, Philologus Supplb. 18, 2, 1926.

[13] Cf. e.g. Plut. *Life of Alexander*, 14; *De Exilio* 605E. In DL, this remark is reported by itself, without context (6. 32).

[14] Solon is, I should say, about as far back in Athenian history as one can go for a subject of *anecdote*, in the sense used in this essay. One cannot tell anecdotes, it seems to me, about essentially mythological figures, such as Theseus, Heracles or Agamemnon.

At quite an early stage of his personal legend, indeed, perhaps already before the end of the sixth century, folk memory had joined him with six other wise men (variously identified) to make up the famous group of Seven Sages, about whom various tales were told which hover interestingly on the borders of anecdote and folktale. Before turning to Solon himself, I would like to look at this group briefly, as it holds something of a place of honour in Greek popular tradition.

Plutarch, in his *Life of Solon* (chapter 4), tells the story of how the Seven Sages Club got started, and it is a tale with a folkloric motif which one might term 'the Contentious Gift'.[15] The story goes that some fishermen of the island of Cos brought up in their nets a valuable object, none other than the golden tripod which Helen of Troy had thrown into the sea there as a dedication, on her voyage back from Troy. The fishermen had sold the catch, sight unseen, to some men of Miletus, but when the tripod was found, a fight broke out about its ownership, and this fight progressively came to involve the states of Cos and Miletus as a whole.

They finally appealed to Delphi for a judgement, and the priestess declared that the tripod was to be given 'to the wisest', which was naturally understood as meaning 'to the wisest man on earth'. The Coans readily acknowledged that this was Solon's contemporary, Thales of Miletus, and presented it to him. Thales, however, declared that Bias of Priene was wiser than he, and sent it on to him. Bias, in turn, declared in favour of another noted sage, and so the tripod was passed on, round a field that included Chilon of Sparta, Kleoboulos of Lindus (in Rhodes), Periander of Corinth, Pittakos of Mytilene, and Solon, who sent it back to Thales. Thales then presented it to Ismenian Apollo in Thebes – or else to Apollo in Didyma.[16]

This, as I say, exhibits the motif of a gift which causes contention, but here with a nice philosophic twist to it, in that the contention

[15] The famous Apple of Discord, which the Goddess Eris threw onto the table at the wedding of Peleus and Thetis, inscribed 'for the fairest', is a good example. It led to the Judgement of Paris, the abduction of Helen, and the Trojan War. This particular tale seems, on Plutarch's own testimony ad loc., to go back at least to Theophrastus, who is represented as giving a variant version, so we may assume it to be far older than him.

[16] There are numerous minor variations, as befits such a story. Theophrastus changes the story to give the priority to Bias of Priene. Others said the prize was not a tripod from the sea, but a bowl left by Bathykles the Arcadian at his death (so Callimachus), or a golden goblet donated by King Croesus of Lydia (so Eudoxus of Cnidus). And there is a variant reported by Diogenes Laertius (I 28), which exalts Solon, but spoils the anecdote, according to which, when the tripod, or whatever it was, reached Solon, he sent it straight to the god at Delphi, saying that Apollo was plainly 'the wisest'.

takes the form of a competition in modesty and mutual regard, as befits wise men. The anecdotal element in what is otherwise a folktale seems to me to lie in the 'punch-line', as it were, according to which the last on the list (usually, though, not always, Solon) sends the prize back to the first one, thus completing the circle – and he in turn presents it to a divine recipient, reinterpreting the meaning of the oracle.

The origin of the notion of a group of seven sages is obscure.[17] A time early in the fifth century, when people were beginning to look back at the period of a hundred years earlier, when so much ferment was taking place in politics, philosophy and literature, and were seeking to identify eponymous sources of traditional wisdom, would commend itself as probable, except that it is strange that that alert recorder of folk-tradition, Herodotus, betrays no inkling of it, though it is a story-pattern that would surely have attracted him.

At any rate, one aspect of Solon's personality is hereby fixed. He was one of the Seven Sages of Hellas. Tradition, preserved by Plato in the same passage of the *Protagoras*, has the sages meet for a banquet or symposium in Delphi, where they each dedicated to Apollo a wise saying, which were then inscribed on the facade of his temple. There is also the tradition of a banquet of the sages convened by Periander in Corinth,[18] but how old that tradition is is not clear. Plutarch constructs a pleasant, Lucianic fantasy on the theme in his *Banquet of the Seven Sages* (*Mor.* 146Bff.). The wisdom of the Seven is essentially folk wisdom, pithy apophthegms to live by: *Know thyself, Nothing in excess, Learn to obey before you command, Give a pledge, and ruin follows, Mercy is better than vengeance, Treat your friends as if they would one day be your enemies, and your enemies as if they would one day be your friends.* The parameters of popular Greek ethics are accurately delimited by these canny, if frequently banal, utterances.

But Solon is not primarily a sage (in the sense of a purveyor of timeless wisdom); he was – as indeed were most of the seven – first

---

[17] The earliest extant mention of the group occurs in Plato, *Protagoras* 343A. Their sevenness may have something to do with the fact that seven is a number sacred to Apollo, and the group is connected with the worship of Apollo; but there is also the possibility of Middle Eastern antecedents.

[18] Periander properly fills the role of the tyrant who is host to sages, not that of a sage himself (though he can be co-opted to the company). Other authors make the sages meet in other courts, Ephorus at that of Croesus, Archetimus of Syracuse at that of Cypselus (Diogenes Laertius, I 40). It had plainly become a literary motif already by the fourth century BC, joining the more general theme (which, of course, had some basis in fact, e.g. Plato at the court of Dionysios) of the philosopher at the court of the monarch.

and foremost an active political figure. His contributions in this area form themselves into four groups: (1) his regaining of Salamis from the Megarians; (2) his political reforms (traditionally connected with his archonship in 594 BC, but probably spread out over the years subsequent to that); (3) his travels (particularly to Egypt and to King Croesus of Lydia); and (4) his opposition to the rise to tyranny of his kinsman Peisistratos. All of these are hedged about thickly by anecdote.

It was the struggle for Salamis (to be located around the turn of the seventh century) that first brought Solon to prominence. What really happened (except that the Athenians eventually won) is obscured beyond recovery, but we have a pretty good idea of what the Athenians themselves liked to remember as having occurred, and Solon figures prominently in that.

First of all, we have the tale[19] that, after a long and unsuccessful struggle, which lost them the island, the Athenians were so depressed that they passed a law forbidding anyone, on pain of death, to reopen the question of reconquering Salamis. The provision is in fact not entirely incredible, since we have a number of well-attested examples of laws ending with dire threats against anyone proposing their repeal.[20] At any rate, Solon, being annoyed at this defeatism, and noting that many of the younger men were also, decided to sidestep the ban on debate by pretending that he had gone mad. He then composed and memorised an elegiac poem on Salamis, and went down one morning into the market-place, acting the fool ('wearing a little cap'),[21] and, when a crowd had gathered, recited the poem. He got away with it. The Athenians repealed the law, and renewed the war, electing Solon general, and putting him in command.

This is rather too diffuse to count as an anecdote in the strict sense, but it is a good piece of oral history, in an anecdotal mode. The niceties

[19] Told by Plutarch in his *Life of Solon*, ch. 8.

[20] Cf. Demosthenes' story about the custom of the Locrians (*Against Timocrates* 139) that 'if any man wishes to propose a new law, he legislates with a halter round his neck. If the law is accepted as good and beneficial, the proposer departs with his life, but if not, the halter is drawn tight, and he is a dead man.' As a consequence, it seems, only one new law had been passed by the Locrians in more than two hundred years.

[21] What is the significance of this wearing of a little cap (*pilidion*)? On this there is a good article by R. Flacelière, in *RÉA* 49 (1947), 235–47. Various suggestions have been put forward, but the best one seems to me to be that it is, not exactly a dunce's cap, but a nightcap, or head-covering for an invalid, which no sane man would wear out of doors, and that it would produce much the same effect as appearing in one's pyjamas. This might gain one at least temporary immunity. The legend seems to be in place at least by the fourth century, since Demosthenes alludes to it in an attack on Aeschines in the *De Falsa Legatione* (251–5), where the point of his gibe requires that wearing a *pilidion* like Solon did might have gained Aeschines immunity from punishment for the lies he has uttered.

of constitutional procedure, and even logic, are ignored. If Solon was pretending to be mad, which presumably is what exempted him from the provisions of the law, how did he get away with reciting a perfectly rational poem? Why not just recite the poem? And then, in what way was he appointed to conduct the war? By being elected polemarch? But the polemarch is an archon, elected at the beginning of each year, and Solon was not an archon at this time – unless, perhaps he played his trick just at election time. But such pedantic considerations should not be allowed to spoil the story, which is anecdotal at least in the detail of Solon's outwitting of the prohibition. Its historical value must be regarded as low, but, as I have noted, it was already firmly fixed in the folk memory of the Athenians by the classical period.

However he came to be war-leader, Solon certainly was remembered as having directed the war, since a further series of stories are preserved on that subject, all involving tricks – trickery being a quality that the Athenians valued in their heroes (as can be seen in the case of Themistocles, to whom I alluded at the outset). One may read of them in chapters 8 to 10 of Plutarch's *Life of Solon*.

One story may perhaps suffice, to illustrate their flavour. Plutarch describes these stories collectively as 'the popular account' (*ta dêmôdê tôn legomenôn*), which accurately characterises them as the oral memory of the people, recorded in writing only much later, perhaps in the fourth century. It is interesting, and typical, that all the stories result in the utter routing of the Megarians and the capture of the island, so that they are really *alternative* exploits. In fact, none of them seems to have led to the capture of Salamis, since history (as attested by Plutarch himself, chapter 10) records that the dispute finally went to arbitration before a commission of Spartans, and they decided in favour of the Athenians.

At any rate, the first story runs as follows. Solon, accompanied by Peisistratos, sailed to Cape Kolias (just south-west of Phaleron), and came upon all the women of the city celebrating ancestral rites in honour of Demeter. This gave Solon an idea. He sent a trusted emissary to the Megarians on Salamis, pretending to be a deserter, and told them, if they wanted to capture all the top ladies of Athens, to head for Cape Kolias without delay. The Megarians fell for this, and sent out an expedition to capture the ladies. Meanwhile, Solon dressed up the younger men who were still beardless as women, and set them to dancing and disporting themselves on the seashore, with daggers under their dresses. The Megarians landed, rushed to capture the 'women', and were all slain. Then the Athenians set sail, and took possession of Salamis.

This is a nice story, and most satisfying to Athenian self-esteem, but there are a number of serious problems with it. The first problem is that it is what may be termed a 'floating anecdote', having been told originally, so far as we can see, about Peisistratos, and in rather more credible circumstances. Aeneas Tacticus,[22] writing in the mid-fourth century BC, tells it as a stratagem of Peisistratos in response to an advance warning that the Megarians were about to launch a night attack on the women of Athens while they were celebrating the Thesmophoria at Eleusis. The Megarian raiders are all killed, whereupon Peisistratos orders the Athenian youths to man the Megarian ships, and they sail back to the port of Megara and slay many unsuspecting Megarians before escaping back to Athens. This is altogether more plausible than the Solonic version, though even so we cannot trust its historicity. What we have in Plutarch is an interesting contamination, in which the story is transferred to Solon (and we have a number of 'pure' forms of that), but with Peisistratos inserted into the plot, in dim recognition of his role in the original version of the story, although he can only have been a child at the time.

The virtue of this tale, then, resides not in its relation to any historical reality,[23] but rather in its revelation of how the Athenian man in the street's mind worked. He dearly loved a neatly turned trick, and he approved of a degree of rascality in his popular heroes, and this is the sort of thing that Solon *ought* to have done, even if the story was more plausibly attached to the much less popular Peisistratos.

The other two stories involve a degree of trickery as well, including the alleged insertion into the text of Homer of a line after *Iliad* 2. 557, in the Catalogue of Ships, to testify that Ajax of Salamis stationed his ships beside those of the Athenians, and was thus by implication closely connected with them. This line (558) is accepted now as part of the text of Homer, and was almost certainly not composed by Solon, but Athenian folklore would have it that he inserted it there.[24]

Solon's legislation (traditionally associated with his archonship in

---

[22] *Poliorcetica*, IV 8–12. It is not clear what the date of this exploit might be. Aeneas says only that it was while Peisistratos 'was general at Athens', so it may date from the time that he was polemarch, c. 565 BC.

[23] Such a trick is not entirely inconceivable, certainly, as we can gather from the very successful trick of a similar nature which Themistocles played on King Xerxes.

[24] If there was any Athenian tampering with the text of Homer (and there probably was) it will much more probably have taken place later, in the time of Peisistratos, in connection with his commissioning of a standard text of the poems – an event which I see no serious reason to doubt.

594 BC) leaves little room for anecdote (though some of his regulations had a homely or paradoxical quality),[25] but the account of his
reasons for his ten years' voluntary exile after completing the legislation smacks of folklore.[26] People would not leave him alone, but
were always bothering him with requests to change or explain his
laws, and so, in exasperation, and to give the laws time to settle into
people's minds, he resolved to absent himself for a period of ten years,
and devote himself to travel, and Herodotean-style *historia*. He went
first to Egypt, where he was reported to have consorted with a
number of learned priests, and then stayed for a few years, it would
seem, in Cyprus, where he helped a local king to reorganise his state;
but the only anecdote to emerge from his travels (which is indeed,
perhaps the most famous story about him) is his discourse with
Croesus, King of Lydia, himself a popular subject of anecdote (as we
have seen in connection with the Seven Sages).

This is too well known, I think, to justify retelling in detail, but we
might consider certain aspects of it.[27] First of all, a point about the
form. It has a triadic structure, so popular in folktale. Croesus, having
shown Solon all his treasures, asks *three times* (with increasing exasperation), who does Solon consider the happiest of men (and who after
that, and who after *that*?). Only after three unexpected replies does he
blurt out: 'And am I not to be counted happy at all?'

Secondly, as to *content*: we may note Solon's first choice, Tellos the
Athenian, since he (much more than runners-up Kleobis and Biton)
exemplifies the ideal of happiness of the man in the street (which is,
after all, very much the ideal emerging from the bulk of Aristotle's
Nicomachean Ethics): Tellos is the happiest of men

> because his country was flourishing in his days, and he himself had
> sons of excellent character [*kaloi k' agathoi*], and he lived to see children
> born to each of them, and these children all survived; and further,
> because, after a life spent in what our people look upon as comfort, his
> end was most glorious; for in a battle between the Athenians and their
> neighbours near Eleusis,[28] he came to the assistance of his countrymen,

---

[25] Such as, for instance, the law that anyone who declined to take either side in the event
of civil war (*stasis*) should be disfranchised (Plut. *Life*, ch. 20) – an excellent way to deal
with the 'Don't Knows'!

[26] Plut. *Life*, ch. 25.

[27] It is to be found in Herodotus, *Histories* I 30, and Plutarch, *Life of Solon*, ch. 27. Plutarch
recognises at the outset that the chronological problems had been raised by some
authorities, but he himself is unwilling to pass up such a good and *appropriate* story.

[28] What is probably being referred to is the conquest of Eleusis by Athens some time in
the first half of the seventh century, about a hundred years before the supposed date of
this mythical conversation.

routed the enemy, and died upon the field most gallantly. The Athenians gave him a public burial on the spot where he fell, and paid him the highest honours.

We have here an anecdote within an anecdote. Tellos had presumably become proverbial for felicity before he became connected with Solon's dialogue with Croesus, but we have no indication that his story (or that of Cleobis and Biton, for that matter) was told separately. An active grandfather (he must have been sixty, at a conservative estimate, to see children 'surviving' – the verb used is *parameinanta* – from his sons), Tellos admirably illustrates both the ideals of the ordinary, non-philosophical Athenian (we may take reasonable health and prosperity as given), and the type of solid, middle-of-the-road citizen that Solon, by his reforms, wished to foster. The emphasis on survival of his name, glorious death in battle, and public honour, reminds us how far Athens was still a sub-Homeric 'shame culture' (well analysed by Arthur Adkins in *Merit and Responsibility*).[29] His death, of course, contributes to the punch-line of the whole anecdote, so redolent of Greek folk-wisdom, 'Count no man happy until he is dead.'

One more anecdote of Solon is worth presenting, this time from the evening of his life (if, indeed, it can be reconciled chronologically at all),[30] since it relates to literature, even as the initial stories about the Seven Sages related him to philosophy. The story concerns the origins of drama. The Athenians liked to tell that, when Thespis, who is credited with the 'invention' of tragedy, first put on a performance of this new art-form – a performance which involved him standing up in front of a chorus, his face smeared with either white lead or wine-lees (the evidence is conflicting), and speaking *in the person of* some great hero of the epic tradition (Achilles, it might be, or Ajax) – the aged Solon came up to him after the performance and scolded him, asking if he was not ashamed to tell such lies in the presence of so many people.

Thespis answered that there was no harm in talking and acting that way in play, whereupon Solon smote the ground sharply with his staff and said, 'Soon, however, if we give play of this sort so much praise and honour, we shall find it in our solemn contracts.'

[29] Oxford, 1960 (repr. Chicago, 1975).
[30] Plut. *Solon*, 29, 6–7. Solon is generally agreed to have died in the early 550s – he survived Peisistratos' first coup *d'état* in 561 by a few years – and Thespis is not thought to have introduced his new art form until the 530s. One would have to suppose that he was already toying with his new idea back before 561 (the incident is placed by Plutarch just before Peisistratos' coup), which is most improbable.

This tale is certainly *ben trovato* rather than *vero*, bringing together as it does the father of Athenian democracy (no mean practitioner of dramatic politics himself, it must be said), and the father of European drama, in a confrontation which reflects very well the probable bafflement of the older generation of Athenians when faced with this curious new art-form, which involves an actor stepping outside himself and assuming a new personality.

However, as we have noted above, there are well-nigh insuperable chronological problems. From our point of view, though, it matters little whether the confrontation ever took place, any more than did that between Solon and Croesus. It is the folk memory of the Athenian people that is important, and the story is certainly embedded in that. The connection of dramatic performance with charlatanry in politics is interesting. Solon's attitude is almost that of Plato two hundred years later, in the *Republic*. In Plutarch's narrative, Solon's fears are dramatically confirmed shortly afterwards by Peisistratos' staging of an assassination attempt against himself, which involved wounding himself, and then riding into the market-place in a chariot and claiming that his enemies had plotted against his life because of his championship of the people, a move which gained him the armed bodyguard he needed to seize power. On that occasion, indeed, Solon is said (*Life*, chapter 30) to have approached him and said, 'Son of Hippokrates, you are acting the Homeric Odysseus badly; for you are doing to deceive your fellow-citizens what he did to deceive his enemies, when he disfigured himself' – a reference to Helen's story about Odysseus' visit to Troy in *Odyssey* 4, 244–64. Solon's words had no effect then, but they fixed themselves in later oral memory, as we can see.

THE LITERARY MAN: SOPHOKLES

The next character that I want to consider is a dramatist, the much-loved figure of Sophokles, son of Sophillos, of the deme Kolonos. I select him rather than Aeschylus or Euripides, or indeed the comic playwright Aristophanes, since only about him are stories preserved that would count as anecdotes. Euripides' character does not seem to have lent itself to anecdote[31] (though it certainly did to personal abuse from comic poets, not least Aristophanes), and even in the case of

---

[31] The story of the cave on Salamis to which he used to like to retire to compose his plays is, I suppose, a sort of anecdote – certainly characteristic of the man – but it lacks a punch-line.

Aeschylus there is nothing that would strictly qualify, I think. The story of his being prosecuted for profaning the Mysteries in a play, and then getting off by proving that he had not been initiated, or his saying that his plays were merely 'slices from Homer's banquets', or even his meeting his death in Sicily from an eagle dropping a tortoise on his bald head, mistaking it for a rock, while containing perhaps some element of the anecdote in them, are not the real thing.

When we come to Sophokles, on the other hand, we have at least a few real specimens. There are none for his early life, though there are some biographical details preserved, of varying degrees of reliability. The first story that I would identify as an anecdote dates from his later middle years. It is told by that excellent raconteur, Ion of Chios, and relates to a visit paid by Sophokles to Chios during his generalship in 441/0, the period of the war against Samos:[32]

> I met Sophokles the poet at Chios, when he was sailing as general to Lesbos. He was full of fun at his wine, and witty to boot. A Chian friend of his, Hermesilaos, who was the *proxenos* of Athens, was entertaining him, when there appeared, standing beside the fire, the wine-pourer, a handsome boy, of a ruddy complexion. Sophokles was plainly attracted by him, and said, 'Do you want me to enjoy my drinking?' When the boy said yes, he said, 'Then don't be too rapid in handing me the cup and then taking it away.' The boy blushed prettily, while pouring the wine, and then tried to pick off a straw on the side of the cup with his little finger. Sophokles asked him whether he could see the straw. When the boy said he could, Sophokles said, 'Then blow it away, for I shouldn't want you to get your finger wet.' As the boy brought his face up to the cup, Sophokles drew the cup nearer to his own lips, that the two heads might come closer together. When he was very near the lad, he drew him close with his arm and kissed him. All present applauded him, amid laughter and shouting, because he had tricked the boy so neatly, and Sophokles said, 'I am practising strategy, gentlemen, since Pericles told me that whereas I could write poetry, I don't know how to be a general. Don't you think my stratagem has turned out happily for me?'

This story is somewhat diffuse, it must be said, to count as an anecdote. Indeed, it might more properly be regarded as the raw material of an anecdote than an anecdote itself. But I am not prepared

---

[32] Preserved in Athenaeus, *Deipn.* XIII 604 = *FGH* 392 F6. Ion's *Memoirs* are unfortunately lost.

to pass it up, as it is a story of peculiar interest, being told by a contemporary and an eye-witness, with considerable circumstantial
detail, and is thus guaranteed to be substantially factual. It also presents
us with an aspect of Sophokles which may be unfamiliar to us, but
one plainly dear to the hearts of the Athenian public, the fun-loving
and mildly lecherous public man, rather than the Olympian playwright, brooding on ultimate problems of the human condition.

That this image of Sophokles is not just something presented to us
by the non-Athenian Ion, and thus not genuinely Athenian, is
indicated by the amusing story put into the mouth of old Kephalos by
Plato in *Republic* I (329C):

> I remember hearing the poet Sophokles greeted by a fellow who said,
> 'How are you off as regards sex these days, Sophokles – are you still
> able to get it on with a woman?' And he replied, 'Hush, man, most
> gladly have I escaped this thing you talk of, as from a raging and
> savage beast of a master!'

The story ends up, in many retellings in later antiquity, as a thoroughly
edifying anecdote. It even encouraged the Emperor Julian to give up
sex altogether after the death of his wife, according to Ammianus
Marcellinus.[33] But I take the point to be rather that Sophokles was
well known to be a man who liked his bit of fun, and this reply of his,
presumably delivered some time later than the period of Ion's story
(when he will have been only fifty-five), thus constitutes a witty put-
down to a member of the 'nudge nudge, wink wink' brigade who
was pestering him on this subject, knowing his proclivities.

There are, of course, more edifying stories about Sophokles, but
most of them do not take on the form of anecdote. He was renowned
for his piety, and various details are given of that in the anonymous
Life prefixed to manuscripts of his plays. One story that approaches
anecdotal status is that after his death (in 406 BC), his body was placed
on his ancestral tomb near the road to Dekeleia, eleven stades outside
the town, and left there unburied, for fear of the Spartans, since the
Spartans were building a wall in the area. However, the god
Dionysos appeared to the Spartan commander, Lysandros, in a
dream, and ordered that the man who had been left on the tomb
should be buried. When Lysandros ignored the dream, Dionysos
appeared to him a second time with the same message. Lysandros then
asked some fugitives who had died, and learned that it was Sophokles;

---

[33] *Hist.* XXV 4, 2

so he sent a herald and allowed the Athenians to bury the body.

This bizarre story has at least the virtue of attempting to give plausible circumstantial details, but it betrays itself in the process. Sophokles died at some time late in 406, as the noose was tightening around Athens, but Lysandros does not seem to have assumed command of the Spartan forces until early 404, in the final months of the siege. However, the point of the story is the reverence in which Sophokles was held by his fellow-citizens (though this story in its present form, because of the chronological vagueness which it exhibits, can hardly have originated less than a few generations after his death).

Of a similar nature is the report that, because of his hospitality to the god Asclepios, in entertaining the statue of the god in his own home while a shrine was being built for it, he was honoured after his death as a hero, with the title of Dexion, 'the hospitable one'.[34] Unfortunately, no trace has turned up of a shrine to a hero Dexion, which might lend some credence to this tale, at least as an aetiological myth, so it is hard to know what to make of it, except to note the testimony it bears to the respect in which Sophokles was held.

More in the nature of an anecdote, though, is what is perhaps the most famous story about Sophokles, relating to a period just before his death at the age of ninety. It is very probably apocryphal as it stands, but may yet have some basis in fact. At any rate, it was a story that the Athenians loved to tell, and that is all that need concern us in the present context. The story as we have it seems to go back to the Hellenistic gossip-writer Satyros,[35] a usually unreliable source much beloved of Diogenes Laertius, but it probably has its roots in Athenian oral tradition (*Life* 13):

> The story is told by many authorities that he became involved in a lawsuit with his son Iophon. Iophon was his son by Nikostrate, but he had a son Ariston by Theoris of Sicyon, and he was especially fond of this son's child, whose name was Sophokles.

The text now becomes corrupt, but reveals, I think, if properly restored, where later gossip-writers got at least part of the anecdote.[36]

---

[34] Plutarch, *Numa* 3.

[35] Satyros' *Life of Sophokles*, like his *Life of Euripides*, will presumably have been in dialogue form, cf. *Pap. Oxy.* 1176.

[36] Specifically, there must be a name omitted as the subject of *eisêgage* in *kai pote en dramati eisêgage ton Iophonta autôi phthonounta* ... Sophokles cannot have himself 'introduced in a play' his son Iophon having a grudge against him. This must surely refer to some comic poet. Naeke suggested Leukon, a poet of Old Comedy, who is known to have written a play called *The Clan-Brothers* (*Phrateres*) but that may be too ingenious. Another suggestion, that of Gottfried Hermann, is that the reference is to

Some comic poet, the text seems to be trying to tell us, brought on Iophon accusing his father before his clansmen (*phrateres*) of senile dementia (*paranoia*) – which was a charge that a son could in fact bring against a father who was no longer capable of managing his affairs. In the anecdote, as reported by Satyros (though not, perhaps, in the scene from the comedy),[37] Sophokles gets the case dismissed by bringing into court the *Oedipus at Colonus*, which he has just composed, and reading some extracts from it, saying, 'If I am Sophokles, I am not out of my mind; if I am out of my mind, I am not Sophokles!'[38]

Such a story as this, as I say, poses us a problem. It does seem to be one of those items which Mary Lefkowitz is able to fasten on in her most useful, if rather *too* sceptical book, *The Lives of the Greek Poets*, as being simply a story fabricated by dim-witted Hellenistic gossip-writers on the basis of a reference, or in this case a story-line, in a comedy. It is possible, I suppose, that there may be slightly more to it than that, though there are serious barriers in the way of the acceptance of its historicity. There was certainly, as I have mentioned above, a procedure in Greek law for deposing one's senile father from control of his property, a *dikê paranoias*. This, however, was not something that could be brought before one's *phrateres*, who were not concerned with litigation at all, but rather before the eponymous Archon, who was concerned with family law.[39] In any case, we seem to have evidence, from immediately after Sophokles' death, in Aristophanes' *The Frogs* (73ff.), that Iophon was regarded as Sophokles' literary heir, who might still be producing plays which had been at least drafted by his father, which would suggest that no serious rift between them had taken place. Iophon is also reported, for good measure, to have composed an epitaph for his father's funerary monument.[40] As for the younger Sophokles, we do, in fact, have inscriptional evidence as to the existence of a grandson of Sophokles named Sophokles,[41] but this grandson was a citizen (he is named with his demotic, *Kolônêthen*), and worse still, he is the son, not of Ariston,

---

Aristophanes, in *one* of his plays (he composed two!) entitled *The Plays* – reading *en Dramasi* for *en dramati* – but we do not know the plots of either of them.

[37] The report of the comedy continues: *hoi de tôi Iophônti epetimêsan*, 'and they [sc. the clan-brothers, who would have constituted the chorus] criticised Iophon for that'. The fact that Satyros is brought in as the authority for the punch-line suggests to me that it was not in the comedy, but one cannot be certain.

[38] I must confess that I do not grasp the point of this remark. It seems to embody some rather deep point about personal identity.

[39] Aristotle, *Ath. Pol.* 56. 6.

[40] Valerius Maximus VIII 7, 12.

[41] *Inscriptiones Graecae* II² 1374–5.

but of Iophon. He does seem to have produced the *Oedipus at Colonus*, and is the author of a number of plays himself.[42]

So the basis in fact of this anecdote is very shaky indeed. On the whole, I am attracted by the suggestion that what we have here is simply a piece of an Old Comedy, possibly even by Aristophanes (despite the counter-evidence provided by *The Frogs*), in which Iophon is introduced complaining against his father before his clan-brothers that he is, in effect, by declining to die at a decent age (or even to cease composing tragedies), depriving his son of his literary patrimony by not allowing him to develop a reputation of his own. The same sort of complaint might have been lodged, in a Gilbert and Sullivan opera, by Edward, Prince of Wales, against his mother, Queen Victoria (or even, indeed, in a modern farce, by the present Prince of Wales against *his* mother!). Hermann's suggestion (cf. above, n. 36) is attractive palaeographically, the only problem being that neither of the two Aristophanic plays entitled *Dramata* sounds very promising from the plot point of view, one being subtitled *Kentauros*, the other *Niobos*. On the other hand, at least one fragment from one or other of them (286 Kock) does mention *phrateres*, while another (290) mentions that Aristophanes introduced Euripides (though not, unfortunately, Sophokles) into the plot, which betokens a fairly wide range of reference. On the whole, if either of these Aristophanic plays is being referred to, we may, I think, assume a passing reference to our story, rather than a full-dress treatment as part of the plot – which may, indeed, have made it easier for a later biographer to assume that something historical was being referred to.

That, I think, is almost enough about Sophokles for our present purpose. The story of his death (*Life* 14) from choking on an unripe grape at the festival of Choes (the second day of the Anthesteria), from a bunch of grapes sent to him by the actor Kallipides, 'who had just returned from an engagement at Opous', hardly qualifies as an anecdote on my strict criteria, but it is worth mentioning, I think, for its curiously detailed quality. It is relayed to us via the Hellenistic historians Istros and Neanthes (ibid.), but there is no obvious reason why such details should be invented out of the whole cloth. We have

---

[42] As for the story of Sophokles' mistress from Sicyon, that has something of a life of its own, and has no doubt been grafted on to the basic story of the lawsuit, to increase the soap-opera quality of the whole. At least from the early Hellenistic period (c. 260 BC), we find this mistress celebrated by the poet Hermesianax in his *Leontion*, so she may have some basis in fact. Whether or not she had a son Ariston, and whether he in turn produced *another* Sophokles junior, is another matter.

no other knowledge, after all, of the actor Kallipides, or of what the nature of his 'engagement (*ergasia*)' may have been in Opous (presumably he was 'on tour', and that is useful evidence for this sort of activity even before the end of the fifth century). It *could* in theory all be dreamed up by some comic poet, but why on earth make such a joke about Sophokles' death?

I would actually be prepared to accept the essential historicity of the story, but for a troublesome chronological problem. If we accept the story of Sophokles bringing on his chorus in mourning, at the *proagon* of the City Dionysia of 406, out of respect for the recently-dead Euripides, he must obviously have died later than this. The Anthesteria of 405 would then have to be the festival in question, at which Aristophanes first produced *The Frogs*, which involves Sophokles being dead for at least some months. The only possibilities then are (a) that Aristophanes only brought in the references to Sophokles at the *second* performance of *The Frogs*, at the Dionysia of 405; or (b) that Sophokles brought on the chorus in mourning at the *Lenaia* of 406, and that he choked on the grape at the Anthesteria shortly afterwards. But I would not, after all, wish to press the historicity of the story that far!

THE PHILOSOPHER: DIOGENES THE CYNIC

However, it is time that we left our representative poet, and turned to our representative philosopher. Here the obvious figure to turn to would perhaps be Plato, but I feel that in the present connection the Cynic philosopher from Sinope, Diogenes, is a more suitable choice. Diogenes, after all, is almost entirely a figure of anecdote, though he may have written at least a few of the various works attributed to him by Diogenes Laertius (VI 80). Diogenes Laertius, indeed, is our main source for his life, though anecdotes about him abound also in such writers as Cicero, Plutarch and Aelian, and even in the Arabic tradition. Diogenes Laertius, unfortunately, as we know, is not a man endowed with a very developed sense of humour, so that the point of many of Diogenes' more off-beat utterances seems to bypass him altogether, but at least he reports a good deal of useful material, even when slightly bemused by it.

Every stage of Diogenes' career is so enmeshed in legend that the historical facts are virtually irrecoverable, but fortunately for our present purpose that does not much matter. We are concerned precisely with Diogenes the legend rather than Diogenes the historical figure (though I will not be able to resist some historical speculations at various points).

Diogenes, we learn,[43] came to Athens as a youngish man from Sinope on the Black Sea, where his father Hikesias had been in charge of the mint. Since we actually have some evidence from coins of his father being in charge of the mint there after 362 BC,[44] this gives us a *terminus post quem* for Diogenes' arrival in Athens. At any rate, a very widespread story, with many embellishments, tells of his father being condemned and driven into exile for adulterating the coinage (*parakharattôn to nomisma*).[45] In some versions, Diogenes himself was involved in this activity as well.[46] One version has him consulting the oracle at Delphi, which gives him the instruction 'to adulterate the coinage', and this is accordingly what he sets out to do, on a metaphorical level.

Somewhere at the back of this farrago, it seems to me, there lurks a witty conceit of Diogenes himself, analogous to those of Socrates about having inherited his skill as a midwife from his mother, and having been commissioned by the oracle at Delphi to aggravate the people of Athens. Diogenes Laertius actually reports (VI 20), with no consciousness of irony, that Diogenes confessed to this 'crime' in a work of his called the *Pordalos* – a title of mysterious purport, but, knowing Diogenes, probably having something to do with farting.[47] Diogenes will, then, have gone on record as remarking that he had inherited his propensity for 'adulterating the coinage' from his father, even as Socrates had inherited his skill at 'midwifery' from his mother. Now Diogenes' father may well have adulterated the coinage of Sinope, even as Socrates' mother may well have been a midwife, at least in an amateur capacity, but in each case the key point is the ironic use made of this circumstance by their offspring. In Diogenes' case, it would be entirely in character for him to declare that he had inherited his occupation from his father, taking *parakharattôn to*

---

[43] DL VI 20–1.

[44] See H. Bannert, 'Numismatisches zu Biographie und Lehre des Hundes Diogenes', *Litterae Numismaticae Vindobonenses* I (1979), pp. 49–63. Defaced coins of Sinope have apparently been found from the period 350–340 BC, and the name of Hikesias is attested on other coins minted after 362 BC.

[45] This version stems from Diocles of Magnesia (2nd cent. BC), in his *Epidromê tôn philosophôn* (ap. DL VI 20).

[46] Notably that of a certain Eubulides, in his work *On Diogenes* (DL ibid.), who may well, however, only be taking seriously Diogenes' own claim in the *Pordalos* to have done so, on which see below.

[47] *Pordaleos*, at any rate, means 'flatulent', from *perdomai*, 'fart'; and *pordôn* is recorded as one of the nicknames for a Cynic in Arrian, *Discourses of Epictetus* 3. 22. 80.

nomisma in the sense of 'undermining established custom'. But this remark would only make much sense, after all, if his father had in fact been involved in some such scandal.

However, Diogenes' 'debasing of the coinage' is not exactly an anecdote in the strict sense. It falls rather into the class of witty sayings, or *chreiai*, of which mention was made at the outset of this chapter. Indeed, Diogenes might be said to be the ancient master of the 'one-liner'. But our business here is properly with anecdotes. More in the nature of an anecdote is the story of his initial confrontation with Antisthenes, the founder of the 'Cynic' movement, to whom he wished to attach himself, but who did not welcome followers (DL VI 22). The historicity of the story is rendered doubtful by reason of chronological difficulties, if Diogenes really did not reach Athens until after 362, since Antisthenes, if still alive, would by then be a very old man, but that does not matter greatly in the present context. It serves to dramatise their real philosophical connection:

> On reaching Athens he fell in with Antisthenes. Being repulsed by him, because he never welcomed pupils, by sheer persistence Diogenes wore him out. Once when he stretched out his staff against him, Diogenes offered him his head with the words, 'Strike, for you will find no wood hard enough to keep me away from you, so long as I think you have something to say.'

Many sayings and stories concern his learning self-sufficiency, particularly from animals and children. One or two will suffice here:

> One day, observing a child drinking out of his hands, he cast away the cup from his wallet with the words, 'A child has beaten me in frugality [*euteleia*].'[48]

or:

> One day, as he was watching the Athenians celebrate a festival, and was inclined to envy them, he saw a mouse creeping up and nibbling the crumbs of his bread, and said to himself, 'Diogenes, for this creature your leavings are a feast', and this encouraged him to be still more frugal.[49]

Diogenes Laertius (VI 22) gives what appears to be a variant of this same story (though it could, I suppose, be regarded rather as a separate 'mouse-anecdote'), which simply involves Diogenes watching a

---

[48] DL VI 37.
[49] Aelian, *VH* XIII 26; a more elaborated version is to be found in Plutarch, *On Progress in Virtue* 77EF.

mouse running about, 'not looking for a place to lie down, not afraid of the dark, and not seeking any of the things which are considered luxuries', and learning from this how to adapt himself to all circumstances. Diogenes gives Theophrastus in his *Megarian Dialogue* as the source for his version of this story, which constitutes almost contemporary testimony, and might thus be regarded as the base from which the more elaborate versions of the story grew. It also serves to remind us of one major use to which anecdotes were put – that is, the provision of *exempla* for orators and philosophers. This process will have begun with the great sophists of the fifth century, and is practised in the fourth century both by the philosopher Plato (as we have seen in the case of the tale about Sophokles mentioned above) and by orators such as Demosthenes and Aeschines, but in later antiquity it becomes a major component of school instruction, the version of this tale told by Plutarch being a case in point.

At any rate, it is plain that one popular cycle of Diogenes stories concerned his attempts to find out how little he could survive on. Another cycle of stories which was obviously popular concerns a curious incident (to which there is an interesting parallel in the life of Plato):[50] Diogenes' being sold as a slave. At least two people, Menippus (or perhaps Hermippus)[51] and Eubulus, wrote works entitled *The Sale of Diogenes* (*Diogenous Prasis*), which they could hardly have done if the story had not been well established by their time (mid-third century BC). Many of the stories simply assume that we know how he came to put up for sale, but one tale[52] speaks of him as being captured by pirates and put up for sale in Crete (we are even told the pirate chief's name – Skirpalos). At any rate, when Diogenes was put up for sale, he was asked what he could do. His reply was, 'Govern men' (DL VI 29). Or alternatively,[53] he shouted out, pretending to be his own auctioneer, 'Who wants to buy a master?' Then (DL VI 29), when he was forbidden to sit down, he said, 'It makes no difference; for, however fishes are laid out, they find a buyer!' Or alternatively

---

[50] In Plato's case all we learn (from DL III 18–20) is that he was captured by the Aeginetans on his way back from his first visit to Syracuse and sold by them as a slave, but bought and freed by Anniceris of Cyrene, and this is in turn tied in with the founding of the Academy; there are no tales, however, as in the case of Diogenes, of the actual process of sale.

[51] Some authorities are concerned that DL himself does not list a *Sale of Diogenes* among the works of Menippus in his *Life* at VI 101, and propose the philosophical biographer Hermippus of Smyrna as an alternative, but the list of works is admittedly incomplete, and it seems a rather suitable work for Menippus to have written.

[52] DL VI 74; a much briefer version in Plutarch, *Can Vice Cause Unhappiness?* 499B.

[53] Plutarch, *On Tranquillity of Mind*, 466E.

(Plut. loc. cit.), he lay down on the ground, and mocked the auctioneer; when this official ordered him to get up, he made fun of him,
saying, 'Suppose you were selling a fish?'

These stories are meant to illustrate the famous Cynic 'freedom of
speech' (*parrhêsia*) – fearless straight-talking, we might term it, a
characteristic which any philosopher worth his salt was expected to
exhibit, but which Diogenes practised to an extreme degree. A good
many of the anecdotes told about him show him taking the great ones
of the earth down a peg or two, Philip or Alexander, Plato or Demosthenes, as the case may be. In the present instance, he is bought by a
certain Xeniades of Corinth (even as Plato is sold on Aegina to
Annikeris of Cyrene). To Xeniades he said, 'You must obey me,
though I am a slave; for if a doctor or a steersman were a slave, he
would be obeyed.'[54] Eubulus, indeed, in his work mentioned above,
gives an extended description of his life in Xeniades' household in
Corinth, his education of Xeniades' sons, and even of his death in the
service of Xeniades (ap. DL VI 30–2), though this is hardly
compatible with the famous tale of his meeting Alexander outside in
his barrel.[55] On the principle, however, of 'no smoke without fire', I
would entertain the possibility of there being some basis for this set of
stories, though fortunately I do not have to pronounce definitively
on this question in the present context. Suffice it to say that the story-
cycle seems to be at least of early Hellenistic provenance.

As one would expect, Diogenes exemplifies well both sub-types of
verbal confrontation which I distinguished at the outset: that with an
anonymous or insignificant foil, and that with a well-known figure.
Of the first type, his victim is often an anonymous 'youth': 'Noticing
a good-looking youth lying down to sleep in an unguarded position,
he nudged him and said, "Rise up, lest some foe thrust a dart into thy
back!"' This last line is in fact a witty adaptation of a line of Homer,
Iliad 8. 95, where Diomede shouts to the fleeing Odysseus, 'Let it not
be that as thou fleest some man plant his spear in thy back.' This
witticism actually forms part of a large class of such sallies, mostly of
no very obvious philosophical significance, attributed to Diogenes,

---

[54] DL VI 30; cf. the more literary version, ibid. 36, where Xeniades quotes a line of
Euripides at him, 'Upwards now flow the streams of rivers', *Medea* 410.

[55] This barrel, or wine-jar (*pithos*), is actually a rather mobile entity. Another story (VI
23) has him deciding to occupy a *pithos* in the agora of Athens, outside the Metrôon.
We would have to assume that he did this again in Corinth; he cannot be supposed to
have encountered Alexander in Athens, since Alexander steered clear of Athens. On
the other hand, in DL's version of this tale, no barrel is mentioned. Diogenes is simply
'taking the sun in the Kraneion' (a gymnasium at the entrance to Corinth).

which involve adaptations of Homer and the poets to some detail of everyday life.[56] It is possible that these are the inventions of some later pedant, but we cannot deny the possibility also that this was a form of humour that appealed to Diogenes. It is, after all, a form of 'adulteration of the coinage'. Such sallies, after all, would be by no means peculiar to Diogenes, and are a natural by-product of the more-or-less universal popular knowledge of Homer, in particular – very much like music-hall uses of tags from Shakespeare in modern times.

Another set of stories have an almost Zen-like quality. Someone wanted to study philosophy with him, so Diogenes gave him a tunny to hold, and told him to follow him. The man in shame threw the tunny away and departed. Some time later, on meeting him, Diogenes said, 'The friendship between you and me was broken by a *saperdes*' – using the unusual, Black Sea name for a tunny. A similar story is told of his asking someone to carry a cheese, with similar results (DL VI 36).

In other stories the interlocutor or interlocutors are left quite vague, as in the famous story of his going round the agora in broad daylight with a lighted lamp. When someone asked what he was doing (which, no doubt, was the reaction he was waiting for), he said that he was looking for a real man (DL VI 41). Or again, in his Dr Johnson-like response to somebody who declared (like Zeno of Elea) that there was no such thing as motion: he got up and walked about. But many stories were also told of his confrontations with the famous. One of his favourite butts seems to have been Plato – or at any rate Athenian popular tradition liked to bring them into confrontation, often with the theme of Plato's consorting with Dionysios of Syracuse in the background – Diogenes being very much the uncompromising democrat:

> Observing Plato one day at a costly banquet taking olives, he said: 'How is it that you, the philosopher who sailed to Sicily for the sake of these dishes, now, when they are before you, do not enjoy them?' 'Nay, by the Gods, Diogenes', replied Plato, 'there also for the most part I lived upon olives and suchlike.' 'Why then', said Diogenes, 'did you need to go to Syracuse? Was it that Attica at that time did not grow olives?' (DL VI 25)[57]

---

[56] VI 36, the more literary version of VI 30 referred to in note 54, is a case in point; others include VI 52 (*Iliad* 10. 343, 387); VI 53 – just following the anecdote quoted above (*Iliad* 5. 40; 18. 95); VI 55 (Eur. *Phoenissae* 40); VI 57 (*Iliad* 5. 83).

[57] This is actually a 'floating anecdote'; DL tells us that Favorinus attributes it to Aristippus, another suitable critic of Plato.

I quote this not so much for any degree of wit it may possess, which is minimal, as for the insight it affords into the attitude of the Athenian man in the street to Plato's activities. Diogenes, in so many of these stories, seems to personify the plain Athenian's view of life, irreverent, sceptical, anti-establishment – indeed, 'cynical' in the original sense of the word.

Other brushes with Plato involve criticisms of the more exalted aspects of his philosophy, such as the Theory of Forms:

> As Plato was conversing about the Forms, and using such terms as 'tablehood' and 'cuphood', he said, 'Table and cup I see, but your tablehood and cuphood, Plato, I in no way see.' (DL VI 53).[58]

In this case, though, Plato has the last word: 'That's readily accounted for', he said, 'for you have the eyes to see the visible table and cup, but not the understanding (*nous*) by which ideal tablehood and cup-hood are discerned.' This does, admittedly, sound like a rather frigid appendage to the anecdote added by a loyal Platonist, since the same basic story, without this addition, is told also of Antisthenes, with 'horse' instead of 'table' and 'cup'[59] – which avoids the problem of postulating forms of artificial objects.

We also have the story of Diogenes plucking a fowl and bringing it into Plato's lecture-room (*scholê*), saying, 'Here is Plato's man!' – this because Plato had defined man as a 'biped, featherless animal'. In consequence of this, we are told, the further specification 'broad-nailed' (*platyônychon*) was added to the definition (DL VI 40).

CONCLUSIONS

My purpose in selecting these three notable subjects of Athenian anecdote to illustrate my theme is to indicate some of the qualities that the Athenians valued in their 'characters'. Plainly they valued trickery – Themistocles, as well as Solon, is a good example of that, as indeed is Pericles. They also admired a certain randy quality in their public figures, such as is exemplified by Sophokles. And lastly, they dearly loved a streak of honest-to-god anarchic insolence (as exemplified in modern times by such a figure as Groucho Marx), which they found in full measure in Diogenes and the other Cynics,

---

[58] This would be evidence, by the way, if it could be trusted, that Plato was prepared to postulate forms of artificial objects (such as the ideal Bed of *Rep.* X 597CD), in accordance with the general principle enunciated at *Rep.* X 596A.

[59] Simplicius, *Commentary on Aristotle's Categories* pp. 208, 30ff.

such as Antisthenes, the founder of the tradition, and Crates.

As to questions of the social context of the anecdote – when and where anecdotes tended to be told – I would suggest as a primary context the symposium, as the Athenians sat around the table with their wine and their nuts, and secondarily the assembly and the lawcourts, where such stories would fill the role of *exempla*, edifying and otherwise. It is notable that when we turn to the orators of the fourth century, we find them appealing for their vision of the past, not to history books, but rather to the oral tradition of the people. Athens may have been literate to an extent never before achieved, but it was still in many ways an oral society, and the Athenians' view of their past – and, deriving from that, their own self-image – was very largely formed by the telling and re-telling of stories such as these about famous figures of the past. What we have, in the pages of Cicero or Plutarch or Diogenes Laertius, is a fossilised record of this process, and we should cherish it as such, rather than throwing out stories merely because they do not conform to our rigid historical standards. If we brush aside these tales, doubtful though their historicity may be, we are in danger of rejecting a host of stories which do at least perform the service of revealing something of the mind of that remarkable anonymous hero of world history, the Athenian fifth- and fourth-century man in the street. And it is essentially such a person, and his long-suffering women-folk and slaves, that this book has been about.

Bibliography

The following list of works is by no means exhaustive, and is mainly confined to works written in English, and of relatively easy access. It is designed chiefly to indicate books that I have found useful, and to suggest further reading in various areas. In the case of ancient texts, I have given the version or versions most easily accessible to the Greekless reader – usually the Penguin and/or the Loeb Classical Library (LCL), but in some cases a good modern edition with useful introduction and/or notes.

PRIMARY (ANCIENT) TEXTS

Aeschines, *Against Timarchos*, trans., with intro. and commentary, by Nick Fisher, Oxford, 2001.

— *Against Timarchus* (*In Tim.*), in *The Speeches of Aeschines*, ed., with Engl. trans., by Charles Darwin Adams, Cambridge, MA and London, 1919 (LCL).

Andocides, *Greek Orators IV – Andocides*, ed., with trans. and commentary, by Michael Edwards, Aris and Phillips, Warminster, 1995.

— *On the Mysteries* (*De Myst.*), in *Minor Attic Orators* I, ed., with Engl. trans., by K. J. Maidment, Cambridge, MA and London, 1941 (LCL).

— *On the Mysteries*, ed. D. M. MacDowell, Oxford, 1962.

Antiphon, *Against the Stepmother*, in *Minor Attic Orators* I, ed., with Engl. trans., by K. J. Maidment, Cambridge, MA and London, 1941 (LCL).

Apollodorus, *Against Neaira* (= [Demosthenes], *Speech* LIX), in *Demosthenes* VI, ed., with Engl. trans., by A. T. Murray, Cambridge, MA and London, 1939 (LCL).

— *Against Neaira*, ed. and trans. by Christopher Carey, Aris and Phillips, Warminster, 1992.

— *Against Nicostratus* (= [Demosthenes], *Speech* LIII), in *Demosthenes* VI, ed., with Engl. trans., by A. T. Murray, Cambridge, MA and London, 1939 (LCL).

Aristophanes, *The Frogs*, in *Aristophanes*, ed., with Engl. trans., by B. B. Rogers, 3 vols, Cambridge, MA and London, 1924, vol. II (LCL).

— *The Frogs and Other Plays*, trans. David Barrett, Penguin Books, Harmondsworth, 1964.

— *The Knights/The Birds/The Assemblywomen/Wealth*, trans. by David Barrett and Alan H. Sommerstein, Penguin Books, Harmondsworth, 1978.

— *The Knights*, in *Aristophanes*, ed., with Engl. trans., by B. B. Rogers, 3 vols, Cambridge, MA and London, 1924, vol. I (LCL).

Aristotle, *Aristotle, Politics*, trans. T. A. Sinclair, Penguin Books, Harmondsworth, 1983.

— *The Nicomachean Ethics*, trans. J. A. K. Thomson, revised by Hugh Tredennick; intro. and bibliography by Jonathan Barnes, Penguin, Harmondsworth, 1976.

— *Nicomachean Ethics* (*Eth. Nic.*), ed., with Engl. trans., by H. Rackham, Cambridge, MA and London, 1926 (LCL).

— *The Politics*, ed., with Engl. trans., by H. Rackham, Cambridge, MA and London, 1932 (LCL).

— *The Politics of Aristotle*, trans., with intro. and notes, by Ernest Barker, Clarendon Press, Oxford, 1946 (revised, with intro. and notes, by R. F. Stalley, Oxford (World's Classics), 1995).

Athenaeus, *The Deipnosophists, or Doctors at Dinner* (*Deipn.*), ed., with Engl. trans., by Charles Burton Gulick, 7 vols, Cambridge, MA and London, 1927 (LCL).

Demosthenes, *Against Aphobus*, I, II, III (= *Private Orations* XXVII–XXIX); *Against Onetor*, I, II (= *Private Orations* XXX–XXXI) in *Demosthenes* IV, ed., with Engl. trans., by A. T. Murray, Cambridge, MA and London, 1936 (LCL).

— *Against Boeotus*, I, II (= *Private Orations* XXXIX–XL), in *Demosthenes* IV, ed., with Engl. trans., by A. T. Murray, Cambridge, MA and London, 1936 (LCL).

— *Against Euergus and Mnesibulus* (= *Private Oration* XLVII), in *Demosthenes* V, ed., with Engl. trans., by A. T. Murray, Cambridge, MA and London, 1939 (LCL).

— *Against Meidias*, in *Demosthenes* III, ed., with Engl. trans., by A. T. Murray, Cambridge, MA and London, 1935 (LCL).

— *Against Meidias*, ed. D. M. MacDowell, Oxford, 1990.

Diogenes Laertius, *Life of Diogenes the Cynic* (= *Lives*, Book VI 20–81), in *Lives of Eminent Philosophers*, 2 vols, ed., with Engl. trans., by R. D. Hicks, Cambridge, MA and London, 1925 (LCL).

Hippocrates, *Airs, Waters, Places*, in *Hippocratic Writings*, ed. G. E. R. Lloyd, trans. J. Chadwick and W. N. Mann, Penguin Books, Harmondsworth, 1978.

Isaeus, *On the Estate of Ciron* (= *Speech* VIII), in *Isaeus*, ed., with Engl. trans., by E. S. Forster, Cambridge, MA and London, 1927 (LCL).

Isocrates, *Areopagiticus* (= *Address to the Areopagus*), in vol. II of *Isocrates*, ed., with Engl. trans., by George Norlin, Cambridge, MA and London, 1929 (LCL).

Lysias, *Against Andocides* (= *Speech* VI); *Against Diogeiton* (= *Speech* XXXII); *Against Simon* (= *Speech* III); *On the Murder of Eratosthenes* (= *Speech* I); *On the Olive Stump* (= *Speech* VII); *On the Property of Aristophanes* (= *Speech* XIX), in *Lysias*, ed., with Engl. trans., by W. R. M. Lamb, Cambridge, MA and London, 1930 (LCL).

Menander, *The Arbitration; The Double Deceiver; The Girl from Samos; Old Cantakerous; The Shield* in *Menander, Plays and Fragments*, trans., with intro., by Norma Miller, Penguin Books, London, 1987.

— *Aspis* (= *The Shield*); *The Bad-Tempered Man*); *Dis Exapatôn* (= *The Twice-Deceived*); *Dyskolos* (= *Epitrepontes* (= *The Arbitration*); *Samia* (= *The Girl from Samos*) in *Menander*, ed., with Engl. trans., by W. G. Arnott, 3 vols, Cambridge, MA and London, 1979–2000 (LCL).

Plato, *Early Socratic Dialogues (Ion, Laches, Lysis, Charmides, Hippias Major, Hippias Minor, Euthydemus)*, ed. T. J. Saunders (*Lysis* trans. by Donald Watt), Penguin Books, Harmondsworth, 1987.

— *Euthyphro; Phaedrus* (*Phaedr.*), in *Plato: Euthyphro, Apology, Crito, Phaedo, Phaedrus*, ed., with Engl. trans., by H. N. Fowler, Cambridge, MA and London, 1914 (LCL).

— *The Last Days of Socrates(Euthyphro/Apology/Crito/Phaedo)*, trans. Hugh Tredennick, Penguin Books, Harmondsworth, 1954.

— *The Laws*, ed., with Engl. trans., by R. G. Bury, Cambridge, MA and London, 1926 (LCL).

— *The Laws*, trans. Trevor J. Saunders, Penguin Books, Harmondsworth, 1970.

— *Lysis; Symposium* (*Symp.*), in *Plato: Lysis, Symposium, Gorgias*, ed., with Engl. trans., by W. R. M. Lamb, Cambridge, MA and London, 1925 (LCL).

— *Phaedrus*, in *Plato, Phaedrus and Letters VII and VIII*, trans. Walter Hamilton, Penguin Books, Harmondsworth, 1973.

— *Symposium*, trans. Walter Hamilton, Penguin Books, Harmondsworth, 1951.

Plutarch, *Life of Alcibiades*, in *Plutarch's Lives*, IV, ed., with Engl. trans., by Bernadotte Perrin, Cambridge, MA and London, 1916 (LCL).

— *Life of Solon*, in *Plutarch's Lives*, I, ed., with Engl. trans., by Bernadotte Perrin, Cambridge, MA and London, 1914 (LCL).

— *Life of Solon; Life of Alcibiades*, in *Plutarch, The Rise and Fall of Athens,* trans. Ian Scott-Kilver, Penguin Books, Harmondsworth, 1960.

Thucydides, *Histories* (*Hist.*), ed., with Engl. trans., by C. F. Smith, Cambridge, MA and London, 1919–23 (LCL).

— *The History of the Peloponnesian War*, trans. Rex Warner, Penguin Books, Harmondsworth, 1954.

Xenophon, *Memoirs of Socrates; The Estate Manager; The Dinner Party*, in *Xenophon, Conversation of Socrates*, trans. Hugh Tredennick and Robin Waterfield, Penguin Books, London, 1990.

— *Memorabilia* (*Mem.*); *Oeconomicus* (*Oec.*); *Symposium*, in *Xenophon IV*, ed., with Engl. trans., by E. C. Marchant and O. J. Todd, Cambridge, MA and London, 1923 (LCL).

SECONDARY WORKS

Adkins, A. W. H., *Merit and Responsibility, A Study in Greek Values*, Oxford, 1960.

Adkins, A. W. H., *Moral Values and Political Behaviour from Homer to the End of the Fifth Century*, London, 1972.

Boegehold, A. L. and Scafuro, A. C. (eds), *Athenian Identity and Civic Ideology*, Baltimore and London, 1994.

Calhoun, G. M., *Athenian Clubs in Politics and Litigation*, Austin, TX, 1913.

Cartledge, P. A., Millett, P. C. and Todd, S. C. (eds), *Nomos: Essays in Athenian Law, Politics and Society*, Cambridge, 1990.

Cartledge, P. A., Millett, P. C. and von Reden, S. (eds), *Kosmos: Essays in Order, Conflict, and Community in Classical Athens*, Cambridge, 1998.

Christ, M. R., *The Litigious Athenian*, Baltimore and London, 1998.

Cohen, David, *Law, Sexuality and Society*, Cambridge, 1991.

Cohen, E. E., 'Whoring under Contract': The Legal Context of Prostitution in Fourth-Century Athens', in V. J. Hunter and J. Edmonson (eds), *Law and Social Status in Classical Athens* (Oxford, 2000), 113–48.

Cox, C. A., *Household Interests: Marriage Strategies and Family Dynamics in Ancient Athens*, Princeton, 1998.

Davidson, J., *Courtesans and Fishcakes*, London, 1997.

Davies, J. K., *Athenian Propertied Families, 600–300 BC*, Oxford, 1971.

Davies, J. K., *Wealth and the Power of Wealth in Classical Athens*, London and New York, 1981.

Dodds, E. R., *The Greeks and the Irrational*, Berkeley/Los Angeles, 1951.

Dover, K. J., *Greek Popular Morality in the Time of Plato and Aristotle*, Oxford, 1974.

Dover, K. J., *Greek Homosexuality*, Harvard, 1978.

Earp, F. R., *The Way of the Greeks*, London, 1929.

Ferguson, J., *Moral Values in the Ancient World*, London, 1958.

Finley, M. I. (ed.), *Slavery in Classical Antiquity*, London, 1960.

Finley, M. I., *Ancient Slavery and Modern Ideology*, London, 1980.

Fisher, N. R. E., *Hybris*, Warminster, 1992.

Fisher, N. R. E., *Slavery in Classical Greece*, Bristol, 1993.

Foxhall, L. and Lewis, A. D. E. (eds), *Greek Law in its Political Setting: Justifications not Justice*, Oxford, 1996.

Garlan, Y., *Slavery in Ancient Greece* (Eng. trans. Janet Lloyd), Ithaca, NY, 1988.

Garland, R., *The Greek Way of Life from Conception to Old Age*, London, 1990.

Golden, M., *Children and Childhood in Classical Athens*, Baltimore and London, 1990.

Golden, M. and Toohey, P., *Sex and Difference in Ancient Greece and Rome*, Edinburgh, 2003.

Hansen, M. H., *The Athenian Democracy in the Time of Demosthenes*, Oxford, 1991.

Harris, E. M., *Aeschines and Athenian Politics*, Oxford, 1995.

Harrison, A. R. W., *The Law of Athens*, 2 vols, Oxford, 1968–71.

Hunter, V. J., *Policing Athens: Social Control in Attic Lawsuits, 420–320*, Princeton, 1994.

Hunter, V. J. and Edmonson, J. (eds), *Law and Social Status in Classical Athens*, Oxford, 2000.

Hutter, H., *Politics as Friendship*, Waterloo, Ontario, 1978.

Jaeger, W., *Demosthenes*, Berkeley and Los Angeles, 1938.

Jaeger, W., *Paideia: The Ideals of Greek Culture* (trans. G. Highet), 3 vols, Oxford, 1946.

Jones, A. H. M., *Athenian Democracy*, Oxford, 1957.

Just, R., *Women in Athenian Law and Life*, London, 1989.

Lacey, W. K., *The Family in Classical Greece*, London, 1968.

Lattimore, R., *Themes in Greek and Latin Epitaphs*, Urbana, 1962.

Lefkowitz, M. and Fant, M. B., *Women's Life in Greece and Rome*, London, 1982.

Lewis, S., *News and Society in the Greek Polis*, London, 1996.

Loraux, N., *The Children of Athena* (trans. C. Lewis), Princeton, 1993.

MacDowell, D. M., *Athenian Homicide Law in the Age of the Orators*, Manchester, 1963.

MacDowell, D. M., *The Law in Classical Athens*, London, 1978.

Mikalson, J. D., *Athenian Popular Religion*, Chapel Hill, 1983.

Millett, P. C., *Lending and Borrowing in Ancient Athens*, Cambridge, 1991.

Mossé, C., *The Ancient World at Work* (trans. Janet Lloyd), London, 1969.

Murray, O. (ed.), *Sympotica: A Symposium on the* Symposion, Oxford, 1990.

Neils, J. (ed.), *Goddess and Polis: The Panathenaic Festival in Ancient Athens*, Princeton, 1992.

North, H., *Sophrosyne: Self-Knowledge and Self-Restraint in Greek Literature*, Ithaca, NY, 1966.

Ober, J., *Mass and Elite in Democratic Athens*, Princeton, 1989.

Osborne, R. G., *Demos: The Discovery of Classical Athens*, Cambridge, 1985.

Osborne, R. G., 'Vexatious Litigation in Classical Athens: Sykophancy and the Sykophant', in P. A. Cartledge, P. C. Millett and S. C. Todd (eds), *Nomos: Essays in Athenian Law, Politics and Society* (Cambridge, 1990), 83–102.

Parker, R. C. T., *Miasma: Pollution and Purification in Early Greek Religion*, Oxford, 1983.

Parker, R. C. T., *Athenian Religion: A History*, Oxford, 1996.

Pearson, L., *Popular Ethics in Ancient Greece*, Stanford, 1962.

Price, A. W., *Love and Friendship in Plato and Aristotle*, Oxford, 1988.

Pomeroy, S., *Goddesses, Whores, Wives and Slaves*, London, 1975.

Rhodes, P. J., 'Enmity in Fourth-Century Athens', in P. A. Cartledge, P. C. Millett and S. von Reden (eds), *Kosmos: Essays in Order, Conflict, and Community in Classical Athens* (Cambridge, 1998), 144–61.

Schaps, D., *Economic Rights of Women in Ancient Greece*, Edinburgh, 1979.

Thomas, R., *Oral Tradition and Written Record in Classical Athens*, Cambridge, 1989.

Trevett, J., *Apollodorus the son of Pasion*, Oxford, 1992.

Wallace, R. W., 'Private Lives and Public Enemies: Freedom of Thought in Classical Athens', in A. L. Boegehold and A. C. Scafuro (eds), *Athenian Identity and Civic Ideology* (Baltimore and London, 1994), 127–55.

Whitehead, D., *The Ideology of the Athenian Metic*, Cambridge, 1977.

Wilson, P. J., *The Athenian Institution of the* Khoregia: *The Chorus, the City and the Stage*, Cambridge, 2000.

Wycherley, R. E. *The Stones of Athens*, Princeton, NJ, 1978.

Index